James R. Moore

Managerial Economics and Operations Research

REVISED AND EXPANDED EDITION

Managerial Economics
and
Operations Research

A Nonmathematical Introduction

REVISED AND EXPANDED EDITION

EDITED BY

Edwin Mansfield

UNIVERSITY OF PENNSYLVANIA

W·W·NORTON & COMPANY·INC·*NEW YORK*

Printed in the United States of America

To Charity L.

A GREAT WOMAN AND A GREAT HORSE

Contents

Preface   xi

PART ONE   The Decision-making Process   1

Alfred P. Sloan · INDUSTRIAL DECISION-MAKING: OLD
STYLE AND NEW   3
Herbert A. Simon · THE DECISION-MAKING PROCESS   8
Eugene Grant and W. Grant Ireson · THE COMPARISON
OF ALTERNATIVES   11
C. Northcote Parkinson · PARKINSON'S LAW   20

PART TWO   Cost and Demand   29

N. E. Harlan, C. J. Christenson, and R. F. Vancil · COST
ANALYSIS   31
Business Week · AN AIRLINE TAKES THE MARGINAL
ROUTE   48
Joel Dean · THE MEASUREMENT OF PROFITS   52
Fortune · A NOTE ON BREAK-EVEN CHARTS   58
Edwin Mansfield · THE IMPORTANCE OF THE PRICE ELAS-
TICITY OF DEMAND   62
Joel Dean · ESTIMATING THE PRICE ELASTICITY OF
DEMAND   66
A. D. H. Kaplan, Joel B. Dirlam, and Robert F. Lanzil-
lotti · PRICING AND THE CHARACTER OF THE PRODUCT   77

PART THREE   Capital Budgeting and Forecasting   81

Pearson Hunt, Charles M. Williams, and Gordon Donaldson · TIME ADJUSTMENTS OF FLOWS OF FUNDS   83

Joel Dean · Measuring the Productivity of Capital 96
Business Week · Business and Economic Forecasting 116
National Industrial Conference Board · Forecasting in
Industry 125
Sidney S. Alexander · Economics and Business
Planning 150

Part Four Linear Programming and Related
Techniques 153

Cyril Herrmann and John Magee · Operations
Research 155
Fortune · Decision Theory and Program Scheduling 163
Alexander Henderson and Robert Schlaifer · Mathe-
matical Programing 179
George Dantzig · Linear Programming: Examples
and Concepts 191
Robert Dorfman · Linear Programming: A Graphical
Illustration 201
W. W. Garvin and others · Applications of Linear
Programming in the Oil Industry 205

Part Five Decision Theory, Game Theory, and
Other Techniques 217

John Pratt, Howard Raiffa, and Robert Schlaifer · Intro-
duction to Statistical Decision Theory 219
Martin Shubik · A Note on Decision-making under
Uncertainty 227
A. A. Walters · Decision Theory: An Example 230
John McDonald · The "Game" of Business 242
J. D. Williams · Introduction to Game Theory 246
Thomson M. Whitin · Introduction to the Lot-size
Formula 255
William J. Baumol · Queuing Analysis and Monte
Carlo Methods 258

PART SIX   The Role of the Computer in Industrial
     Management   **265**

Gilbert Burck · "ON LINE" IN "REAL TIME"   267
Harold J. Leavitt and Thomas C. Whisler · MANAGE-
  MENT IN THE 1980's   273
John Dearden · COMPUTERS AND PROFIT CENTERS   289
Herbert A. Simon · THE CORPORATION: WILL IT BE
  MANAGED BY MACHINES?   303

PART SEVEN   Operations Research in the Public
     Sector   **311**

Charles J. Hitch and Roland N. McKean · ECONOMIC
  CHOICE IN MILITARY PLANNING   313
Edwin Mansfield · THE ALLOCATION OF FISSIONABLE
  MATERIALS AND THE THEORY OF EXCHANGE   320
Charles Schultze · THE PLANNING, PROGRAMMING, AND
  BUDGETING SYSTEM IN THE FEDERAL GOVERNMENT   329
Roland N. McKean · COST-BENEFIT ANALYSIS   343
Alan R. Prest and Ralph Turvey · APPLICATIONS OF
  COST-BENEFIT ANALYSIS   356
Jack Hirshleifer, James De Haven, and Jerome Milli-
  man · THE UTILIZATION OF EXISTING WATER SUPPLIES   381

Preface

The postwar period has witnessed exciting and important developments in economics and related disciplines, with the invention or adaptation of new techniques and concepts for solving major managerial problems of business firms, the military services, and other organizations. In the first place, traditional economic analysis has been extended to meet the need for greater precision in the management of the business enterprise. In the process a new field, *managerial economics,* has emerged. In developing a more rigorous approach to executive decisions, managerial economics draws upon economic analysis for such concepts as cost, demand, profit, and competition. It attempts to bridge the gap between the purely analytical problems that intrigue many economic theorists and the problems of policy that management must face. It now offers powerful tools and approaches for managerial policy-making.

In recent years another new field—*operations research* or *management science*—has been opened up. Its boundaries are not easy to define. According to one definition, operations research involves "the use of systematic quantitative analysis to aid in the making of management decisions." [1] Emphasis is placed on a scientific approach to decision-making, with considerable reliance on advanced mathematical techniques and a computer-based technology. First used on a sustained and significant scale in connection with military activities during World War II, operations research has spread rapidly throughout American industry, and is now a very important managerial tool.

This book provides an elementary description of important facets of these new fields. Aimed primarily at students of eco-

1. Charles Hitch, "Economics and Military Operations Research," *Review of Economics and Statistics,* August 1958, p. 200.

nomics and business administration with modest training in mathematics, it provides a general introduction to the nature, purpose, and potential usefulness of various concepts and techniques in managerial economics and operations research without going far into their technical details. Much material is available for the advanced student with some mathematical sophistication, but little is available for the beginner. Hopefully, this book will help to fill the gap.

The papers in Part One explore the nature of the decision-making process. The papers in Part Two deal mainly with costs and demand, while those in Part Three are concerned with capital budgeting and forecasting. In Part Four, linear programming and related techniques are examined in theory and in practice, and in Part Five the focus shifts to decision theory, game theory, and other aspects of operations research. The part played by the computer in modern management is considered in Part Six. The volume closes with Part Seven, which deals with the use of economics and operations research in solving important problems in the public sector of the economy.

In this revised edition, I have tried to alter the book's contents in the light of the reactions of the many instructors who have used the book in their courses. The length of the book has been increased considerably, with the result that much more attention is devoted to the role of the computer and to the uses of economic techniques in the public sector of the economy. Also, some of the weaker articles have been removed, new ones have been added, and some have been reprinted in expanded form. About 30 percent of this edition is new. In carrying out this revision, I have been particularly grateful for the useful suggestions of Professors Sidney Turoff and John Clair Thompson of the University of Connecticut.

E. M.

Part One

The Decision-making Process

SINCE managerial economics and operations research deal with decision making, we begin by considering the nature of the decision-making process as it presently exists in most industrial organizations. Alfred P. Sloan describes some of his experiences as a top executive of General Motors and concludes that the great difference in decision-making between today and yesterday "is what might be referred to as the necessity of the scientific approach, the diminution of operation by hunches; this affects men, tools, and methods." Herbert Simon then discusses the various phases of the decision-making process, which he characterizes as: finding occasions for making a decision, finding possible courses of action, and choosing among courses of action.

In the next article, Eugene Grant points out that many managerial decisions are made improperly because the decision-maker fails to reason clearly about the costs and benefits of alternative courses of action. To arrive at a realistic cost figure for decision-making, it is necessary to define the alternatives clearly; otherwise some costs that are common to both alternatives may influence the choice. Grant notes two important corollaries of this: average and marginal costs should not be confused, and "sunk costs are sunk." The concluding paper in this part is Parkinson's Law. This famous, and amusing, law is based on the proposition that "work expands so as to fill the time available for its completion." Although Parkinson is writing about the British bureaucracy, his observations also provide interesting insights into the decision-making process and the growth of bureaucracies in large industrial organizations.

Industrial Decision-making:
Old Style and New

ALFRED P. SLOAN

*One of America's leading industrialists,
Alfred P. Sloan was president of General
Motors from 1923 to 1937 and chairman of
its board of directors from 1937 to 1956.
This short piece is taken from his book,*
Adventures of a White-Collar Worker.

[When I was vice-president of General Motors and Mr. Durant was president,] I was constantly amazed by his daring way of making decisions. My business experience had convinced me facts are precious things, to be eagerly sought and treated with respect. But Mr. Durant would proceed on a course of action guided solely, as far as I could tell, by some intuitive flash of brilliance. He never felt obliged to make an engineering hunt for facts. Yet at times he was astoundingly correct in his judgments.

One legend concerning him goes back to 1912, when a gathering of automobile manufacturers pooled guesses on the next year's production, each man dropping his slip of paper into a derby hat. That year 378,000 cars had been made. Mr. Durant guessed that in the next year they would manufacture half a million cars.

The others gasped. They said, "People can't buy that many

cars. Our industry will be ruined by such overproduction before it really gets started."

Mr. Durant mildly rebuked them, saying, "Gentlemen, you don't realize the purchasing power of the American people. I look forward to the time we'll make and sell one million cars a year."

Those men thought he was being fantastic. Actually, his vision was clear. In 1929 the industry was to make, and sell, 5,621,000 automobiles. However, this example of Mr. Durant's vision does not alter the fact that many costly errors would have been avoided had his practice been to base decisions on a comprehensive analysis of all facts and circumstances. He was invariably optimistic. It was easy to be optimistic, though, if you had been in a position to observe the booming growth of Detroit, Flint, and other places where cars were being made; and Durant had seen all of it.* * *

Although I had important responsibilities under Mr. Durant, our methods of approaching operating problems were entirely different. But I liked him even when I disagreed with him. Durant's integrity? Unblemished. Work? He was a prodigious worker. Devotion to General Motors? Why, it was his baby! He would have made any sacrifice for it, and he did make for it almost the ultimate sacrifice. But the question constantly in my mind was whether the potential industrial force under the General Motors emblem could be realized by the same boldness and daring that had been needed to enlist the units of that force. General Motors had become too big to be a one-man show. It was already far too complicated. The future required something more than an individual's genius. In any company I would be the first to say that William C. Durant was a genius. But General Motors justified the most competent executive group that could possibly be brought together.

In bringing General Motors into existence, Mr. Durant had operated as a dictator. But such an institution could not grow into a successful organization under a dictatorship. Dictatorship is the most effective way of administration, provided the dictator knows the complete answers to all questions. But he never does and never will. That is why dictatorships eventually fail. If

General Motors were to capitalize its wonderful opportunity, it would have to be guided by an organization of intellects. A great industrial organization requires the best of many minds.* * *

After forty years of experience in American industry, I would say that my concept of the management scheme of a great industrial organization, simply expressed, is to divide it into as many parts as consistently can be done, place in charge of each part the most capable executive that can be found, develop a system of coordination so that each part may strengthen and support each other part; thus not only welding all parts together in the common interests of a joint enterprise, but importantly developing ability and initiative through the instrumentalities of responsibility and ambition—developing men and giving them an opportunity to exercise their talents, both in their own interests as well as in that of the business.

To formalize this scheme, I worked out what we speak of in industry as an organization chart. It shows how the business functions from the standpoint of the relationship of the different units, one to another, as well as the authority delegated to the executives, also in relation to one another. I grouped together those operations which had a common relationship, and I placed over each such group for coordinating purposes what I termed a Group Executive. These group executives were the only ones that reported to me. Then I developed a General Staff similar in name and purpose to what exists in the army. The general staff was on a functional basis: engineering, distribution, legal, financial affairs, and so on. Each of these functions was presided over by a vice-president, the purpose being twofold: first, to perform those functions that could be done more effectively by one activity in the interests of the whole; and second, to coordinate the functional activities of the different operating units as well as to promote their effectiveness. In the General Motors scheme, for instance, the vice-president in charge of sales is a coordinating executive. He has a staff at his command. His contribution is in developing better and more advanced policies of distribution technique through research and in other ways.

He cooperates with the sales departments of the different operating units. But he has no direct authority over their operations; that exists exclusively in the chief executive of the operation itself.

There is no need of repeating the story of how Chevrolet grew and grew, until it gained world leadership among the motorcars in the low-priced field, and how it has successfully maintained that leadership.

As I proudly make that observation there comes into my mind a rather interesting incident.

At the time Mr. du Pont became president, someone had the idea of having a survey made of the General Motors properties, with recommendations as to what might be done in the way of a reconstruction program. The job was entrusted to a firm of consulting engineers of high standing. The most illuminating recommendation was that the whole Chevrolet operation should be liquidated. There was no chance to make it a profitable business. We could not hope to compete. I was much upset because I feared the prestige of the authors might overcome our arguments to the contrary. So I went to Mr. du Pont and told him what we thought we might accomplish if we built a good product and sold it aggressively. We urged upon him the fact that many more people always could buy low-priced cars than Cadillacs and even Buicks. That it was an insult to say we could not compete with anyone. It was a case of ability and hard work. He listened most patiently, and finally said, "Forget the report. We will go ahead and see what we can do." Mr. du Pont was always that way. He had the courage of his convictions. Facts were the only things that counted. So Chevrolet was saved and General Motors avoided what would have been a catastrophe.

The great difference in managerial technique between the industry of today as compared with that of yesterday is what might be referred to as the necessity of the scientific approach, the elimination of operation by hunches; this affects men, tools and methods. Many associate the word scientific with physics. But it means much more than that. Scientific management means a constant search for the facts, the true actualities, and their intelligent, unprejudiced analysis. Thus, and in no other way, policies and their administration are determined. I keep saying to the General Motors organization that we are prepared to spend any proper amount of money to get the facts. Only by increased knowledge can we progress, perhaps I had better say survive. That is really research, but few realize that research can and should be just as effectively used in all functional branches of industry as in physics. Research into the problem of distribution, for instance, has paid General Motors big dividends. Again it is the scientific approach. I keep mentioning it because it seems to me the willingness and ability to apply such methods might well determine the extent of success of any enterprise, and the larger the enterprise, the more vital it becomes. I had thought much about all this as an executive working under Mr. Durant; hence it was natural, as chief executive of the corporation, that I should turn to that type of managerial approach. The answer would be found in the facts.

The Decision-making Process

HERBERT A. SIMON

*Herbert A. Simon is Associate Dean of the
Graduate School of Industrial Administra-
tion at Carnegie Institute of Technology.
The following paper comes from his book,*
The New Science of Managerial Decision
Making, *published in 1960.*

Decision making comprises three principal phases: finding
occasions for making a decision; finding possible courses of action; and choosing among courses of action. These three activities account for quite different fractions of the time budgets of
executives. The fractions vary greatly from one organization level
to another and from one executive to another, but we can make
some generalizations about them even from casual observation.
Executives spend a large fraction of their time surveying the
economic, technical, political, and social environment to identify
new conditions that call for new actions. They probably spend
an even larger fraction of their time, individually or with their
associates, seeking to invent, design, and develop possible courses
of action for handling situations where a decision is needed. They
spend a small fraction of their time in choosing among alternative
actions already developed to meet an identified problem and already analysed for their consequences. The three fractions, added
together, account for most of what executives do.[1]

1. The way in which these activities take shape within an organization
is described in some detail in James G. March and Herbert A. Simon, *Organizations* (New York: John Wiley & Sons, Inc., 1958), chapters 6 and 7.

8

The first phase of the decision-making process—searching the environment for conditions calling for decision—I shall call *intelligence* activity (borrowing the military meaning of intelligence). The second phase—inventing, developing, and analysing possible courses of action—I shall call *design* activity. The third phase—selecting a particular course of action from those available—I shall call *choice* activity.

Let me illustrate these three phases of decision. In the past five years, many companies have reorganized their accounting and other data processing activities in order to make use of large electronic computers. How has this come about? Computers first became available commercially in the early 1950s. Although, in some vague and general sense, company managements were aware that computers existed, few managements had investigated their possible applications with any thoroughness before about 1955. For most companies, the use of computers required no decision before that time because it hadn't been placed on the agenda.[2]

The intelligence activity preceding the introduction of computers tended to come about in one of two ways. Some companies—for example, in the aircraft and atomic energy industries—were burdened with enormously complex computations for engineering design. Because efficiency in computation was a constant problem, and because the design departments were staffed with engineers who could understand, at least in general, the technology of computers, awareness of computers and their potentialities came early to these companies. After computers were already in extensive use for design calculations, businesses with a large number-processing load—insurance companies, accounting departments in large firms, banks—discovered these new devices and began to consider seriously their introduction.

Once it was recognized that computers might have a place in modern business, a major design task had to be carried out in each company before they could be introduced. It is now a commonplace that payrolls can be prepared by computers. Programs in both the general and computer senses for doing this are relatively

2. Richard M. Cyert, Herbert A. Simon, and Donald B. Trow, "Observation of a Business Decision," *Journal of Business,* Vol. 29 (1956), pp. 237-248.

easy to design in any given situation.[3] To develop the first computer programs for preparing payroll, however, was a major research and development project. Few companies having carried their investigations of computers to the point where they had definite plans for their use, failed to install them. Commitment to the new course of action took place gradually as the intelligence and design phases of the decision were going on. The final choice was, in many instances, almost *pro forma*.

Generally speaking, intelligence activity precedes design, and design activity precedes choice. The cycle of phases is, however, far more complex than this sequence suggests. Each phase in making a particular decision is itself a complex decision-making process. The design phase, for example, may call for new intelligence activities; problems at any given level generate subproblems that, in turn, have their intelligence, design, and choice phases, and so on. There are wheels within wheels within wheels. Nevertheless, the three large phases are often clearly discernible as the organizational decision process unfolds. They are closely related to the stages in problem solving first described by John Dewey:

What is the problem?
What are the alternatives?
Which alternative is best?[4]

3. For a good discussion on the use of the computer for such purposes, see Robert H. Gregory and Richard L. Van Horn, *Automatic Data-Processing Systems* (San Francisco: Wadsworth Publishing Company, Inc., 1960).
4. John Dewey, *How We Think* (New York: D. C. Heath & Company, 1910), chapter 8.

The Comparison of
Alternatives

EUGENE L. GRANT AND
W. GRANT IRESON

*Eugene Grant is Professor of Economics of
Engineering at Stanford University. In 1960
he, together with W. Grant Ireson, wrote* Principles of Engineering Economy, *from which
this article is taken.*

The conduct of a business enterprise requires a successive series of business decisions—decisions between possible alternatives with reference to the future. These decisions are of all degrees of importance, varying from trivial matters to matters of major policy. Some of them are made by intuitive judgments or "hunches" without any conscious attempt to express the alternatives to be compared in commensurable terms, or perhaps even to see clearly what these alternatives really are. Others, however, involve choices between definite alternatives which have been made commensurable by reducing them to terms of money and time. There is much evidence that many of these latter decisions, based on conscious economy studies involving estimates of expected costs (and possibly of revenues) are incorrectly made because of the failure of the estimator to reason clearly about the *differences* between alternatives which involve common elements.

WHAT IS THE "COST" OF AN AUTOMOBILE TRIP?

To illustrate the type of error that may occur if alternatives are not clearly defined, let us consider a familiar and relatively simple situation. Suppose it is desired to estimate the cost of a 600-mile automobile trip.

Bill Jones, who has agreed to "share the cost" of such a proposed trip to be taken in the car of his friend Tom Smith, may calculate merely the expected out-of-pocket expense for gasoline. If Smith's car makes 15 miles to the gallon, and gasoline costs 25 cents per gallon, this is 1⅔ cents per mile. He therefore concludes that the trip will cost $10.

Tom Smith, on the other hand, may estimate all of the costs associated with the ownership and operation of his automobile over its expected life in his service, in order to find an average cost per mile. His car has a first cost of $2,000; he expects to drive it 10,000 miles per year for four years; at the end of this time he hopes to realize $1,000 from its sale. His estimates of total cost might be as follows:

1. Gasoline (40,000 miles at 1⅔¢ per mile)	$ 667
2. Oil and grease	163
3. Tires	150
4. Repairs and maintenance	600
5. Insurance	400
6. Storage (48 months at $5 per month)	240
7. License fees and property taxes	120
8. Total depreciation in 4 years ($2,000-$1,000)	1,000
9. Interest on investment in car	260
(This is based on average interest at 4% per annum.)	
	$3,600

Divided among 40,000 miles of travel, this is an average cost of 9 cents per mile. At this rate a 600-mile trip appears to cost $54.

The Concept of Cost Must Be Related to Specific Alternatives if It Is to Be a Reliable Guide to Decisions · The second of these two figures for the cost of a given service is 540 percent of the first one. At first glance it would appear that one or the other of the two figures must be wide of its mark. However, a more critical consideration will disclose that the simple question "What is its cost?" with reference to a particular service does not define any mark for the estimator to shoot at.

To use a cost figure as a basis for a decision, it is necessary to have clearly in mind the alternatives between which it is desired to decide. Otherwise, certain costs which, after a clear definition of alternatives, would be recognized as common to both, may be given weight in influencing the choice. It is dangerous to base conclusions on average costs without regard to the specific alternatives which it is intended to compare. The fact that widely differing cost figures may be required for different decisions about a given service may be illustrated by examining some of the different pairs of alternatives which might arise relative to the service of a given automobile.

A Situation in Which It Is Necessary to Estimate Total Cost of Ownership and Operation · If Tom Smith did not own an automobile, and wanted to decide whether or not to purchase one, he might set up the following alternatives for comparison:

Alternative A. Buy a $2,000 car and operate it approximately 10,-000 miles per year for the next four years.

Alternative B. Do not buy a car. Use some others means of transportation as railway, street car, bus, taxicab, his friends' automobiles, and his own legs for part of the contemplated mileage and do without the rest.

If these are the alternatives, all of the items included in his estimate of $3,600 for four years' service are disbursements[1] which will take place if Alternative A is selected, and which will not take place if Alternative B is selected. Thus, the unit cost of 9 cents per mile is relevant to Smith's decision whether or not to own a car. The total cost (which in this case is more important than the average cost per unit of service) of $3,600 should be compared with the costs associated with Alternative B. The higher cost of A, if any, should then be judged in the light of differences which are not reducible to money terms, and in the light of Smith's prospective ability to pay this higher cost.

A Situation in Which It Is Necessary to Estimate the Increment Cost of an Added Service · On the other hand, if Smith has

---

1. That is, they are all disbursements with the possible exception of interest which might in some cases be a disbursement and in others an income given up—an opportunity foregone.

already purchased an automobile and intends to continue to own and operate it, but is undecided about the annual mileage he will drive, the kinds of alternatives to be compared are quite different. In order to determine the effect on cost of driving extra miles, he might set up two alternatives differing only in annual mileage:

Alternative A. Continue to own the car, driving it 12,500 miles per year for four years before disposing of it.

Alternative B. Continue to own the car, driving it 10,000 miles per year for four years before disposing of it.

In comparing these alternatives, it is necessary to consider the various elements of total cost of ownership which have already been listed, item by item, and estimate the effect on each of a total increase of 10,000 miles in the mileage driven over the life of the car.

Item 1, gasoline, and item 2, oil and grease, may be expected to increase at least in proportion to the increase in mileage. It is likely that the increase would be somewhat more than in direct proportion, because of the tendency of the rate of consumption of fuel and lubricants to increase after a car has been driven a good many miles. Perhaps if the car had averaged 15 miles per gallon in its first 40,000 miles, it might average only 14.3 miles per gallon in the following 10,000 miles. In general, item 3, tires, may be expected to increase in proportion to driving mileage; the actual effect of any proposed increase in mileage will depend on whether it requires the purchase of tires and tubes during the extended period of service. Item 4, repairs and maintenance, will doubtless tend to increase somewhat more than in direct proportion to mileage.

On the other hand item 5, insurance, item 6, storage, and item 7, license fees and property taxes, will be unchanged by an increase in mileage driven in any given time. Because the second-hand price of automobiles seems to depend almost entirely on age and not on miles driven, it is probable that the estimated realizable value after four years will be affected very little, if at all, by an increase of 25 percent in total mileage. If this is the case, neither item 8, total depreciation, nor item 9, interest, will be changed by the contemplated increase in mileage.

Smith might make his estimate of the extra costs associated

with increasing his total expected mileage from 40,000 to 50,000 somewhat as follows:

1.	Gasoline (10,000 miles at 1¾¢ per mile)	$175
2.	Oil and grease	50
3.	Tires	50
4.	Repairs and maintenance	225
		$500

If this estimate is correct, so that an increase of 10,000 miles would increase total costs by $500, then the average cost for each increased mile of travel is 5 cents. This unit increment cost might then be applied to the mileage of any proposed trip, in order to get an idea of how the proposed trip will affect automobile costs in the long run. If this is done for a proposed 600-mile trip, the conclusion will be that this trip ultimately will be responsible for $30 of extra expense.[2]

It will be noted that although this estimated unit increment cost of 5 cents per mile is much less than the estimated 9 cents per mile for ownership and operation over the life of the automobile, it is three times the 1¾ cents per mile estimate that Bill Jones made for the out-of-pocket expense of a short trip. The difference between the 5-cent and the 9-cent figures lies in those costs that are "fixed" by the decision to buy and to continue to own and operate the car, and which are, therefore, independent of its miles of operation. On the other hand, the difference between the 1¾-cent and the 5-cent figures is the difference between short-run and long-run viewpoints. It may well be true that the only out-of-pocket expenses of a 600-mile trip will be for gasoline; nevertheless, the long-run effect of increasing the number of miles of

2. Incidentally, it may be noted that the question of what, in equity, Bill Jones ought to pay when he rides in Tom Smith's car "sharing the cost" of a trip is a question of social conduct which cannot be answered by an economy study. All an economy study can do is to disclose the expected differences between alternatives. Thus, if Tom is making the trip in any event, an economy study might indicate that the least he could afford to accept from Bill without loss would be nothing at all; this is the difference between the alternatives: (a) make the trip, taking Bill along, and (b) make the trip, leaving Bill behind. On the other hand, if he is making the trip entirely for Bill's convenience, his estimates would appear to indicate that the least he could afford to take for a 600-mile trip is $30; here the alternatives are: (a) make the trip with Bill and (b) do not make the trip at all.

operation of an automobile will be to increase the expenditures for lubricants, tires, and repairs.

A Situation in Which It is Necessary to Estimate the Costs of Continuing a Machine in Service · If Smith purchases an automobile, and then has misgivings as to whether or not he can afford to continue to own and operate it, the alternatives which present themselves to him are still different, and different cost figures from any we have yet discussed will be required as a basis for his decision. Suppose he sets up the following alternatives for comparison:

Alternative A. Continue to own the car, driving it 10,000 miles per year for four years.

Alternative B. Immediately dispose of the car for the best price obtainable, thereafter using other means of transportation.

In considering the difference between these two alternatives, it is necessary to recognize that the $2,000 purchase price of the car has already been spent, no matter which alternative is chosen. The important question here is not the past outlay for the car, but rather the "best price obtainable" for it if Alternative B is selected. If Smith's decision had been made, say, in 1947, when it was possible to sell certain makes of new cars in a so-called used car market at several hundred dollars more than the purchase price, this best price obtainable might have been $2,500. If so, Smith's question would obviously have been whether or not he could afford to continue to own an automobile that he could sell for $2,500. On the other hand, if his decision is to be made under the more normal conditions where the resale price of a new automobile is substantially below its purchase price, even though the car may have been driven only a few miles, the best price obtainable might possibly be $1,700. Under these circumstances, Smith's question is whether or not he can afford to continue to own an automobile that he could sell for $1,700. The $300 difference between the $2,000 purchase price and the $1,700 resale price is gone whether he keeps the car or disposes of it at once.

The principles underlying financial calculations to determine whether or not to continue to own a given asset enter into a wide variety of engineering economy studies. . . . At this point it is sufficient to note that there is a substantial difference in principle between a decision whether or not to acquire an asset and a decision whether or not to continue to own and operate that asset once it is acquired. To guide the latter type of decision intelligently, attention must be focused on the net realizable value of the machine (that is, on the prospective net receipts from its sale if it should be disposed of). Once an asset has been purchased, its purchase price has been paid regardless of whether it is continued in service or disposed of at once. This past investment may be thought of as a "sunk cost" that, generally speaking, has no relevance in decisions for the future.

COMPARING ALTERNATIVES IN BUSINESS SITUATIONS

These examples from the familiar situation of automobile ownership have illustrated the necessity for recognizing definite alternatives to be compared before using cost as a basis for decisions. No doubt the different kinds of relevant "costs" which should be considered in automobile ownership and operation are recognized in their qualitative aspects by many automobile owners. However, even in these relatively simple situations which have been discussed, it will be noted that in order to express differences quantitatively we were obliged to make assumptions which, in order to be definite, were somewhat arbitrary. For instance, in order to estimate increment costs per mile of operation, we found it necessary to assume two definite total mileages, and to assume that the four-year period of ownership would be unchanged by a change in the total miles of operation.

In industry, the circumstances in which comparisons are made are likely to be more involved. The machines and structures which are the subjects of engineering economy studies are generally parts of a complex plant, and this complexity may create difficulties in differentiating the effects of alternatives. As has been stated, industrialists are often misled as to the costs which are relevant to particular decisions by failure to define alternatives clearly. In industrial situations, even more than in the automobile cost illustration, it is necessary to make definite assumptions in order to have a basis for decisions.

Irreducible Data in Comparing Alternatives · In the case of the alternatives involving Tom Smith's decision whether or not to purchase a car, we noted briefly that there would be certain advantages and certain hazards incident to the ownership of an automobile which could not be reduced to money terms, but which, nevertheless, would have considerable influence on Smith's choice.

This is characteristic of many economy studies. Although the reduction of units which would otherwise be incommensurable (for example, tons of coal, pounds of structural steel, barrels of cement, gallons of oil, kilowatt-hours of electric energy, hours of skilled machinists' labor, hours of common labor) to terms of money and time is essential to all business decisions which are not made entirely on "hunch," some differences between alternatives will generally remain which cannot be reduced to money terms. In an economy study, it is as much a part of the estimator's duty to note these irreducibles as it is to predict the money receipts and disbursements at various dates. The final decision must give weight to the irreducible differences, as well as to the money differences.

Differences Between Alternatives Are in the Future · If it is recognized that only those matters which are different as between two alternatives are relevant to their comparison, it should be obvious that everything that has happened in the past is irrelevant, except as it may help in the prediction of the future. Whatever has already happened is past and gone, regardless of which of two future alternatives is selected. This implies, among other things, that apportionments against future times of expenditures already past should not be included in economy studies. It also implies that economy studies are based on forecasts, and that their conclusions are dependent on predictions of future events, predictions which are either conscious forecasts or implied ones.

The Limitations of Accounting as a Basis for Estimates in Economy Studies · Generally speaking, the accounts of an enterprise constitute the source of information which has the greatest potential value in making estimates for economy studies. Nevertheless, the uncritical use of accounting figures is responsible for many errors in such estimates. There are a number of important differences between the point of view of accounting and that which should be taken in an economy study.

Accounting involves a recording of past receipts and expenditures. It deals only with what happened regarding policies actually followed and is not concerned with alternatives that might have been followed; it is concerned more with average costs than with differences in cost. It involves apportionment of past costs against future periods of time, and apportionment of joint costs between various services or products. It does not involve consideration of the time value of money.

Engineering economy, on the other hand, always involves alternatives; it deals with prospective differences between future alternatives. It is concerned with differences between costs rather than apportionments of costs. It does involve consideration of the time value of money.

Parkinson's Law

C. NORTHCOTE PARKINSON

*C. Northcote Parkinson is Raffles Professor
of History at the University of Singapore.
This article first appeared in the* Economist
in November 1955.

It is a commonplace observation that work expands so as to
fill the time available for its completion. Thus, an elderly lady
of leisure can spend an entire day in writing and dispatching
a postcard to her niece at Bognor Regis. An hour will be spent
in finding the postcard, another in hunting for spectacles, half-an-
hour in a search for the address, an hour and a quarter in composition, and twenty minutes in deciding whether or not to take an
umbrella when going to the pillar-box in the next street. The
total effort which would occupy a busy man for three minutes
all told may in this fashion leave another person prostrate after
a day of doubt, anxiety and toil.

Granted that work (and especially paper work) is thus elastic
in its demands on time, it is manifest that there need be little or
no relationship between the work to be done and the size of the
staff to which it may be assigned. Before the discovery of a new
scientific law—herewith presented to the public for the first time,
and to be called Parkinson's Law[1]—there has, however, been
insufficient recognition of the implication of this fact in the field
of public administration. Politicians and taxpayers have assumed

1. Why? Why not?—Editor.

(with occasional phases of doubt) that a rising total in the number of civil servants must reflect a growing volume of work to be done. Cynics, in questioning this belief, have imagined that the multiplication of officials must have left some of them idle or all of them able to work for shorter hours. But this is a matter in which faith and doubt seem equally misplaced. The fact is that the number of the officials and the quantity of the work to be done are not related to each other at all. The rise in the total of those employed is governed by Parkinson's Law, and would be much the same whether the volume of the work were to increase, diminish or even disappear. The importance of Parkinson's Law lies in the fact that it is a law of growth based upon an analysis of the factors by which the growth is controlled.

The validity of this recently discovered law must rely mainly on statistical proofs, which will follow. Of more interest to the general reader is the explanation of the factors that underlie the general tendency to which this law gives definition. Omitting technicalities (which are numerous) we may distinguish, at the outset, two motive forces. They can be represented for the present purpose by two almost axiomatic statements, thus:

Factor I. An official wants to multiply subordinates, not rivals; and

Factor II. Officials make work for each other. We must now examine these motive forces in turn.

THE LAW OF MULTIPLICATION OF SUBORDINATES

To comprehend Factor I, we must picture a civil servant called *A* who finds himself overworked. Whether this overwork is real or imaginary is immaterial; but we should observe, in passing, that *A*'s sensation (or illusion) might easily result from his own decreasing energy—a normal symptom of middle-age. For this real or imagined overwork there are, broadly speaking, three possible remedies:

(1) He may resign.

(2) He may ask to halve the work with a colleague called *B*.

(3) He may demand the assistance of two subordinates to be called *C* and *D*.

There is probably no instance in civil service history of *A* choosing any but the third alternative. By resignation he would lose his pension rights. By having *B* appointed, on his own level in the hierarchy, he would merely bring in a rival for promotion to *W*'s vacancy when *W* (at long last) retires. So *A* would rather have *C* and *D*, junior men, below him. They will add to his consequence; and, by dividing the work into two categories, as between *C* and *D*, he will have the merit of being the only man who comprehends them both.

It is essential to realize, at this point, that *C* and *D* are, as it were, inseparable. To appoint *C* alone would have been impossible. Why? Because *C*, if by himself, would divide the work with *A* and so assume almost the equal status which has been refused in the first instance to *B*; a status the more emphasized if *C* is *A*'s only possible successor. Subordinates must thus number two or more, each being kept in order by fear of the other's promotion. When *C* complains in turn of being overworked (as he certainly will) *A* will, with the concurrence of *C*, advise the appointment of two assistants to help *C*. But he can then avert internal friction only by advising the appointment of two more assistants to help *D*, whose position is much the same. With this recruitment of *E*, *F*, *G* and *H*, the promotion of *A* is now practically certain.

THE LAW OF MULTIPLICATION OF WORK

Seven officials are now doing what one did before. This is where Factor II comes into operation. For these seven make so much work for each other that all are fully occupied and *A* is actually working harder than ever. An incoming document may well come before each of them in turn. Official *E* decides that it falls within the province of *F*, who places a draft reply before *C*, who amends it drastically before consulting *D*, who asks *G* to deal with it. But *G* goes on leave at this point, handing the file over to *H*, who drafts a minute, which is signed by *D* and returned to *C*, who revises his draft accordingly and lays the new version before *A*.

What does *A* do? He would have every excuse for signing the thing unread, for he has many other matters on his mind. Knowing now that he is to succeed *W* next year, he has to decide whether *C* or *D* should succeed to his own office. He had to agree to G going on leave, although not yet strictly entitled to it. He is worried whether H should not have gone instead, for reasons of health. He has looked pale recently—partly but not solely because of his domestic troubles. Then there is the business of F's special increment of salary for the period of the conference, and E's application for transfer to the Ministry of Pensions. A has heard that D is in love with a married typist and that G and F are no longer on speaking terms—no one seems to know why. So A might be tempted to sign C's draft and have done with it.

But A is a conscientious man. Beset as he is with problems created by his colleagues for themselves and for him—created by the mere fact of these officials' existence—he is not the man to shirk his duty. He reads through the draft with care, deletes the fussy paragraphs added by C and H and restores the thing back to the form preferred in the first instance by the able (if quarrelsome) F. He corrects the English—none of these young men can write grammatically—and finally produces the same reply he would have written if officials C to H had never been born. Far more people have taken far longer to produce the same result. No one has been idle. All have done their best. And it is late in the evening before A finally quits his office and begins the return journey to Ealing. The last of the office lights are being turned off in the gathering dusk which marks the end of another day's administrative toil. Among the last to leave, A reflects, with bowed shoulders and a wry smile, that late hours, like grey hairs, are among the penalties of success.

THE SCIENTIFIC PROOFS

From this description of the factors at work the student of political science will recognize that administrators are more or less bound to multiply. Nothing has yet been said, however, about the period of time likely to elapse between the date of A's appointment and the date from which we can calculate the pensionable service of H. Vast masses of statistical evidence have been collected and it is from a study of this data that Parkinson's Law has been deduced. Space will not allow of detailed analysis, but research began in the British Navy Estimates.

These were chosen because the Admiralty's responsibilities are more easily measurable than those of (say) the Board of Trade.

The accompanying table is derived from Admiralty statistics for 1914 and 1928. The criticism voiced at the time centered on the comparison between the sharp fall in numbers of those available for fighting and the sharp rise in those available only for administration, the creation, it was said, of "a magnificent Navy on land." But that comparison is not to the present purpose. What we have to note is that the 2,000 Admiralty officials of 1914 had become the 3,569 of 1928; and that this growth was unrelated to any possible increase in their work. The Navy during that period had diminished, in point of fact, by a third in men and two-thirds in ships. Nor, from 1922 onwards, was its strength even expected to increase, for its total of ships (unlike its total of officials) was limited by the Washington Naval Agreement of that year. Yet in these circumstances we had a 78.45 percent increase in Admiralty officials over a period of fourteen years; an average increase of 5.6 percent a year on the earlier total. In fact, as we shall see, the rate of increase was not as regular as that. All we have to consider, at this stage, is the percentage rise over a given period.

ADMIRALTY STATISTICS

	1914	1928	Percentage increase or decrease
Capital ships in commission	62	20	—67.74
Officers and men in Royal Navy	146,000	100,000	—31.50
Dockyard workers	57,000	62,439	+ 9.54
Dockyard officials and clerks	3,249	4,558	+40.28
Admiralty officials	2,000	3,569	+78.45

Can this rise in the total number of civil servants be accounted for except on the assumption that such a total must always rise by a law governing its growth? It might be urged, at this point, that the period under discussion was one of rapid development in naval technique. The use of the flying machine was no longer confined to the eccentric. Submarines were tolerated if not approved. Engineer officers were beginning to be regarded as almost human. In so revolutionary an age we might expect the storekeepers would have more elaborate inventories to compile. We might not wonder to see more draughtsmen on the payroll, more designers, more technicians and scientists. But these, the dockyard officials, increased only by 40 percent in number, while the men of Whitehall increased by nearly 80 percent. For every new foreman or electrical engineer at Portsmouth there had to be two or more clerks at Charing Cross. From this we might be tempted to conclude, provisionally, that the rate of increase in administrative staff is likely to be double that of the technical staff at a time when the actually useful strength (in this case, of seamen) is being reduced by 31.5 percent. It has been proved, however, statistically, that this last percentage is irrelevant. *The Officials would have multiplied at the same rate had there been no actual seamen at all.*

It would be interesting to follow the further progress by which the 8,118 Admiralty staff of 1935 came to number 33,788 by 1954. But the staff of the Colonial Office affords a better field of study during a period of Imperial decline. The relevant statistics are set down below. Before showing what the rate of increase is, we must observe that the extent of this department's responsibilities was far from constant during these twenty years. The colonial territories were not much altered in area or population between 1935 and 1939. They were considerably diminished by 1943, certain areas being in enemy hands. They were increased again in 1947, but have since then shrunk steadily from year to year as successive colonies achieve self-government.

COLONIAL OFFICE OFFICIALS

1935	1939	1943	1947	1954
372	450	817	1,139	1,661

It would be rational, prior to the discovery of Parkinson's Law, to suppose that these changes in the scope of Empire would be reflected in the size of its central administration. But a glance at the figures shows that the staff totals represent automatic stages in an inevitable increase. And this increase, while related to that observed in other departments, has nothing to do with the size— or even the existence—of the Empire. What are the percentages

of increase? We must ignore, for this purpose, the rapid increase
in staff which accompanied the diminution of responsibility
during World War II. We should note rather the peacetime rates
of increase over 5.24 percent between 1935 and 1939, and 6.55
percent between 1947 and 1954. This gives an average increase
of 5.89 percent each year, a percentage markedly similar to that
already found in the Admiralty staff increase between 1914 and
1928.

Further and detailed statistical analysis of departmental staffs
would be inappropriate in such an article as this. It is hoped,
however, to reach a tentative conclusion regarding the time likely
to elapse between a given official's first appointment and the
later appointment of his two or more assistants. Dealing with
the problem of pure staff accumulation, all the researches so far
completed point to an average increase of about 5¾ percent per
year. This fact established, it now becomes possible to state
Parkinson's Law in mathematical form, thus:

In any public administrative department not actually at war
the staff increase may be expected to follow this formula:

$$x = \frac{2k^m + p}{n}$$

where k is the number of staff seeking promotion through the
appointment of subordinates; p represents the difference between
the ages of appointment and retirement; m is the number of man-
hours devoted to answering minutes within the department; and
n is the number of effective units being administered. Then x
will be the number of new staff required each year.

Mathematicians will, of course, realize that to find the percentage increase they must multiply x by 100 and divide by the
total of the previous year, thus:

$$\frac{100 \, (2k^m + p)}{yn} \%$$

where y represents the total original staff. And this figure will
invariably prove to be between 5.17 percent and 6.56 percent,
irrespective of any variation in the amount of work (if any) to be
done.

The discovery of this formula and of the general principles upon which it is based has, of course, no emotive value. No attempt has been made to inquire whether departments ought to grow in size. Those who hold that this growth is essential to gain full employment are fully entitled to their opinion. Those who doubt the stability of an economy based upon reading each other's minutes are equally entitled to theirs. Parkinson's Law is a purely scientific discovery, inapplicable except in theory to the politics of the day. It is not the business of the botanist to eradicate the weeds. Enough for him if he can tell us just how fast they grow.

Part Two

Cost and Demand

MANAGERIAL economics is concerned with the application of economic concepts and economic analysis to the problem of formulating rational managerial decisions. The essays in Part Two describe some of these basic economic concepts and techniques and illustrate how they can be useful to the manager. Although the concepts are elementary, they often turn out to be important in pointing up fundamental ways of viewing problems and in showing the way to well-reasoned conclusions.

The papers in Part Two deal with costs and demand. Neil E. Harlan, Charles J. Christenson, and Richard F. Vancil, like Eugene Grant in Part One, are concerned with the proper measurement of the costs of alternative courses of action. Using a hypothetical case, they describe the different cost concepts used by accountants and economists, and conclude that the economist's notion of opportunity cost is more appropriate for decision-making than the accountant's notion of acquisition cost. The following paper, an article from *Business Week*, describes how Continental Air Lines has used marginal analysis to increase its profits. Joel Dean also contrasts accounting and economic concepts but places his emphasis on profits rather than costs. Focusing on the meaning of depreciation, the treatment of capital gains, and the valuation of assets, he concludes that, for purposes of managerial decision-making, a profit statement based on economic concepts is more useful than one based on the conventions of fiscal accounting. His paper is followed by one taken from *Fortune* which describes the break-even chart, the diagram that projects a firm's revenues and costs at various levels of sales. To illustrate its use, two hypothetical cases are taken up.

The next three papers are concerned with demand and pricing. One of the first things a firm must consider in pricing its product is the price elasticity of demand. The editor's paper discusses the nature and determinants of this elasticity and describes why it is of major importance. Joel Dean's paper suggests various ways in which the firm can estimate the price elasticity of demand, using controlled experiments, consumer questionnaires, engineering estimates, and correlation analyses. He describes in some detail a study of this sort done for a large New York department store. Then A. D. H. Kaplan, Joel B. Dirlam, and Robert F. Lanzillotti show how a firm's pricing policy is influenced by the character of its product—the type of demand to which it caters, its physical attributes, production requirements, amenability to differentiation, and stage of maturity.

Cost Analysis

Neil E. Harlan,
Charles J. Christenson,
and Richard F. Vancil

Neil Harlan is Professor of Business Administration at Harvard University. In 1962 he, together with Charles Christenson and Richard Vancil, wrote Managerial Economics, *from which the following article is taken.*

Why is cost analysis so important in making business decisions? The answer lies in the objectives of the business enterprise and in the way its accomplishments are measured in our economy.

In a narrow, simplified sense it might be said that business administration consists of the twin tasks of (1) allocating resources among alternative uses and (2) supervising the activities of people to insure that the resources are efficiently utilized toward achieving the assigned goals. While there is nothing wrong with this definition as a theoretical concept, it glosses over the uncertainties of the complex world of business. Business administration is an art. While there have been rapid advances in scientific, professional management during the last half-century, successful business administration still requires an intangible ability best described as *skill*.

The success of a commercial enterprise in allocating its resources effectively is usually measured by the profit it earns, and

31

a primary goal of most firms is, therefore, to earn a profit, either the maximum possible profit or a satisfactory profit consistent with other goals of the firm. But what is profit? Both the accountant and the economist use this word to mean the difference between the revenues earned from the sale of goods and services and the costs incurred in earning these revenues. Yet, despite this agreement on the basic concept of profit, the accountant and the economist would generally disagree if each were asked to measure the profit of a particular business enterprise.

The disagreement would arise primarily because of a difference between the accounting concept and the economic concept of cost, Even here, however, there is an element of agreement: both the accountant and the economist consider cost as a measurement in monetary terms of the resources consumed by the firm in producing its revenue. The accountant usually measures the *acquisition cost* of these resources, in the sense of the money amount which the firm had to pay when it initially acquired the resources. The economist, in contrast, thinks in terms of the *opportunity cost* of the resources. The opportunity cost of devoting a resource to a particular use is the return that the resource could earn in its best alternative use. The economist's concept of cost, therefore, involves an explicit recognition of the problem of choice faced by the businessman in the utilization of resources.

Opportunity cost may be either greater or less than acquisition cost. Suppose, for example, that a firm is considering the production of an item which would require the use of material on hand for which $100 was originally paid; the acquisition cost, then, is $100. If the material could currently be sold on the market for $125, however, its opportunity cost must be $125, since the use of the material requires the firm to forego the opportunity of receiving $125. If, on the other hand, the material currently has no market value nor any alternative use, its opportunity cost is zero.

The businessman lives with both these concepts of cost. For decision-making purposes, the economist's concept of opportunity cost is the relevant one, since a rational decision must involve the comparison of alternative courses of action. The accountant's role as a "scorekeeper" for outside investors is also important to the businessman. Moreover, accounting records are often a primary source of information for decision-making purposes.

Types of Resources · The basic resource of business is money, or perhaps more precisely, the power that money has in our society to command the primary resources, the labor provided by men and the materials provided by nature. Money by itself is powerless, however, without a manager or entrepreneur to decide how to put it to work. Even then, capital does not become productive until it is exchanged for more tangible resources than imagination: labor, raw materials, and combinations of labor and materials in the form of products manufactured by other business. In the "raw" state, as money, the wise utilization of resources is difficult; it becomes even more difficult once the money resource has been exchanged for a wide variety of heterogeneous resources, each with a specialized productive capability.

An operating business possesses a variety of resources in addition to money: a building which is adaptable to a greater or lesser variety of uses, equipment which can be used to produce a range of products with varying degrees of efficiency, and employees whose productive skills may embrace a broad spectrum. At first glance, the problem of allocating physical resources might not seem vastly different from that of allocating money. All of these resources have been purchased with money, and their values can be measured in monetary terms. Why, then, did Henry J. Kaiser, a man with adequate capital resources and a reputation as an efficient shipbuilder during World War II, fail in his attempt to establish a new line of passenger cars in the late 1940's? It is not an easy task to convert raw capital into an efficient combination of productive resources. And the converse is also true: It is very difficult to measure the value of an existing set of productive resources in monetary terms.

In the "long run," money is the basic business resource. But business decisions are made in the short run, and money, the best available common denominator for all resources, is an imperfect yardstick. At the core of the broad problem of resource allocation, therefore, is the problem of measurement. Actually, the measurement problem can usefully be broken into two parts for purposes of analysis: (1) what types of resources will be required in order to carry out each course of action being considered? and (2) what is the value (or cost) of the combination of resources required for each alternative?

Classification of Problems · As a practical matter, businessmen rarely refer to their problems as problems in resource allocation. Rather, they say, "I've got a make-or-buy problem," or a "capital expenditure problem," or a "lease-or-buy problem," or a "pricing problem," and so forth. This "specific problem" orientation is not necessarily due to a failure to recognize the resource allocation characteristic of the problem, it is simply an attempt to find a practical way to begin the analysis that will eventually lead to a decision.

Dividing business decisions into problem categories has two advantages:

1. From his prior experience with similar problems in the past, the businessman may have observed the kinds of resources that typically are involved in the evaluation of alternatives, and may be familiar with some of the most common problems in measuring the cost of the resources required. Categorizing the problem facilitates making maximum use of this experience.

2. Some types of problems may be best resolved using analytical techniques that have been developed specifically for that class of problems. Identifying the type of problem thus serves also to identify the techniques which may aid in the solution.

There is a danger, too, in the classification of business problems: the danger of a closed mind that can only follow familiar decision patterns used in the past rather than searching imaginatively for new and better ways to grapple with the problems of today and tomorrow.

FORMULATING THE PROBLEM

In order to illustrate some of the most common problems of cost analysis, let us examine the decision process in a simple example. The Webber Company manufactures industrial equipment in a small plant with fifty employees. A recent increase in orders has taxed the one-shift capacity of the plant, and management can see that the company will fail to meet its delivery schedules unless some action is taken. What should be done?

The first step in analyzing this problem, and the most important step by far, is to determine the alternative courses of action that might solve the problem. The list is longer than one might first suppose. There are three main types of actions which might be taken: restricting the quantity sold to the present capacity of the plant; increasing the plant capacity on a permanent or semipermanent basis; or increasing capacity on a temporary basis. Under each of these broad headings, further actions can be identified, as the list below demonstrates.

1. Restricting the quantity sold by:
   (*a*) Refusing to accept orders in excess of present plant capacity.
   (*b*) Accepting all orders and apologizing to customers when deliveries are late.
   (*c*) Raising prices enough to reduce volume of orders down to present plant capacity.
2. Increasing plant capacity by:
   (*a*) Building an addition to the present plant.
   (*b*) Operating the present plant on two shifts.
3. Providing temporary capacity by:
   (*a*) Using overtime.
   (*b*) Buying some components from another manufacturer rather than making them.

This initial stage of formulating the problem is vital to wise decision making. It is a waste of time to do a careful analysis of three alternatives and to select the best of the three if a fourth course of action which is far better is completely overlooked. Analysis is no substitute for imagination. A few extra minutes devoted exclusively to the preparation of an exhaustive list of alternatives will nearly always be time well spent.

So that the exhaustive list does not become exhausting, the next (and sometimes simultaneous) step in problem formulation is to select those alternatives that merit further investigation. Several alternatives on Webber Company's list may be eliminated in this screening process. Items 1(*a*) and 1(*c*) would have the effect of reducing the demands placed on the factory. If the company had long-run growth in sales volume as one of its objectives, these two actions might be rejected as incompatible with the goal. Even if the company's only goal were "maximization of long-run profits" (as we will usually assume, in the absence of a specific statement of goals), alternative 1(*a*) is not acceptable if the additional product could be produced profitably. The profit effect of raising prices is more difficult to assess. Let us simply assume that we are interested in determining the best course of action at the present price in order to compare it with the results obtainable at a higher price.

Alternative 1(*b*) might appear attractive as a method of accepting the available orders without incurring additional production costs. Evaluation of this alternative should, however, recognize that it involves the consumption of an intangible business resource, customer "goodwill." Depending upon competition and normal trade practices in Webber's industry, it may be that stretching out of delivery schedules is the best solution to the problem. In most industries, however, this practice might be a costly one, and we will eliminate it from further consideration here.

The remaining four alternatives are ways to provide increased production in order to meet the increased demand. It is difficult to reject any of these solutions based only on a cursory analysis. It may be useful, however, to realize that there are major differences in type and magnitude of the resources required for each course of action. Expanding the plant or adding a second shift will cause significant changes in Webber's fixed costs as well as in its productive capacity. Even a second shift is a semipermanent action that involves hiring new supervisors as well as laborers, and may require a heavy expenditure of the vital *management* resource. Neither of these two actions would be wise unless Webber's management believed that the increase in demand was a relatively permanent one.

As a temporary solution to their problem, therefore, Webber's management might decide to narrow their analysis to a choice between alternatives 3(*a*) and 3(*b*), the use of overtime in the plant or the purchase of some components from outside vendors. The selection of either of these solutions can easily be changed in the future, and a few months from now management may be in a better position to assess the permanence of the current spurt in demand.

The final stage in formulating the problem is now at hand. How shall we evaluate the alternatives that we have decided to examine? What is the criterion on which we shall make our decision? A careful restatement of the problem at this point may help us to see the best way to point our subsequent analysis. It is little help at this point to say that we have a problem in resource allocation. It may be of more use to define the problem as "fulfilling our production requirements while minimizing the consumption of our resources." The businessman would say simply, "Which parts, if any, would it be cheaper to buy outside?"

In situations such as this where the decision has no revenue implications (we have already decided to accept all orders and deliver them on time), the best course of action is the one that costs the least. Realizing that we are equating "cost" with "resource consumption," therefore, we may say that our decision rule will be to choose the "least cost" alternative, and may then turn our attention to measuring the cost of pursuing each course of action.

RELEVANT COSTS

Before we can begin a detailed analysis, we need a more precise statement of the alternatives. For this purpose, we will assume that the anticipated capacity problem will arise only in the machining department of the Webber Company. Normally this department does the machining of all the component parts in the Webber product. Most of the parts are produced in small lots and require specialized skills not possessed by many outside vendors. Two parts, however, are produced in rather large quantities and the machining operations on them are routine. Clearly these parts are the best candidates for outside purchase. If they were purchased outside, the machining department would have no trouble making all the remaining components on schedule.

Having identified the alternatives, we must next determine the resources required to execute them. According to engineering estimates, the production of one unit of Part A requires raw materials costing $3.00 and a half hour of the time of a machine operator, while the production of one unit of Part B requires $8.00 of raw materials and one hour of operator time. The purchasing agent, after checking with several vendors, informs us that the Smithy Corporation, a reliable source, will deliver Part A for $4.50 each and Part B for $11.50 each.

The next step is to determine the cost of the resources required.

Earlier we referred to the different cost concepts used by accountants and economists and we argued that the economist's notion of opportunity cost is more appropriate for decision making than the accountant's notion of acquisition cost. Accounting records provide a useful source of cost data, however, and so we will begin by presenting the costs of the alternatives to the Webber Company as its accountants might prepare them; then we will indicate how these accounting costs must be analyzed and modified to reflect opportunity costs.

Accounting Costs · After being supplied with the list of resources required as given above, the accounting department of the Webber Company provides the following schedule of manufacturing costs:

| | Cost per Unit | |
	Part A	Part B
Prime Cost:		
Raw materials	$3.00	$ 8.00
Direct labor @ $2.00/hour	1.00	2.00
Total prime costs	$4.00	$10.00
Factory overhead @ 100% of labor	1.00	2.00
Normal manufacturing cost	$5.00	$12.00
Overtime premium @ 50% of labor	0.50	1.00
Overtime manufacturing cost	$5.50	$13.00

The accounting department explains its calculations as follows. The purchase of raw materials is, of course, a direct out-of-pocket cost. The machine operators are paid $2.00 per hour and this rate is applied to the time requirements to arrive at the direct labor cost. The total of raw materials and direct labor costs, representing the cost of resources directly consumed in the manufacture of the parts, is called *prime cost*.

Production of the parts would also require the use of certain common resources of the company: plant, equipment, supervision, and the like. The acquisition costs of these resources, called *overhead costs*, allocated to the machining department are given in Exhibit 1. Since total allocated overhead costs are equal to total direct labor costs, a charge of 100 percent of direct labor is made to cover these overhead costs. Finally, if work were done on overtime, an additional cost of 50 percent of direct labor would be incurred for overtime premium pay.

EXHIBIT 1
WEBBER COMPANY
MONTHLY BUDGET FOR MACHINING DEPARTMENT

Direct labor (2,000 hours @ $2.00)		$4,000
Overhead:	Indirect labor—materials handling	$ 300
	Department foreman	400
	Payroll taxes, vacation and holiday pay, pension contributions, and other fringe benefits	900
	Heat, light, and power	250
	Shop supplies	150
	Depreciation of machinery	800
	Repairs and maintenance—machinery	600
	Allocated share of plant-wide costs (superintendent, building depreciation and maintenance, property taxes and insurance, watchman, etc.)	600
	Total overhead	$4,000

If we look at accounting costs, therefore, both parts are apparently cheaper to buy from Smithy than to produce in our own plant—even ignoring the premium paid for overtime work! But we must take a closer look at the behavior of manufacturing costs.

Another classification of manufacturing costs often used by accountants is into *direct costs* and *fixed costs*. This classification is a little closer to the economist's way of thinking about costs. Direct costs include those which vary at least approximately in proportion to the quantity of production. Prime costs are usually direct costs, but not all direct costs are prime costs: some overhead costs may also vary with production. Analysis of the overhead costs listed in Exhibit 1, for example, might reveal the following facts about the behavior of overhead costs under two circumstances: (*a*) at present volume if one man is laid off and parts are purchased outside; (*b*) at the anticipated increased volume, if overtime is used.

1. *Indirect Labor.* One man is employed as a materials handler in the department. If a machinist were laid off there would be no saving in the wages paid to this man; he would just be a little less busy. If the department worked overtime, however, the materials handling function would have to be performed by someone, either the machinist himself (thereby lowering his productive efficiency) or by the materials handler also working overtime.

2. *Department Foreman.* This cost probably would not vary with either a small decrease or small increase in production. The

machining work to be performed on overtime might not require the presence of a supervisor; if it did, the overtime paid to the supervisor would be relevant.

3. *Payroll Taxes, etc.* These costs amount to nearly 20 percent of Webber's expenses for labor and supervision. If a man were laid off, the entire 20 percent might be saved. There would be some increase in these costs on overtime, but the workers would not get more holidays or longer vacations. The variable portion, using overtime, might be 10 percent of the labor cost.

4. *Heat, Light, Power, and Shop Supplies.* These costs are difficult to analyze. There might be an insignificant saving in power if one machine were shut down. On overtime, additional power and light would be required.

5. *Depreciation.* This cost is not a cash expenditure but a pro rata portion of the original cost of the equipment. This cost, caused simply by the passage of time, will not be changed by management's decision to either lay off a man or use overtime.

6. *Repairs and Maintenance.* This expense is made up of two components: routine, preventive maintenance and the repair of breakdowns. The former is the larger expense, and might be reduced somewhat if one machine were shut down completely. The latter probably bears some relationship to the volume of work put through the equipment and would vary for either a decrease or increase in production.

7. *Allocated Plant Costs.* These overhead costs occur at the next higher level in the company, and would not change as a result of a minor change in production volume in the department.

We may now recapitulate the results of our analysis. Direct labor seems to be a useful measure of volume in this department because each man operates one machine and costs that vary in relation to machine utilization will also vary with labor costs. In Exhibit 2, therefore, we have computed the direct overhead cost for each of the two circumstances mentioned above (laying off one man or using overtime).

How variable are overhead costs? The preceding analysis illustrates how difficult it is to answer that question in a practical way. It seems safe to say that overhead is not completely variable, as might be inferred from the accountant's allocation mechanism. Saving $1.00 in labor cost will not save $1.00 in overhead in the machining department. But any further general statement about overhead variability is useless. For decision-making purposes, the most useful answer is one based on an analysis of the specific cost items in the specific situation in which a specific decision is

EXHIBIT 2

WEBBER COMPANY

Overhead Cost Analysis

Overhead Item	Monthly budget cost		Variable cost as a % of direct labor cost changes if	
	Amount	% of direct labor	one man laid off	overtime used
Indirect labor—materials handler	$ 300	7.5%	...	7.5%
Department foreman	400	10.0	...	...
Payroll taxes, etc..............	900	22.5 *	19.1%	10.8
Heat, light, and power........	250	6.2	1.0	2.0
Shop supplies	150	3.8	...	...
Depreciation of machinery	800	20.0	...	...
Repairs and maintenance......	600	15.0	12.0	5.0
Allocated plant costs.........	600	15.0	...	...
Total	$4,000	100.0%	32.1%	25.3%

* Stated as a percentage of total departmental payroll, this cost is $\frac{900}{4,700}$ = 19.1%. On overtime, it is estimated here that direct payroll taxes would be 10% of wage costs, but would also apply to the materials handler (10% of 7.5%).

to be made. Fortunately, it is possible to gain skill in this kind of analysis, with a concomitant reduction in the analytical time required. This is a skill worth developing, because reliance on rules of thumb or general cost variability classifications is a poor, and sometimes dangerous, substitute for such skill.

Opportunity Costs · The accountant measures the cost of resources consumed in terms of the outlay originally made to acquire them. The economist, in contrast, measures their cost in relation to alternative opportunities for their employment. Let us see how these two concepts differ in the Webber Company example.

On some costs, the accountant and the economist would agree. This would probably be true, for example, of the cost of buying the parts from the Smithy Corporation or the cost of the raw materials if the parts are manufactured. In these cases, the foregone opportunity is to refrain from buying the parts or the raw material, so that the opportunity cost and the acquisition cost would be identical.

It might seem, in fact, that opportunity cost is identical with the accounting concept of direct cost. While there is a close relationship between opportunity cost and direct cost and while they are often identical, there are important differences which must be borne in mind.

We can illustrate this point using the direct labor cost in the company example. The company employs eleven machinists in the machining department; approximately 2,000 hours of production labor are available each month. Before the company's anticipated sales volume increase, these men spent about 1,550 hours per month on machining the special, low-volume parts and used the balance of their time, as available, to turn out Parts A and B. Forgetting for the moment about the increase in volume, how would you decide whether or not to have Parts A and B made by Smithy? Are the labor costs true opportunity costs? The answer depends on what action Webber's management would take if the parts were purchased outside. A total of 450 labor hours could be saved. Would two and one-half machinists be laid off? Such action might mean reducing the range of skills now available in an eleven-man force, and might cause morale problems for the man working a short week. If, in fact, only one man would be laid off, then we should not say that the entire labor cost used in producing the parts is an opportunity cost of the parts. The relevant cost in this situation is the *total* amount of money that will be spent for labor under each course of action. If labor costs $2.00 per hour, the cost would be $4,000 if both parts are manufactured inside, and about $3,660 if one man is laid off and some parts were purchased. Although Webber's accountant would say that $900 is spent each month on machining labor for Parts A and B, the *opportunity cost* of that labor is only $340. The other $560 is spent primarily to maintain a balanced labor force with the necessary variety of skills—skills that may be a vital resource in Webber's overall success.

On the other hand, now that the demand for Webber's product is expected to increase, what is the relevant labor cost in deciding whether to use overtime to meet the requirements? With a 10 percent increase in demand, 1,705 hours per month are needed for low-volume parts and 495 hours of machining are needed for Parts A and B. Hiring a twelfth man might provide most of the 200 extra hours needed, but there is no room in the plant for another machine. If overtime is used, the additional labor will cost $3.00 per hour, or $600. This cost is relevant to the decision because its expenditure depends upon the course of action management selects.

Even in the relatively simple case of direct labor, therefore, opportunity cost is not necessarily identical with direct cost. In the example just considered, opportunity cost was less than direct cost, but the reverse could also be true, as we will demonstrate shortly. While the acquisition cost of fixed resources (i.e., accounting fixed overhead) is neither a direct cost nor an opportunity cost, there may be an opportunity cost associated with employing these facilities in one use rather than in an alternative. This opportunity cost is relevant in making decisions regarding the use of the fixed resources although it is not an acquisition cost.

Opportunity cost, then, depends upon the context of a particular decision whereas direct cost does not. The two concepts are similar enough to create both an advantage and a danger: an advantage in that direct cost can often be used to estimate opportunity cost, a danger in that this process can be carried farther than appropriate.

COMPARISON OF ALTERNATIVES

After the problem has been formulated and the relevant costs determined, the next step in the analysis of a decision problem is to recapitulate the results of our analysis to determine which alternative is least costly. If the problem has been formulated properly and the cost analysis done systematically, this ranking task is a simple one. Illustrative calculations for the Webber Company's make-or-buy decisions are shown in Exhibits 3 and 4.

Exhibit 3 is an evaluation of the alternatives that faced Webber under its "normal" demand conditions, i.e., before the anticipated increase in demand. As a result of our analysis, the most promising alternatives have now been more sharply defined. Only one man would be laid off if any parts were purchased outside, eliminating 170 labor hours per month. If this were done, Webber would then have to buy outside either 340 units of A or 170 units of B. In terms of total costs, the best alternative is to continue to manufacture all our requirements inside. The only difficult cost calculation is the overhead cost. If all parts were made inside, the labor and overhead budgets would be unchanged at $4,000 each per month. If one man were laid off, labor cost would decline by $340 and the overhead budget would fall by 32.1 percent of that amount (Exhibit 2).

An alternative analysis in Exhibit 3 arrives at the same conclusion in terms of opportunity costs. According to the cost accountant's statement on page 31, the "normal" cost of one unit of Part A was $5.00. We have seen that this figure is not useful

EXHIBIT 3

WEBBER COMPANY

MAKE-OR-BUY ANALYSIS

CONDITION NO. 1: NORMAL DEMAND

	Make 500 units of A and 200 of B	Lay off one machinist and	
		Buy 340 units of A	Buy 170 units of B
Raw material costs:			
Part A	$ 1,500	$ 480	$ 1,500
Part B	1,600	1,600	240
Purchased parts	. . .	1,530	1,955
Direct labor	4,000	3,660	3,660
Overhead costs	4,000	3,891	3,891
	$11,100	$11,161	$11,246

ALTERNATIVE ANALYSIS

	Opportunity cost of manufacturing	
	Part A	Part B
Raw material costs.........................	$ 3.00	$ 8.00
Direct labor—one man.....................	1.00	2.00
Overhead at 32.1% of labor.................	0.32	0.64
Total opportunity cost...................	$ 4.32	$ 10.64
Purchase price	4.50	11.50
Saving due to manufacturing..............	$ 0.18	$ 0.86
Number of units produced in 170 hours........	340	170
Total savings	$61.00	$146.00

for decision-making purposes; we are interested in the opportunity cost of manufacturing Part A. To measure opportunity cost, we must answer the question, "What costs (resources) will be saved if the parts are purchased outside?" For Part A, we will save $3.00 of raw material for each unit, the labor cost of one man divided by the units he could produce, and approximately 32 percent in overhead costs related to labor. What costs (resources) will be required to achieve those savings? Part A must be purchased at a price of $4.50 each. The savings are less than the additional cost, indicating that outside purchase is not the cheapest course of action. It is no coincidence that the total saving due to manufacturing is equal to the difference in the total costs of the alternatives as computed in the upper part of Exhibit 3.

Exhibit 4 is a similar set of calculations after a 10 percent increase in demand. The overhead cost increase of $138 was computed in two stages as follows: Variable overhead was estimated as 25.3 percent of labor in Exhibit 2, and this percentage was applied to the $400 straight time cost of the added labor. In addition, indirect labor and payroll taxes (18.3 percent of labor) would vary as a function of cost (not time), so that percentage was applied to the $200 of overtime premium pay. The best alternative is to buy 400 units per month of Part A rather than to use overtime.

We have said that most decision problems are basically problems in resource allocation. Cost analysis is used to solve these problems because money is the best common denominator for resources, and because money is the basic "scarce resource" which the business would like to utilize in an optimal fashion. In the Webber Company's overtime decision it is useful to conceive of the problem somewhat differently. The company has 2,000 hours of machining capacity available, and our analysis in Exhibit 3 has shown that this capacity should not be reduced. As demand increases, Webber's real question is, "How should the 2,000 hours be allocated among the available jobs?" The special, low-volume parts are of first priority, and require 1,705 of the available hours. The remaining 295 hours should be used in such a way as to maximize their value to Webber.

EXHIBIT 4

WEBBER COMPANY

MAKE-OR-BUY ANALYSIS

CONDITION NO. 2: INCREASED DEMAND

	Use 200 hours of overtime; make 550 units of A and 200 units of B	*Use no overtime and buy 400 units of A*	*buy 200 units of B*
Raw material costs:			
Part *A*	$ 1,650	$ 450	$ 1,650
Part *B*	1,760	1,760	160
Purchased parts	...	1,800	2,300
Direct labor—straight time	4,400	4,000	4,000
Overhead costs	4,000	4,000	4,000
Overtime premium	200	....	....
Overhead costs applied to premium pay	138	....	....
Total cost	$12,148	$12,010	$12,110

ALTERNATIVE ANALYSIS

	Opportunity cost of manufacturing	
	Part A	*Part B*
Raw material costs	$ 3.00	$ 8.00
Direct labor—200 hours	1.00	2.00
Overhead at 25.3% of labor	0.25	0.51
Overtime premium	0.50	1.00
Overhead at 18.3% of premium	0.09	0.18
Total opportunity cost	$ 4.84	$11.69
Purchase price	4.50	11.50
Saving due to purchase	$ 0.34	$ 0.19
Number of units produced in 200 hours	400	200
Total savings from purchase	$138.00	$38.00

In Exhibit 5 we have computed the contribution per labor hour that would be earned by using the available hours to manufacture Part A or Part B. Labor and its related overhead costs are ignored in this calculation since these costs will not change as a result of our decision. They are part of the fixed resources we desire to allocate optimally. We will spend a total of $4,000 for labor and $4,000 for overhead; our decision is to determine *how* to use this capacity. Additional cash resources are required only

EXHIBIT 5

WEBBER COMPANY

CALCULATION OF CONTRIBUTION PER LABOR HOUR

Hours available:

Total	2,000
Required for low-volume, special parts........	1,705
Available for Parts A or B..................	295

	Part A	Part B
Purchase price per unit......................	$ 4.50	$11.50
Raw material cost per unit...................	3.00	8.00
Materials savings per unit...................	$ 1.50	$ 3.50
Number of units produced per labor hour.....	2	1
Contribution per labor hour..................	$ 3.00	$ 3.50

Cost of adding additional labor hours:

Labor per hour.....................	$2.00		
Overhead at 25.3%..................	0.51		
Overtime premium per hour...........	1.00		
Overhead at 18.3% of premium........	0.18		
Total cost	$3.69	3.69	3.69
Excess cost per hour of making rather than buying		$ 0.69	$ 0.19
Total excess cost for 200 hours............		$138.00	$38.00

for materials. For every unit of Part A manufactured we will pay only $3.00 for materials rather than $4.50 for the completed part, a saving of $1.50 per unit or $3.00 per labor hour. Manufacturing Part B is even more attractive because we will save $3.50 per labor hour. In order to get maximum value from our scarce resource (capacity), we should manufacture all of our requirements of Part B before we use any of the capacity to manufacture Part A.

Next, we must decide whether it would be worthwhile to buy additional capacity by using overtime. The cost of adding capacity is $3.69 per hour (Exhibit 5). Since this cost exceeds the contribution earned by the labor hours, the use of overtime is not warranted. The last calculation on Exhibit 5 is proof that this method of analysis is consistent with the two methods shown in Exhibit 4.

Optimal allocation of scarce resources is a primary task of the businessman. The Webber Company example is a simple illustration of what is involved in this task.

An Airline Takes the Marginal Route

BUSINESS WEEK

This article is from Business Week, *April 20,1963.*

Continental Air Lines, Inc. filled only half the available seats on its Boeing 707 jet flights in 1962, a record some fifteen percentage points worse than the national average.

By eliminating just a few runs—less than 5 percent—Continental could have raised its average load considerably. Some of its flights frequently carry as few as thirty passengers on the 120-seat plane. But the improved load factor would have meant reduced profits.

For Continental bolsters its corporate profits by deliberately running extra flights that aren't expected to do more than return their out-of-pocket costs—plus a little profit. Such marginal flights are an integral part of the over-all operating philosophy that has brought small, Denver-based Continental—tenth among the eleven trunk carriers—through the bumpy postwar period with only one loss year.

This philosophy leans heavily on marginal analysis. And the line leans heavily on Chris F. Whelan, vice-president in charge of economic planning, to translate marginalism into hard, dollars-and-cents decisions.

Getting management to accept and apply the marginal concept probably is the chief contribution any economist can make to his company. Put most simply, marginalists maintain that a company should undertake any activity that adds more to revenues than it does to costs—and not limit itself to those activities whose returns equal average or "fully allocated" costs.

The approach, of course, can be applied to virtually any business, not just to air transportation. It can be used in consumer finance, for instance, where the question may be whether to make more loans—including more bad loans—if this will increase net profit. Similarly, in advertising, the decision may rest on how much extra business a dollar's worth of additional advertising will bring in, rather than pegging the advertising budget to a percentage of sales—and, in insurance, where setting high interest rates to discourage policy loans may actually damage profits by causing policyholders to borrow elsewhere.

Whelan finds all such cases wholly analogous to his run of problems, where he seeks to keep his company's eye trained on the big objective: net profit.

Last summer, Whelan politely chewed out a group of operational researchers at an international conference in Rome for being incomprehensible. "You have failed to educate the users of your talents to the potential you offer," he said. "Your studies, analyses, and reports are couched in tables that sales, operations, and maintenance personnel cannot comprehend."

Whelan's work is a concrete example of the truth in a crack by Prof. Sidney Alexander of MIT—formerly economist for Columbia Broadcasting System—that the economist who understands marginal analysis has a "full-time job in undoing the work of the accountant." This is so, Alexander holds, because the practices of accountants—and of most businesses—are permeated with cost allocation directed at average, rather than marginal, costs.

In any complex business, there's likely to be a big difference between the costs of each company activity as it's carried on the accounting books and the marginal or "true" costs that can determine whether or not the activity should be undertaken.

The difficulty comes in applying the simple "textbook" marginal concept to specific decisions. If the economist is unwilling to make some bold simplifications, the job of determining "true" marginal costs may be highly complex, time-wasting, and too expensive. But even a rough application of marginal principles may come closer to the right answer for business decision-makers than an analysis based on precise average-cost data.

Proving that this is so demands economists who can break the crust of corporate habits and show concretely why the typical manager's response—that nobody ever made a profit without meeting all costs—is misleading and can reduce profits. To be sure, the whole business cannot make a profit unless average costs are met; but covering average costs should not determine whether any particular activity should be undertaken. For this would unduly restrict corporate decisions and cause managements to forego opportunities for extra gains.

Management overhead at Continental is pared to the bone, so Whelan often is thrown such diverse problems as soothing a ruffled city council or planning the specifications for the plane the line will want to fly in 1970. But the biggest slice of his time goes to schedule planning—and it is here that the marginal concept comes most sharply into focus.

Whelan's approach is this: He considers that the bulk of his scheduled flights have to return at least their fully allocated costs. Overhead, depreciation, insurance are very real expenses and must be covered. The out-of-pocket approach comes into play, says Whelan, only after the line's basic schedule has been set.

"Then you go a step farther," he says, and see if adding more flights will contribute to the corporate net. Similarly, if he's thinking of dropping a flight with a disappointing record, he puts it under the marginal microscope: "If your revenues are going to be more than your out-of-pocket costs, you should keep the flight on."

By "out-of-pocket costs" Whelan means just that: the actual dollars that Continental has to pay out to run a flight. He gets the figure not by applying hypothetical equations but by circulating a proposed schedule to every operating department concerned and finding out just what extra expenses it will entail. If a ground crew already on duty can service the plane, the flight isn't charged a penny of their salary expense. There may even be some costs eliminated in running the flight; they won't need men to roll the plane to a hangar, for instance, if it flies on to another stop.

Most of these extra flights, of course, are run at off-beat hours, mainly late at night. At times, though, Continental discovers that the hours aren't so unpopular after all. A pair of night coach flights on the Houston–San Antonio–El Paso–Phoenix–Los Angeles leg, added on a marginal basis, have turned out to be so successful that they are now more than covering fully allocated costs.

In conclusion, here is the relevant marginal analysis in a nutshell:

Problem: Shall Continental run an extra daily flight from City X to City Y?

The facts: Fully-allocated costs of this flight $4,500

Out-of-pocket costs of this flight $2,000

Flight should gross $3,100

Decision: Run the flight. It will add $1,100 to net profit—because it will add $3,100 to revenues and only $2,000 to costs. Overhead and other costs, totaling $2,500 ($4,500 minus $2,000), would be incurred whether the flight is run or not. Therefore, fully-allocated or "average" costs of $4,500 are not relevant to this business decision. It's the out-of-pocket or "marginal" costs that count.

The Measurement of Profits

JOEL DEAN

Joel Dean is Professor of Business Economics at Columbia University's Graduate School of Business. This paper is taken from the Accounting Review.

Profits must be measured differently for different purposes, and the kind of measurement that is needed for many executive decisions is not provided by the conventional income statement. The Bureau of Internal Revenue, the stockholders, and the banks, all want special kinds of information, and generally have custom-made income statements designed to fit their requirements. Management also has peculiar demands to make of income analysis in reaching executive decisions; and the profit statement used by executives to run a business generally conforms more closely to the concepts of economic analysis than to the conventions of fiscal reporting. Many executives are unhappy about the kind of income statement produced by conventional accounting methods and feel that decision-making could be raised to a more sophisticated plane by relating income statements more closely to management's purposes.

This article attempts to examine from the managerial standpoint the major issues of profit measurement on which economists and accountants have generally taken different positions. Their most important points of difference center on: (1) the meaning of depreciation; (2) the treatment of capital gains and losses, and perhaps most important in these times (3) the price level basis for valuation of assets (i.e., current vs. historical costs).

DEPRECIATION

Treatment of depreciation is an important instance of this basic conflict. Only in the last fifty years has depreciation been a generally accepted charge against income. As businessmen came to realize that some provision must be made for the future replacement of equipment, some kind of depreciation reserve accounting was needed. The accountants' insistence that the reserve be related to the original cost rather than to the cost of replacement—which is usually quite different—gives depreciation accounting full economic usefulness only under the simplest hypothetical conditions of stable prices and foreseeable obsolescence.

The objective of depreciation in accounting is to allocate the total cost of equipment to production during the period in which it will be used. The effect is to insure that revenues equal to original cost are not distributed as dividends, but are rather put back into assets, such as more equipment or cash. Whether the amount that is thus put out of reach of dividends will actually be enough for replacement is not considered part of this accounting problem. Replacement is viewed by accountants as having no bearing on measurement of profits.

For economists, there are two distinct kinds of depreciation charge. The first is the opportunity cost of equipment, that is, the most profitable alternative use of it that is foregone by putting it to its present use. The alternative involved in using the asset for one year may be viewed as selling it at the beginning instead of the end of the year. The opportunity cost could then be measured by the fall in value of the equipment during the year. This shrinkage in disposal value, which measures the capital-wastage from postponing its disposal for one year, produces a depreciation cost estimate which is quite different from straight-line depreciation for an individual year. For example, it is common to charge as annual depreciation one-fifth of an automobile's original cost. Yet the decline in disposal value during the first year is normally nearer to 40 percent than to 20 percent of original cost. Inherently it has no relation to cost; disposal value rose during some postwar years, producing negative depreciation costs from an economic viewpoint.

The opportunity-cost of depreciation depends upon the nature of the alternative. The alternative may be to keep the equipment idle and save it for later years. Or there may be no alternative uses in other places or times, and thus no real cost of using it in its present function. A hydroelectric dam is perhaps an illustration of this kind of specialized and immobile sunk investment. The economic cost of using the equipment for one year, in any case, has nothing to do with original cost and nothing to do with eventual disposal of the equipment—the two important factors in accounting depreciation.

The second kind of depreciation cost is the exhaustion of a year's worth of limited valuable life. In the case of the dam, where there is no opportunity cost, the future useful life (which measures its unique value to the going concern) is nevertheless continually running out. To preserve owner's capital, enough of the dam's gross earnings must be saved and reinvested to shift capital out of the dam into equally profitable ventures, perhaps a replacement dam. The amount of this kind of economic depreciation is not determined by the historical cost of the equipment. It is better measured by replacement value of equipment that will produce comparable earnings. This kind of depreciation is not a cost; the cost was incurred when capital was originally frozen into the plant. Rather, it is an act of saving, and the amount to charge each year is a financial problem related to past, present, and future patterns of gross earnings, as well as to price level expectations.

Both of these economic concepts of depreciation are important to management. The first, opportunity cost, is needed for operating problems of profit-making, the second, replacement of eroded earnings ability, is needed for financial problems of preserving and administering capital. For neither, however, does original cost play any role in estimates.

TREATMENT OF CAPITAL GAINS AND LOSSES

Capital gains and losses, or "windfalls," as they are often called, may be defined loosely as unanticipated changes in the value of property relative to other real goods. That is, a windfall reflects a change in someone's anticipation of the property's earning power. Fluctuations in stock market prices are almost all of this nature.

"Property" should be interpreted broadly here to include executive ability, organizational structure, brand names, and market connections. All the assets that comprise the value of the firm are vulnerable to windfall changes. For instance, the value of cash deteriorates in inflation; accounts receivable are hit by defaults not allowed for in bad debt reserves; inventory is subject to fire, flood, price drops, and substitute competition; the value of plant facilities is slashed when competitors install new, cost-cutting equipment; and patent protection can be made worthless by a court decision. The list of possibilities is endless.

These are capital losses, which, in a progressive society, are probably larger on balance than capital gains. Many of these risks can be diluted by insurance-type charges, such as surplus reserve appropriations or high depreciation rates. And when conservative managements actually over-insure, the excess eventually appears as capital gains.

A sound accounting policy to follow concerning windfalls is to avoid recording them until they turn into cash by a purchase or sale of assets, since it is never clear until then *exactly* how large they are in dollar terms. Occasionally major write-downs are made when value has apparently been wiped out; but the chastening experience of 1929–1932 has virtually eliminated the practice of write-ups beyond original cost.

How the windfall is reported in financial statements is not a matter of interest to economists (as long as they are explained). They are concerned with the future, not the past. The important thing is that gains and losses usually can be foreseen for some time before they are realized in cash. A fact-minded management must have some sort of balance sheet, if only an estimated one that realizes surprises long before they have become exact enough to be acceptable to accountants. For example, if prices are to be determined with the objective of producing a "reasonable" rate of return on the valuation of investment, they should reflect projectable windfalls even though not yet cashed. Otherwise, a target rate of return based on an historically "factual," but nevertheless fictitious capital value, may lead to later and unpleasant surprises from the resulting price policies.

CURRENT VS. HISTORICAL COSTS

In measuring income, accountants typically state costs in terms of the price level at the time of the purchase, by recording the historical outlay, rather than in terms of the current price level. Various reasons for this have been advanced by accountants: (1) because historical costs produce more accurate measurement of income; (2) because historical costs are less debatable (more objective) than the calculation of present replacement value; (3) because the function of the accountant is to record history whether or not history has relevance for future business or economic problems, but presumably in the hope that it has.

Arguments on historical cost accounting have been going on for decades, but never was the debate more vigorous than during the 1941–1948 inflation. This was an extremely turbulent time: business was scrambling to fill postwar demand and was jockeying for new market positions; there was a rush to get new products on the market; capital expenditures were being made at a tremendous rate. The situation was rich with windfall gains and losses, resulting from the violent changes in demand, supply, and price structure. Management needed the best kind of information to keep track of conditions and to plan astutely. Inflation carried prices to nearly double their level of ten years before; a general revision of ideas was called for on the value of a dollar and the meaning of the older assets on the books. One of the significant by-products of inflation was a bitter controversy among accountants, lawyers, economists, and politicians on the truth or fiction of accounting practice in such a period. The argument was a cross-hatch of speculations on legal and moral obligations to investors, tax liabilities, established accounting traditions, future price levels, and political convenience. Out of the controversy came income statements with a rash of special reserves and footnote explanations, and some extraordinary depreciation treatments.

The implied assumption of most depreciation policies was that we would eventually get back to prewar prices. This assumption seemed quite unreal and irrelevant to most economists, and it was clear that published income statements had only begun to recognize the basic change in the purchasing power of the dollar. With prices on a new high plateau, depreciation charges in terms of prewar prices were carrying only about half the load of financing postwar replacements, and it was almost impossible to determine what part of the capital investment boom was really adding to the nation's productive capacity.

Statistics of corporate earnings were probably gross overstatements of economic earnings, although the amount of the distortion was difficult to estimate. In a period of inflation, cost of living goes up for corporations as well as for persons. The cost of refilling inventories, replacing worn equipment, and expanding capacity all go up. Yet accounting procedures generally fail to take adequate account of these increases. When inventories and depreciation are charged at original costs, rather than at the higher replacement cost, inventory and plant are revalued as they are turned over. Orthodox accounting vigilantly keeps ordinary revaluations from getting into the profit and loss account—by treating them as surplus adjustments. But when revaluations find their way into the accounts indirectly, by the process of turnover of assets during inflation, they *do* get into the earnings account. These revaluation profits are treated as ordinary business income and cannot in the books be distinguished from other income. Hence, accounting profit overstates real business income, not only during an inflation but for some time after prices have reached stability. It is clearly not enough to deflate the reported income figure by dividing money profits by some cost-of-living index after the manner in which real wages are found. Profits are a residual in a calculation that uses dollars of many different dates—today's cash dollars, last year's inventory dollars, and equipment dollars of many years of prosperity and depression. To measure real profits, all these assets must be stated in dollars of the same purchasing power. This is an elaborate operation, and the desirable data on prices, products, and dates are usually hard to estimate. With some expediting assumptions, however, usable approximations can be made.

A Note on Break-even Charts

Fortune MAGAZINE

This article appeared in the February 1949 issue of Fortune.

Essentially, the break-even chart is a graphic presentation of the relationship between revenue and expense, projected for all levels of sales. There is nothing complicated or novel about such a chart. Progressive managements have used this or similar visual aids for years. The break-even chart is no substitute for either detailed accountancy or management judgment.

The basic chart (Chart 1) was developed some forty years ago by Professor Walter Rautenstrauch of the Industrial Engineering Department of Columbia University. It is the great granddaddy of the many sales-profit charts in use today, and is, in some respects, superior to them. The 45-degree sales line makes it possible to plot the break-even points for any number of years or months on a single chart, and to compare charts for different companies, products, etc. A prerequisite to the construction of this or any other break-even chart, however, is a knowledge of which business expenses are constant and which are variable with changes in volume. Once that is known a total-expense line can be drawn for all levels of sales. Few firms customarily break down their costs in this manner, however. Take, for example, the remuneration paid a salesman. Normal accountancy would probably lump his commissions, salary, and bonus together as sales expense. Actually, however, his commission is a variable

CHART 1 FINDING XYZ COMPANY'S BREAK-EVEN POINT

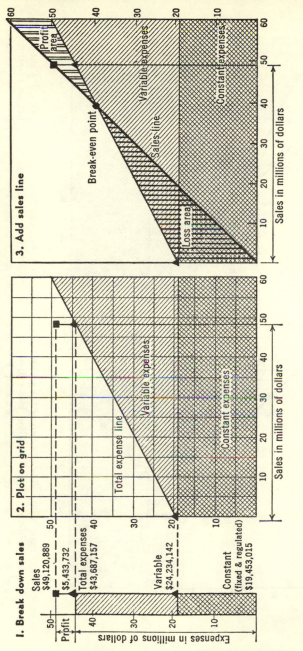

The construction of a break-even chart involves three simple steps. Step 1: Expenses that vary directly with volume (materials, sales commissions, etc.) are segregated from constant expenses (real-estate taxes, depreciation, interest, etc.). Step 2: The total expense line is then plotted on a grid with identical horizontal and vertical dollar scales. Step 3: A sales line is superimposed on this grid forming a 45-degree angle with both scales. That this method of plotting the break-even point is accurate is attested by the fact that the computed break-even volume for the company above (an actual firm) was $38.4 million.

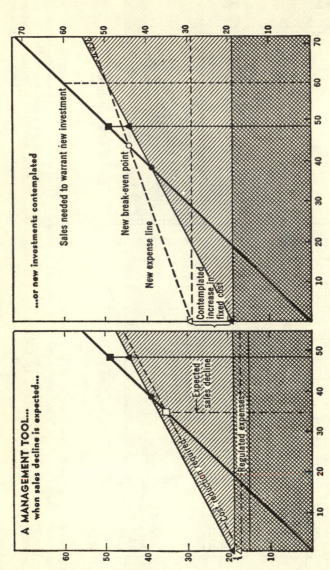

CHART 2

The hypothetical cases above illustrate two of the many ways a break-even chart can be used in management planning. If sales decline $15 million (left) a $4-million loss will result unless costs are cut. If, on the other hand, an investment is contemplated that will increase constant expense by $10 million (right) it can be seen that sales of $60 million are needed to justify the new expense structure.

expense, his salary a constant expense, and his bonus a regulated expense; i.e., although constant in that it is not directly related to sales, it is nevertheless subject to management discretion. The trick of constructing an accurate break-even chart, then, is largely dependent upon proper cost analysis, but that is equally true when the break-even point is computed.

The break-even chart is like a household tape measure. It has many practical uses and yet does not pretend to be microscopically accurate. The total-expense line, for example, is simply a straight line drawn from fixed costs at volume zero through total cost at current volume. No attempt is made at curvilinear refinement because cost figures are themselves mere approximations. Nor can valid deductions be drawn from a break-even chart at volumes widely different from that on which the chart is based. It is important to remember that the chart represents expense at a given moment and under given conditions and that any change in price, wages, *et al.*, will alter the sales-expense relationship. If these limitations are borne in mind, however, the break-even chart can be used to analyze and control costs and to estimate profits under a variety of assumptions.

In Chart 2, the effect of a sales decline or of an additional capital outlay are considered. A decline in sales of $15 million would obviously put the firm into the red unless regulatable expenses (research, promotion, the president's salary, etc.) were cut $4 million. In the other case it is assumed that a contemplated investment will increase constant cost by $10 million but will reduce variable expenses. The chart quickly shows at what volume the new investment becomes profitable. Although these charts are for an entire company, break-even charts can also be constructed for individual departments, plants, products, or even salesmen.

The Importance of the Price Elasticity of Demand

EDWIN MANSFIELD

Edwin Mansfield is Professor of Economics at the Wharton School, University of Pennsylvania. This article was written for the present volume.

The price elasticity of demand is the percentage change in the quantity demanded that results from a 1 percent increase in price. A sharp distinction should be made between an industry's elasticity and a particular firm's elasticity. Whereas the former gauges the sensitivity of total industry demand to industry-wide changes in price, the latter shows the sensitivity of demand for a particular firm's product to changes in its price, the price set by other firms in the industry being held constant. A firm's elasticity depends heavily on the similarity of its product to that of competitors. For instance, a Gulf station is likely to lose a considerable share of its market to a neighboring Esso station whose price is half a cent a gallon less.

The price elasticity of demand is of great importance to the firm. When costs are increasing, it is tempting for the firm to pass on the increases by raising the price to the consumer. If demand for the product is relatively inelastic,[1] this action may succeed.

1. Demand at a particular price is said to be inelastic if the price elasticity is less than one in absolute value. In this case, total revenue decreases with decreases in price.

However, when there are many substitutes and demand is quite elastic,[2] increasing prices may lead to a reduction in total revenues rather than an increase. The result may be lower rather than higher profits. Similarly, businessmen are sometimes surprised by a lack of success of price reductions, this merely being a reflection of the fact that demand is relatively inelastic.

Most businessmen intuitively are aware of the elasticity of demand of the goods they make, although they may not have a detailed, precise estimate. Nonetheless, some firms tend to be conservative and underestimate the elasticity of demand. For example, classical phonograph records were high-priced luxury items for a long time. In 1938, Columbia cut the price per record from $2 to $1, and the response was overwhelming. To the surprise of much of the industry, total expenditure on classical records rose greatly, the price elasticity of demand being relatively large.

Using techniques like those described in "Estimating the Price Elasticity of Demand," it is possible to estimate the price elasticity of demand for a particular product. Some of the results are shown in Table 1. As would be expected, the price elasticity of demand for basic foodstuffs is relatively low. For sugar, potatoes, hay, and wheat, it is less than 0.5 percent in absolute value. That is, a 1 percent increase in the price of these products will result in less than a 0.5 percent decrease in the quantity consumed. On the other hand, the demand for millinery is quite elastic, a 1 percent increase in price leading to a 3 percent decrease in quantity consumed.

One of the most important factors influencing the price elasticity of demand is the availability of substitutes. If a product is faced with extremely close substitutes, its demand will be very elastic. For example, take the case of the Gulf and Esso dealers cited above. Their products, location, and services are so similar that a very small differential in price will result in a considerable shift in sales. On the other hand, in the case of basic foodstuffs such close substitutes do not exist, the result being that the price elasticity of demand is much lower.

2. Demand at a particular price is said to be elastic if the price elasticity is greater than one in absolute value, in which case total revenue increases with decreases in price.

TABLE 1

ESTIMATED PRICE ELASTICITIES OF DEMAND FOR SELECTED
COMMODITIES, UNITED STATES

Product	Price elasticity
beef	—0.92
millinery	—3.00
gasoline	—0.52
sugar	—0.31
corn	—0.49
cotton	—0.12
hay	—0.43
wheat	—0.08
potatoes	—0.31
oats	—0.56
barley	—0.39
buckwheat	—0.99

Source: H. Schultz, *Theory and Measurement of Demand* (Chicago: University of Chicago Press, 1938), and M. Spencer and L. Siegelman, *Managerial Economics* (Homewood, Ill.: Richard D. Irwin, 1959).

Finally, to illustrate very briefly the sorts of studies that have been made of the price elasticity of demand, consider a study of the fare structure of the New York subway and its effect on passenger travel. Table 2 gives forecasts of demand and revenues

TABLE 2

ALTERNATIVE ESTIMATES OF DEMAND CURVE FOR SUBWAY
SERVICE

(passengers and revenues in millions per year)

Fare (cents)	Case A		Case B		Case C		Case D	
	Passengers	Revenues	Passengers	Revenues	Passengers	Revenues	Passengers	Revenues
5	1945	$97.2	1945	$97.2	1945	$97.2	1945	$97.2
10	1683	168.3	1683	168.3	1683	168.3	1683	168.3
15	1421	213.2	1458	218.7	1530	229.5	1547	232.0
20	1159	231.8	1262	252.4	1421	284.2	1457	291.5
25	897	224.2	1092	273.0	1347	336.8	1390	348.2
30	635	190.5	945	283.5	1278	383.4	1340	402.0

Source: W. S. Vickrey, *The Revision of the Rapid Transit Fare Structure of the City of New York* (Technical Monograph No. 3, Finance Project, Mayor's Committee on Management Survey of the City of New York), p. 87.

TABLE 1

ESTIMATED PRICE ELASTICITIES OF DEMAND FOR SELECTED COMMODITIES, UNITED STATES

Product	Price elasticity
beef	—0.92
millinery	—3.00
gasoline	—0.52
sugar	—0.31
corn	—0.49
cotton	—0.12
hay	—0.43
wheat	—0.08
potatoes	—0.31
oats	—0.56
barley	—0.39
buckwheat	—0.99

Source: H. Schultz, *Theory and Measurement of Demand* (Chicago: University of Chicago Press, 1938), and M. Spencer and L. Siegelman, *Managerial Economics* (Homewood, Ill.: Richard D. Irwin, 1959).

Finally, to illustrate very briefly the sorts of studies that have been made of the price elasticity of demand, consider a study of the fare structure of the New York subway and its effect on passenger travel. Table 2 gives forecasts of demand and revenues

TABLE 2

ALTERNATIVE ESTIMATES OF DEMAND CURVE FOR SUBWAY SERVICE

(passengers and revenues in millions per year)

	Case A		Case B		Case C		Case D	
Fare (cents)	Passengers	Revenues	Passengers	Revenues	Passengers	Revenues	Passengers	Revenues
5	1945	$97.2	1945	$97.2	1945	$97.2	1945	$97.2
10	1683	168.3	1683	168.3	1683	168.3	1683	168.3
15	1421	213.2	1458	218.7	1530	229.5	1547	232.0
20	1159	231.8	1262	252.4	1421	284.2	1457	291.5
25	897	224.2	1092	273.0	1347	336.8	1390	348.2
30	635	190.5	945	283.5	1278	383.4	1340	402.0

Source: W. S. Vickrey, *The Revision of the Rapid Transit Fare Structure of the City of New York* (Technical Monograph No. 3, Finance Project, Mayor's Committee on Management Survey of the City of New York), p. 87.

Estimating the Price Elasticity of Demand

JOEL DEAN

Joel Dean is Professor of Business Economics at Columbia University's Graduate School of Business. This article comes from his book, Managerial Economics, *published in 1960.*

CONTROLLED EXPERIMENTS

The most promising method of estimating short-run price elasticity for the product of an individual firm is usually by controlled experiments. The essence of this method is to vary separately certain determinants of demand which can be manipulated, e.g., prices, advertising, packaging, and try to conduct the experiment so that other market conditions either remain fairly constant or can be allowed for. Geographic differentiation is one way to manipulate prices or marketing strategy, comparing sales in separate localities, and usually reversing the arrangement as a check to eliminate the effects of other factors. Or prices and promotion can be manipulated through time in the same market, although this is usually less informative.

The Parker Pen Co. conducted a price experiment recently to determine whether they should raise the price of Quink, which was then selling at a loss to the company and at little profit to the dealer. The increase in price from 15¢ to 25¢ was tested in four cities. Results indicated such low elasticity of demand that the sales loss was more than offset by the added profit margin. After the price was advanced, experimentation was continued in cooperation with fifty dealers. In some stores the old package priced at 15¢ was placed next to a package marked "New Quink, 25¢." Two out of five customers bought the 25¢ package. In other stores Quink was placed on display beside competitive inks priced at 15¢ and at 10¢. In order to test specifically cross-elasticity of demand Quink was sold at 15¢ for two weeks, then at 25¢ for another two weeks. At the higher price there was a slight decline of Quink sales in relation to sales of two competitive inks. Consumer panel reports indicated that volume declined at first and then began to rise both absolutely and relative to competitors. Several competitors followed the price advance of Parker, which is the largest ink manufacturer.

Another example of field tests of competitive cross-elasticity is the Simmons Mattress experiment. Identical mattresses, some bearing the Simmons brand and others an unknown brand, were offered for sale, first at the same prices and then at various price-spreads, to determine the effect on sales. With parity prices the Simmons brand outsold the other fifteen to one; with a five dollar premium, sales were eight to one; and with a 25 percent premium, sales were equal. A parallel experiment with Cannon towels produced similar results.

Field testing of prices is sometimes used in connection with the introduction of new products. Thus, a manufacturer of duplicating supplies introduced a new product in two supposedly comparable geographic areas at different prices. The indicated demand elasticity was less than unity so the product was priced at the higher level. A similar case is that of a large food manufacturer who was faced with the problem of setting the price for frozen orange juice when it was first introduced. He experimented with three different prices in different cities. All three prices were below the then parity level of fresh oranges. Sales did not appear to differ significantly among the three price levels.

To cite another example, a new type of roll-around shopping cart which collapses into an eminently portable form was developed recently. Experimental probing for the right price included an effort to sell it house-to-house for $4.98. But it wouldn't go. Simultaneously, a large Chicago department store was supplied with a lot to be offered at $3.98. At this price and through this channel the shopping carts sold well. Efforts to pare the costs enough to make it profitable to sell at this price through department stores were unsuccessful, however, so the product had to be withdrawn from the market.

For products that are normally sold by mail order, opportunities for experimental analysis of demand are rich. Price, promotion, and even product design, can be varied among keyed mailings, chosen as successive samples of the same prospect population. Several years ago a mail-order house sent out a batch of catalogs in which the price of one item varied from $1.88 to $1.99 and then observed the relation of sales to the range of prices to find the price elasticity.

A new product that is not to be permanently sold by mail can be experimentally offered by direct mail at different prices to carefully controlled and geographically separated sectors of a mailing list. By analyzing the actual order response to each of the series of prices, some conception of demand elasticity can be obtained. This approach may be viewed as a variant of the prospect questionnaire method, but it avoids the difficulty of bridging the gap between declaration of intention and actual purchasing action. It has limitations both in the difficulty of getting satisfactory comparability of the market sectors and in the failure to duplicate the actual purchasing environment.

There are serious problems in determining demand schedules by controlled experiments. Such experiments are expensive, hazardous and time-consuming. In planning the study it is not always clear just what conditions should be held constant. Moreover, it is difficult, costly, and dangerous to set up a pricing experiment that will include all the effects of a price change that you want to measure, and exclude all the effects of other factors that you don't want. It is hard to reflect realistically the reaction of rivals to the price change. And dealers' responses are often atypical since they are privy to the experiment. The temporary impact of a local price raid may be all that is measured, whereas the problem concerns the effect of full-scale and more permanent price reductions. For example, the great responsiveness of sales to price-cuts in the Macy experiment conducted by Whitman (discussed below) probably measures stocking-up to take advantage of a short-lived opportunity and also reflects lags by competitors in meeting Macy's prices. Sufficient reaction time to feel the full effect of price is seldom possible before other conditions change significantly. Thus, the results often have limited generality, since they are tied to the particular conditions of the experiment.

Pricing experiments are costly and hazardous. They run risks of unfavorable side-reactions of dealers, consumers, and competitors. Nonetheless, this method deserves wider use than it has had, and constitutes one of the most promising implements for demand analysis in current markets.

CONSUMER QUESTIONNAIRES

Personal interviews and written questionnaires are widely used to probe the buying motives, intentions and habits of customers and prospects. They are sometimes helpful (in the absence of better measurements) in guessing at the sensitivity of demand to price. Little confidence can be placed in answers to questions that ask consumers what they think they would pay, or how much they would buy if prices were lower, or if price-spreads over competitors and substitutes were different. This kind of frontal attack on the intricate psychological problem of buyers' intentions and actions is still a highly dubious method of analysis, even when the market consists of a few large industrial customers. Not until the psychometric techniques of depth interviewing have advanced far beyond their present status can much be expected from such direct probing.

But collateral information obtained from such interviews can brace up a guess at price sensitivity. For example, interviews revealed that most buyers of a branded baby food chose it on their doctor's recommendation, and that most were quite ignorant about substitutes and about prices. This knowledge, together with other information, led the manufacturer to guess that demand for his product was quite inelastic.

Occasionally questionnaire research can indicate the outer limits of price. For example, an automatic timer developed for photographers was never commercialized because questionnaires indicated that the lowest profitable price was far above what most photographers *said* they would pay. But in general such research is a frail foundation for pricing decisions.

ENGINEERING ESTIMATES

For producers' goods, it is sometimes possible to guess at the effect of price upon the sales of a capital good by making engineering estimates of the cost savings and other benefits that can be produced by the product for a sample of prospects. By applying some standard of capital earnings, e.g., a three-year crude pay-out, it is possible to translate estimates of savings into demand for equipment.

The cost savings of customers will vary because prospects differ in size, wage rate, efficiency of displaced equipment, and other such conditions. To estimate the way these divergent conditions affect the quantity of equipment that will be purchased, a sample of prospects that is representative of various strata of customer size, wage rates, equipment efficiency, etc., is selected. From estimates of the cost savings and the number of prospects in each category, the sample results can be blown up to yield a projected schedule of equipment sales at various prices. Estimates of the cost savings of new equipment types can be supplemented and verified by test installations in major prospect categories.

The most difficult practical problems usually arise not in estimating the cost savings in a particular situation, but in translating these savings into a demand schedule that reflects a composite of all situations. Comprehensive knowledge of the operations of a buying industry are required for the equipment, both to determine the appropriate conversion factors for capitalizing cost savings and to select the sample and blow it up.[1]

---

1. This approach concentrates on obsolescence replacement, since it is here that pricing affects engineering feasibility. Cultural lags of ignorance, uncertainty, and speculation contaminate this relationship. Buying equipment on the basis of its prospective earnings on capital is unfortunately not yet sufficiently common to be the sole basis for analysis of demand. The age, distribution, and the status of depreciation reserves of existing equipment, though they should be irrelevant, may properly enter into forecasts of the rate of displacement of obsolete machinery.

CORRELATION ANALYSIS

Often, information on price elasticity can be found by applying a correlation technique to historical records of prices and sales. The important problem in this method is to design a function that can sift out the price relations from data that show the composite effect of all sales determinants.

Correlation analysis of price elasticity has been applied most extensively to demand for agricultural products, notably by Henry Schultz. Using very simple relationships[2] Schultz found fairly high correlations of price and consumption for most farm products[3] over periods of about fifteen years.

Farm products have economic characteristics that make them particularly susceptible to this kind of analysis: they are homogeneous and staple, so that their demand curves change very slowly over the years; they are sold in highly competitive markets, where prices are flexibly adjusted to demand and supply; supply varies widely from year to year, but annual production, once under way, is hard to control by producers. Wide swings in supply plus highly stable demand can in these conditions be assumed to produce a series of prices that, when plotted against consumption, trace out the shape of the demand curve.

These are far different pricing conditions from those prevailing in manufacturing industry, where prices are a combination of rigid, official quotations and undercover concessions, where products are rarely comparable, and where current demand is more closely matched by current production. Nevertheless, in some industries, price data for this kind of analysis is produced inadvertently. Price wars, regional differences in competitive

2. For instance, he used functions in the forms

$$x = a + by + ct$$
$$x = Ay^m e^{nt}$$

where x is per capita consumption, y is the deflated price, and t is time, while $a,b,c,A,m,n,$ and e are constants. In another form of analysis, price and consumption were used not in absolute terms but as deviations from a long-term trend; time was omitted as an explicit variable. Another variant of the analysis was a correlation of year-to-year changes in price with corresponding changes in consumption, a method first used by Henry Moore (*Economic Cycles: Their Law and Cause*, New York, 1914).

3. An important exception was wheat, for which price behavior was largely governed by a world market rather than a national one.

and substitute price spreads, and the distortion of relative prices caused by inflation create research opportunities that are too often neglected. Statistical analysis of such price experience can sometimes provide usable knowledge about how prices and price spreads affect both the company's market share and the industry's battle with substitutes. A state sales tax on soft drinks recently created data inadvertently that demonstrated a high price elasticity for one bottling company. This company found that a one cent per bottle tax could not be added to the wholesale price without cutting volume enough to lower total revenue. Differences in state taxes on gasoline, together with geographical differences in laid-down cost, have furnished oil companies with data for making correlation analyses of the relationships between price and volume.

When a product's price is rigid, changes in substitutes' prices shift the relative price of the product and give data on price elasticity. For example, in studying the price elasticity of policy-loans made by an insurance company, it was found that the policy-loan rate stayed constant while competing lenders reduced their rates. Thus the relative price of policy-loans was rising in a way that was measurable and could be related to changes in loan volume, both absolutely and relative to competitors' volume.

PRICE ELASTICITY—AN ILLUSTRATIVE STUDY

One of the best studies of the short-run relation of price to sales was done for Macy's department store by R. H. Whitman.[4] In several respects this is an ideal field for such research: (1) prices are an important sales factor—they are featured in advertising, and customers shop between stores; (2) prices are unusually flexible—seasonal patterns and style cycles make careful price administration a must for managing large inventories profitably; (3) there is substantial and regular competition among stores, but with some leeway for price policy; (4) there is keen competition between substitute products on the same counter, which presents the raw material for well controlled experiments.

4. "Demand Functions for Merchandise at Retail," *Studies in Mathematical Economics and Econometrics* (Chicago: University of Chicago Press, 1942), pp. 208-221.

Whitman was thus able to sidestep some of the obstacles discussed earlier in the chapter. For instance, he used a very short time period (two and one-half months), which stabilized consumer income, but which nevertheless saw many price changes. He analyzed only staple products in order to obviate the style cycles problem. He assumed that when Macy's changed its price the pattern of reactions of other stores during the analysis period would be repeated under similar conditions in the future. These simplifying circumstances neutralized the effect of several independent variables that must be used in most demand situations, and permitted him to use simple correlation of price and quantity sold to find price elasticity.

Whitman created his data by systematically manipulating price over a wide range during a short period. Parallel experiments were performed for a number of staples.

When correlation analysis is worked out in its mathematical (least-squares) form, the first step is to set up an algebraic function to express the relation. There is usually room for judgment in deciding on the best form to use. In choosing his demand equation, Whitman rejected the common form, $q = a + bp$ and used instead $q = Ap^a$. (q=quantity sold; p=price; A, a, and b are constants.)[5]

CHART 1

ALTERNATIVE FORMS OF DEMAND FUNCTION

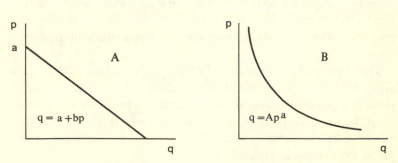

5. Exponential functions of this type are used in logarithmic form for correlation analysis:

$$\log q = \log A + a \log p.$$

An important feature of the hyperbolic demand curve is its constant elasticity: regardless of the level of price, the ratio of a small fixed percent change in price to the resulting percent change in quantity sold is constant. This ratio is equal to the constant a, which is the price elasticity of demand, and which is negative. For example, if a is -5, a drop in price of 1 percent will increase sales by 5 percent and revenue by 4 percent. In the simplest case, where $a = -1$, sales vary inversely with price just enough to keep total revenue constant for all values of p.

In the straight-line demand curve, on the other hand, a \$1 change in price will produce a constant absolute change in quantity sold regardless of the level of price. In this case there is a price which gives a maximum revenue, namely $a/2$.

Whether the hyperbola is more realistic is not clear *a priori:* there is certainly a price where none at all can be sold, and the amount that can be given away is also finite. But for the relevant range of actual prices, Whitman found it a better fit to the facts than a straight line.

The price elasticities that resulted from this analysis told a significant story and were surprisingly reliable in a statistical sense. Chart 1 presents the demand schedule for one product, showing a price elasticity of about -6 (with a standard error of .78) and a correlation coefficient of $-.89$, which indicates a close relation between sales and prices. Other commodities showed comparable price elasticities and correlations. Moreover, by comparing results for the same calendar months in two successive years, Whitman found that the change during the year was relatively slight compared to the margin of probable error.

These price elasticities are relatively high, and mean that sales are sensitive to prices for these products. For these products, price is a powerful weapon in competition—probably too powerful to be used freely. Low elasticity, in contrast, shows products where price competition is too ineffective to be important, compared to the returns from advertising.

Whitman also ran a multiple correlation analysis to find the relation of sales to prices of other products, using as independent variables both the product's price and an index of competing

CHART 2

DEPARTMENT STORE DEMAND FUNCTION

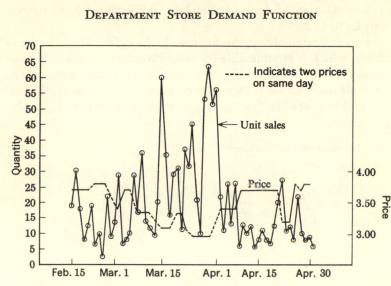

(Source: R. H. Whitman, "Demand Functions for Merchandise at Retail," *Studies in Mathematical Economics and Econometrics*, Chicago, University of Chicago Press, 1942, pp. 210, 214.)

CHART 3

DEPARTMENT STORE PRICES AND SALES. ORIGINAL DATA

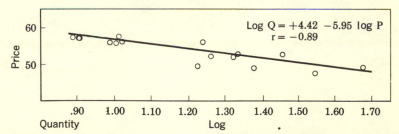

(Source: R. H. Whitman, "Demand Functions for Merchandise at Retail," *Studies in Mathematical Economics and Econometrics*, Chicago, University of Chicago Press, 1942, pp. 210, 214.)

products.[6] The closeness of fit for this equation was not impressively high, but the analysis did contribute some information on cross elasticity of demand, which for different products ranged from 1.4 to 16.2.

As we indicated above, this analysis had a rather ideal short-run setting, which is unattainable for most products. It is much more common for prices to change from year to year than from day to day, and for reaction patterns to be much slower. Nevertheless, it is highly probable that there are other areas where it can be useful.

6. The equation took the form: $Q = Ap^a P^b$.

Pricing and the Character of
the Product

A. D. H. Kaplan, Joel B. Dirlam,
and Robert F. Lanzillotti

*A. D. H. Kaplan is a senior economist at the
Brookings Institution. Together with Joel
Dirlam and Robert Lanzillotti, he wrote*
Pricing in Big Business *from which the fol-
lowing paper is taken.*

The character of the product—the type of demand to which it
caters, as well as its physical attributes, production requirements,
amenability to differentiation, and stage of maturity—sets boundaries to the pricing discretion of the company, big or little. When
interpreting the role of product characteristics, however, the
possibility that reaction may run both ways must be kept in mind.
These characteristics are not fixed or unadjustable. They themselves may be affected by price. But the basic concern at this
point is with pricing policies that seem to be imposed by the
nature of the product, rather than vice versa.

With a product like fresh meat, perishable and subject to unpredictable output and shipments of the primary commodity, even a
firm of the importance of Swift & Company has a limited opportunity to bend wholesale prices to company policy. A durable
product with controlled raw material output, and production
based on orders, better lends itself to fairly stable price quotations, as in steel or crude oil. Copper, on the contrary, with its

volatile price behavior points up the effect on the manageability of prices of a widely diffused raw material supply and a world market. Limitations on the transportability of the product (transportation cost in relation to product value) may give locational advantage in pricing even when there are business giants in the industry.

New products, with varying degrees of marketable uniqueness, provide opportunities for pricing discretion not generally available in standardized goods. Large companies whose resources are concentrated in established standard products are aware of the general unprofitability of price wars when confronted with similarly large and resourceful competitors; hence they keep in step with the competition on price and depend on such factors as favorable location, or availability of adequate supplies and satisfactory service to customers, for their competitive strength at the going price. In the use of these devices, however, product features (*e.g.*, vulnerability to substitution) may determine how successful a stable price policy can be, even for the large and resourceful company.

New Products and Matured Products · The natural frame of reference for pricing a new product is the price range of existing substitutes. For example, it was recognized that nylon was capable of penetrating the markets of a variety of textile fibers. The problem of effectively introducing this new fiber resolved itself through a compromise between pricing for the widest possible use and pricing for the more limited, but in the long run, more sustainable and profitable quality market. In cellophane, the same company reached more aggressively for more extensive market penetration without undermining the profit potential. Apparently, the cost elasticity of volume output and the price elasticity of growing demand were sufficiently high to permit a more rapid rate of expansion than was possible in nylon. The introduction of a major consumer appliance, for which demand is as yet an expectation rather than a reality, has entailed elaborate market research to select a price niche that will permit the inclusion of features required for optimum acceptance. In the pricing of a major piece of farm machinery such as the cotton picker, the decision settles on a middle ground between the estimated maxi-

mum economic value as a replacement for hand labor and a
sufficiently low price to give assurance of widespread adoption.
Prices determined in this manner may well limit the components
that can be selected for incorporation in the assembled product;
automobiles and other consumer durables considered earlier were
cases in point. With the accumulation of know-how and the
lowering of costs, subsequent pricing turns on whether the
product can readily be imitated, whether the prestige acquired
in its pioneering can be prolonged through improvement and
product differentiation, or whether lower cost reflected in lower
price will open up a highly profitable volume increase.

An established standard product, be it a metal, flour, or heavy
chemical, does not entail such conscious balancing of alternative
possibilities to fix its price levels. The price may start from a
fairly well-recognized cost base, but the profit is a residual reflecting the current willingness or ability of the market to keep the
capacity employed. Large firms with heavy investments in established areas of primary production have constantly feared that
price changes will lead to hazards of unpredictable magnitude.
This fear has often been justified in the past—witness the gyra-
tions of price with accompanying demand fluctuations in copper,
lead, or zinc; and even with price leadership, boom and depression fluctuations in steel prices have not been unknown. There
is in consequence an undercurrent of antipathy in the firms inter-
viewed to policies that would disturb the pattern of stable and
infrequently changing prices. The instability of copper prices is
certainy not due to lack of desire on the part of Kennecott and
other primary producers to keep firm the price of their metal.
The volatility issues rather from the fickleness of a world market,
in which fluctuation is accentuated by extremes of overflow or
scarcity in the supply of copper scrap.

At least until the Second World War, Alcoa supplied and
priced aluminum in the United States with some regard to the
fact that it had to penetrate the markets of copper and other
metals as well as some non-metallic products. Its technical development in a capital-intensive form with integrated production
and standardization of finished products now tends to assert itself;
so that while product promotion remains vigorous, pricing in the

basic aluminum lines is showing resemblances to steel's pattern of base prices and extras.

The type of use to which a product is put also has a bearing on the importance attached to price variations. The stable pricing of containers carried by American Can and Continental Can has met with little resistance by their customers, and this is not solely because of the duopoly leadership in can manufacture; it is largely due to the fact that what the final user is buying is not the container but the contents. Similarly, flexible packaging materials, aluminum fabrications, special electrical equipment items, and industrial gases permit the manufacturer a minimum of concern with price competition because these are products sold as part—an incidental part—of the larger end product in which the cost of the contributing item is not a prime consideration.

Cost Structure · Production and cost characteristics of the main product play a primary role in conditioning pricing policies. The overriding importance of certain materials in the total cost structure, as in the case of tin plate for can manufacture; the leanness of the ore, and the consequent magnitude of the mining operations of Kennecott Copper; the relatively small runs and large number of items, as in the case of Alcoa's fabricated operations; and of course the high proportion of indirect cost in basic steel production—all these distinctive features are transmuted into pricing policy. U. S. Steel seeks to avoid cutthroat price competition, and evolves a fair return philosophy. Alcoa finds a standard cost system unusable for many items. Kennecott, when prices drop, has to pile up inventory and await more settled prices; it looks with favor on stabilized prices. American Can, and perhaps even the oil companies, in the long run, become transmission belts for passing material and labor costs on to consumers with an inelastic demand. Thus a large part of price policy may be the response to the cost pattern inherent to the product.

Part Three

Capital Budgeting and Forecasting

THE papers in Part Three deal with capital budgeting and forecasting. To solve most investment and capital budgeting problems, it is necessary to reduce funds received or spent at different points in time to comparable terms. Because a firm can realize a positive return from the investment of its funds, a dollar now is worth more than a dollar later. Pearson Hunt, Charles Williams, and Gordon Donaldson provide the solutions to various investment problems and show how to compute an investment's rate of return.

In a paper which is now a classic in this field, Joel Dean discusses various ways of measuring the economic worth of investment proposals. He evaluates the three most commonly used yardsticks of investment worth—degree of necessity, payback period, and rate of return—and concludes that rate of return is the best. After discussing some of the mistakes that are made in estimating the rate of return, he describes and illustrates the use of the discounted-cash-flow method of computing rates of return, a method which he regards as "demonstrably superior to existing alternatives in accuracy, realism, relevance, and sensitivity."

The next three papers deal with economic forecasting and long-run business planning. Practically all problems in managerial economics involve forecasting. The decision of whether or not to build a new plant may depend crucially on forecasts of demand. Whether or not to cut price may depend crucially on forecasts of the price of materials. The article from *Business Week* describes the various techniques that are commonly used to forecast economic magnitudes: trend extrapolation, leading series, econometric models, and others. The article by the National Industrial Conference Board describes the forecasting methods used by five major companies—Kellogg, Eli Lilly, American Radiator, Long Island Lighting, and B. F. Goodrich. Turning to the role of the economist in a large corporation, Sidney Alexander argues that the economist can make his most valuable contribution in long-term planning.

Time Adjustments of Flows of Funds

PEARSON HUNT,
CHARLES M. WILLIAMS, AND
GORDON DONALDSON

Pearson Hunt is Professor of Business Administration at Harvard University. In 1961, together with Charles Williams and Gordon Donaldson, he published Basic Business Finance *from which this paper is taken.*

Many decisions involve in some way a comparison of the usefulness of receiving or paying funds at one time rather than another, and we need a means of evaluating the effect of the time span involved. The procedure of *time adjustment* provides a consistent and accurate means for the needed evaluation.

One basic assumption must be made before application of the mathematical procedure, which involves nothing more than compound interest. We assume that a firm always can find some way to invest funds to produce some net gain, or *rate of return*. The rate may be very low, as when funds are temporarily placed in short-term treasury bills, or it may be as high as the gain from some new product greatly in demand. In fact, if a firm does not act to obtain some return from the use of its funds, we speak of the *opportunity cost,* which is the loss of revenue because an opportunity was not taken. Therefore, since there can always be earnings from the investment of funds, we can say as a general rule that whenever a business has a choice of the time when it will obtain certain funds, the rule should be "the sooner, the better."

The first step to an understanding of time adjustment is to relate the amounts involved to one another along a scale of time. The time is divided into periods (e.g., days, months, years), and a particular point in time is selected as the starting point from which the effect of compound interest on the funds will be regarded. This time is named the *focal date*. Periods later than this date are designated by the plus sign, periods earlier by the minus sign, and the focal date is designated by zero. To the mathematician, it is unimportant what actual time is chosen as the focal date. The financial analyst can choose any date, past or present, most convenient for his purposes. In fact, for many problems of financial planning, it is convenient to have the focal date in the future, usually the date at which a specific sum will be received or paid, or at which a certain periodic flow of funds will terminate.

It is necessary to calculate the changing values of flows of funds as they occur both before and after the focal date. We first turn to *compounding*, that is, the subsequent growth in the value of funds initially invested at the focal date, because this process is one with which most readers will be familiar from such well-advertised operations as savings accounts on which interest is compounded. We shall then turn to *discounting*, which looks in the other direction from the focal date along the time scale.

COMPOUNDING

There are three quantities necessary for the calculation:

1. *The rate of return.* In the following exposition, to show the effects of different rates, we shall use two that are well within the range of business experience.
2. *The amount of funds in question.* It is convenient to use the sum of $1.00 to develop the formulas, since if one knows how the values of this sum are affected by time, one can compute the values of any other sum by simple multiplication.
3. *The length of time from the focal date.* This may be measured in days, weeks, etc., so that for the sake of generality,

one refers to the *period* rather than to some specific unit of time. One warning is necessary here. The rate of return used must be stated consistently with the actual length of the time period. Thus, 6 percent per year becomes 0.5 percent per month, and so on.

The growing amount that will be found at later times from an investment of $1.00 at the focal date is referred to as the *compound amount* (of a single sum). Interest is computed on the original sum and then added to the original sum at the end of the first period. The new and larger principal is then the base for the interest calculation in the second period, and so on. Jumping over the detailed mathematics, we can turn to any set of tables for business computations, among which we shall find values for the compound amount of a single sum invested at a given time. See Table 1 for a portion of such a table.

DISCOUNTING

The process of compounding discloses how the value of an investment made at the focal date grows in later time. We now turn to *discounting*, a process which looks at times preceding the focal date and answers the question: How much must be invested before the focal date to produce a desired sum at the time of the focal date?

The answers to such questions are determined by using the reciprocals of the values in the table of compound amounts, for the reasons exemplified in the following instance. Take four periods and 4 percent. Table 1 shows that if $1.00 is compounded

TABLE 1

COMPOUND AMOUNT OF $1.00

Periods	Rate 4%	Rate. 10%
0	1.000	1.000
+1	1.040	1.100
+2	1.082	1.210
+3	1.125	1.331
+4	1.170	1.464
+5	1.217	1.611

for this time and rate, it will increase to $1.17. To have only $1.00 at the end of four periods of compounding, we obviously need to invest less than $1.00. The calculation is:

$$\frac{1.000}{1.170} = \frac{x}{1.000}$$

$$x = 0.855$$

The number so produced is known as the *present value* (at the selected time and rate) which will produce $1.00 at the focal date. The term *discounted value* is also used, although less frequently.

Since present values are often used in financial calculations, a table of present values is provided in most books on finance. For convenience, we reproduce a portion of such a table in Table 2.

Having shown how to evaluate a sum both before the focal date (by discounting) and after the focal date (by compounding), we are in a position to picture the changing value of the sum of $1.00 at the time of the focal date over a time scale. This is presented graphically in Chart 1, where the figures from Tables 1 and 2 are used.

The basic relationships to be observed are simple but very important:

1. The value of a sum invested at any time grows as time passes.
2. The necessary investment to produce a future sum decreases as the time to produce it is increased.
3. Both these effects are magnified as the rate of return increases.

TABLE 2

PRESENT VALUE OF $1.00

Periods	Rate 4%	Rate 10%
0	1.000	1.000
—1	0.962	0.909
—2	0.925	0.826
—3	0.889	0.751
—4	0.855	0.683
—5	0.822	0.621

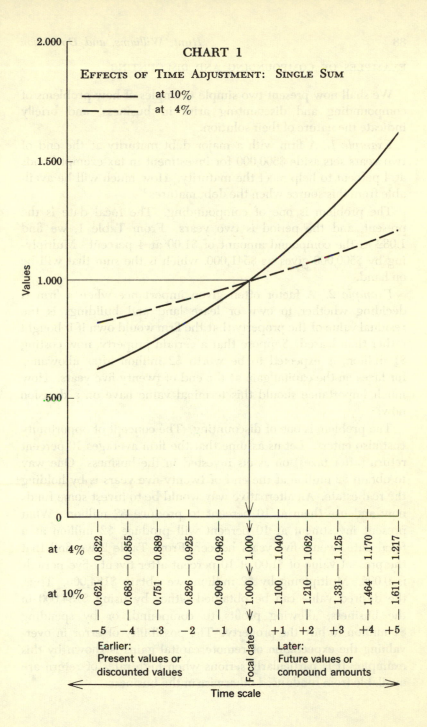

CHART 1

EFFECTS OF TIME ADJUSTMENT: SINGLE SUM

—— at 10%

– – – at 4%

Values

2.000

1.500

1.000

.500

0

at 4%	0.822	0.855	0.889	0.925	0.962	1.000	1.040	1.082	1.125	1.170	1.217
at 10%	0.621	0.683	0.751	0.826	0.909	1.000	1.100	1.210	1.331	1.464	1.611
	−5	−4	−3	−2	−1	0	+1	+2	+3	+4	+5

Earlier:
Present values or
discounted values

Focal date

Later:
Future values or
compound amounts

Time scale

EXAMPLES OF COMPOUNDING AND DISCOUNTING

We shall now present two simple examples of how problems of compounding and discounting arise in business, and briefly indicate the nature of their solution.

Example 1. A firm with a major debt maturity at the end of two years sets aside $500,000 for investment in tax-exempt bonds at 4 percent to help meet the maturity. How much will be available from this source when the debt matures?

The problem is one of compounding. The focal date is the present, and the period is two years. From Table 1, we find 1.082 as the compound amount of $1.00 at 4 percent. Multiplying by $500,000 gives us $541,000, which is the sum that will be on hand.

Example 2. A factor often given importance when a firm is deciding whether to own or lease land and buildings is the residual value of the property that the firm would own if it bought rather than leased. Suppose that a certain property, now costing $1 million, is expected to be worth $2 million after allowance for taxes on the capital gain at the end of twenty-five years. How much importance should this terminal value have on a decision now?

The problem is one of discounting. The concept of opportunity cost also enters. Let us assume that the firm averages 10 percent return (after taxes) on assets invested in the business. One way to obtain $2 million at the end of twenty-five years is by holding the real estate. An alternative way would be to invest some funds now and use them at 10 percent to produce $2 million. What present investment at 10 percent will produce $2 million at a focal date twenty-five years hence? From Table 2 we find that the present value of $1.00 at 10 percent after twenty-five periods is 0.092. Multiplying by $2 million, we obtain $184,000. Thus, the desired value can be obtained either by using $184,000 in the business, allowing profits to compound, or by spending $1 million to buy the property. The possibility of error in over-valuing the expectation of remote capital gains is shown by this example. It is particularly serious when high rates of return are available from funds used otherwise in the business.

FINDING THE RATE OF RETURN

There is another use to which tables of present values are often put in financial work. Given values at two dates, one is sometimes required to find the rate of return that will produce a desired change in value. Using the figures from Example 2 above, the problem can be stated as follows: At what rate of return will \$1 million grow to \$2 million in twenty-five years?

The focal date is the end of the twenty-five-year period, when the present value table expects \$1.00 to be paid. Converting the data from the actual case therefore requires division of the initial and terminal value by \$2 million:

$$\frac{2,000,000}{2,000,000} = 1.000$$

and

$$\frac{1,000,000}{2,000,000} = 0.500.$$

The question has become: At what rate of discount will 0.50 become 1.00 at the end of twenty-five periods?

Looking at a table of present values for twenty-five periods, we find:

Rate 2%..................... 0.610
Rate 4%..................... 0.375

By the process of interpolation,[1] we find the answer, which is 2.9 percent (much lower—and therefore less desirable—than the use of funds to produce 10 percent).

ANNUITIES

Our explanation of the effects of time on the value of funds has so far dealt only with single sums. That is, we have confined ourselves to watching the growth in value of a single in-

1. 2% = 0.610   2% = 0.610 $\frac{110}{235}$ (2%) = x = 0.9%
   4% = 0.375 x = 0.500
   ‾‾‾‾‾‾‾‾‾‾‾   ‾‾‾‾‾‾‾‾‾‾‾
   2% = 0.235   0.110

vestment, once it is made. We now turn to what is perhaps more frequently experienced in business, namely, the receipt or payment of a series of sums periodically over a stated number of time periods. Examples are rent and the flow of funds attached to a tax shield arising from depreciation.

There is much similarity between the mathematics already used and that which is necessary for *annuities,* as this type of periodic payment is termed by mathematicians. The focal date, however, takes on a new meaning, which the conventions of financial mathematics make even more complex. If one is looking into periods following the focal date, that date is the beginning of the first period of the annuity. In this case the applicable value at the focal date is zero, for the first payment of the annuity will take place only at the end of the first time period. If one is looking at times which are earlier than the focal date, however, the focal date is defined as the end of the last period, just after the moment of the final payment of the annuity. Again, the value is zero.

We shall introduce the annuity tables in the same order as before; that is, we first look ahead in time to consider the *compound amount* of an annuity, and then back to consider the *present value* of an annuity.

Compounding · Any annuity can be separated into a series of single payments and evaluated by the table of compound interest already described.

Suppose $1.00 is to be received at the end of each period, and that each $1.00 is to be invested at compound interest. How much will be the amount of the annuity a specified number of periods after the focal date? Let us take 4 percent and five years. The answer can be built up from Table 1, of compound amount, as follows:

$1.00 received at time $+1$ at 4% for 4 years becomes $1.170
1.00 received at time $+2$ at 4% for 3 years becomes 1.125
1.00 received at time $+3$ at 4% for 2 years becomes 1.082
1.00 received at time $+4$ at 4% for 1 year becomes 1.040
1.00 received at time $+5$ at 4% for 0 year becomes 1.000

Total Value, Amount of Annuity $5.417

From this example, we can see that a table of the desired values for annuities can be obtained by accumulating values from compound interest tables. See Table 3 for a brief portion of such a table.

TABLE 3

AMOUNT OF ANNUITY OF $1.00 PER PERIOD

Periods	Rate 4%	Rate 10%
0	0	0
+1	1.000	1.000
+2	2.040	2.100
+3	3.122	3.310
+4	4.246	4.641
+5	5.416*	6.105

* The difference between this figure and 5.417, the amount of annuity given above, is due to rounding.

The question answered by such a table is: How much will the periodic receipt of $1.00 grow if all payments are held at compound interest at a specified rate and for a specified number of periods? In business terms, we are dealing with an annuity that is to be received.

Discounting · We now look at an annuity that is being paid out by the business, asking the question: How much must be invested in period $-n$ at the specified rate to permit the payment of an annuity of $1.00 per period, leaving nothing at the focal date? As before, this can be broken down into separate payments, which can be evaluated from the table of the present value of single sums. Let us take 4 percent and five years once more. Table 2 can be used.

At the beginning of period −5:
it takes 0.822 to produce $1.00 in 5 years,
it takes 0.855 to produce $1.00 in 4 years,
it takes 0.889 to produce $1.00 in 3 years,
it takes 0.925 to produce $1.00 in 2 years,
it takes 0.962 to produce $1.00 in 1 year.

Total 4.453, Value of Annuity at Period −5

This example shows how the desired present values of annuities can be obtained by accumulating values from the table of the present values of a single sum. Such a table is included in most books on finance. For convenience, we reproduce a portion in Table 4.

TABLE 4

PRESENT VALUE OF $1.00 RECEIVED PERIODICALLY FOR *n* PERIODS

Periods	Rate 4%	Rate 10%
0	0	0
−1	0.962	0.909
−2	1.886	1.736
−3	2.775	2.487
−4	3.630	3.170
−5	4.452*	3.791

* The difference between this figure and 4.453, the value of the annuity given above, is due to rounding.

When we were dealing with the changing values of a single sum over time, we ended our explanation with a diagram. A similar one, Chart 2, can be presented for annuities, although the situation is more complex. The reader will note, in studying the charted annuities, that the values get larger as one proceeds in either direction from the focal date. This is because of the periodic payments of $1.00 that are involved. The reader will also note here, as in the more simple case, that changing the rate of return has considerable influence on the values, especially as time becomes more remote. In each instance the higher the rate, the greater the advantage to the user of the funds. That is, if 10 percent is applied, an annuity will cost less, or produce more, than if a lower rate were applied.

Before we leave the subject of the present values of annuities, we shall describe in another way the operation of the investment of $4.452 at 4 percent to permit paying $1.00 per year for five years. This will not add to the theoretical structure, but it will picture the process in a way that is more useful in financial thinking.

At the beginning of year −5, invest $4.452.
At the end of year −5, take interest of $0.178, and withdraw $0.822.
At the beginning of year −4, remainder invested becomes $3.630.

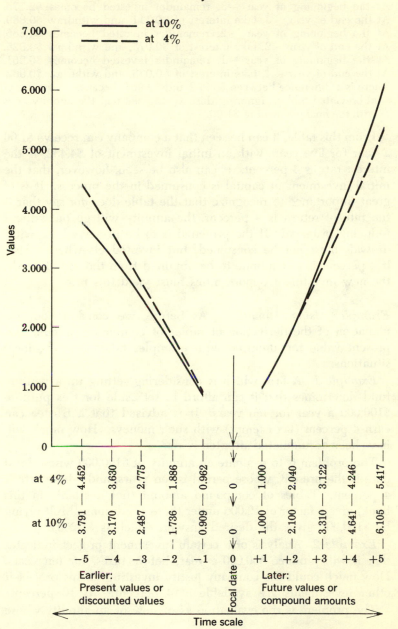

CHART 2

EFFECTS OF TIME ADJUSTMENT: ANNUITY

at 10%
at 4%

at 4%	4.452	3.630	2.775	1.886	0.962	0	1.000	2.040	3.122	4.246	5.417
at 10%	3.791	3.170	2.487	1.736	0.909	0	1.000	2.100	3.310	4.641	6.105
	−5	−4	−3	−2	−1	0	+1	+2	+3	+4	+5

Earlier:
Present values or
discounted values

Focal date

Later:
Future values or
compound amounts

Time scale

At the end of year −4, take interest of $0.145, and withdraw $0.855.
At the beginning of year −3, remainder invested becomes $2.775.
At the end of year −3, take interest of $0.111, and withdraw $0.889.
At the beginning of year −2, remainder invested becomes $1.886.
At the end of year −2, take interest of $0.075, and withdraw $0.925.
At the beginning of year −1, remainder invested becomes $0.961.
At the end of year −1, take interest of $0.038, and withdraw $0.962.
There is a difference between $0.962 and $0.961, because of the use of
  abbreviated tables. Ignoring this, we can see that the annuity ends
  with the final payment of $1.00.

From this table, it can be seen that a company can receive $1.00
a year for five years with an initial investment of $4.452, if the
interest rate is 4 percent. It can also be seen, however, that the
initial investment of capital is consumed in the process. It is of
great importance to recognize that the table does *not* say that if
the rate of return is 4 percent, the annuity will go on without
reducing principal. If the principal is to be preserved, its with-
drawals must not be consumed, but invested elsewhere. Also,
if 4 percent is to continue to be obtained from the use of funds,
the new investment opportunities must yield this rate.

Examples Using Annuities · As before, we conclude our explanation of the derivation of tables of compound amount and
present value for annuities with examples taken from business
situations.

Example 1. A firm which is considering setting up a pension
fund determines that it can afford to set aside for this purpose
$100,000 a year for ten years. It is advised that a trustee can
earn 4 percent (tax exempt) with such moneys. How much will
have been accumulated after ten years?

The problem is to evaluate an annuity of $100,000 whose focal
date is the present, whose period is ten years, and whose rate is
4 percent. Tables of compound amount (not available in this
book) give a factor of 12.006 under these conditions. Multiplying
by $100,000 gives the desired answer, which is $1,200,600.

Example 2. Analysis of a certain investment project indicates
that it will produce $50,000 a year, before taxes, for ten years.
How much could the company justify investing in this project if
other investments are available at 4 percent? At 10 percent?

The problem is the evaluation as of now of an annuity whose

focal date is ten years from the present. We find the present value factor for ten periods to be 8.111 for 4 percent, and 6.145 for 10 percent. Multiplying by $50,000, we find $405,550 for 4 percent and $307,250 for 10 percent. These are the sums that could be invested at the specified rates to produce $50,000 a year for ten years.

Example 3. Taking the figures as developed in Example 2, assume that the firm finds that $350,000 is required as an investment to establish the project. Since this number is more than the present value at 10 percent, the firm should not undertake the project if it has other opportunities on which 10 percent can be earned. The firm should, however, consider the project an excellent one if the alternative opportunities are offering 4 percent return.

Finding the Rate of Return · One last step in the use of present value tables will be illustrated here. Given the periodic amount of an annuity and the original investment, what is the rate of return? Using the figures from Example 3, above, what rate of return will produce a ten-year annuity of $50,000 from the investment of $350,000?

The focal date is the end of the ten-year period, when the last payment will be received. The present value table is based on annuities of $1.00 per period, so the figures in the actual case must be converted by dividing through by $50,000:

$$\frac{50,000}{50,000} = 1.000$$

and

$$\frac{350,000}{50,000} = 7.000.$$

Looking at the table of present values of an annuity for ten periods, we find:

Rate 6% 7.360
Rate 8% 6.710

By interpolation, the answer can be computed. It is 7.1 percent.

Measuring the Productivity of Capital

JOEL DEAN

Joel Dean is Professor of Business Economics at Columbia University's Graduate School of Business. This article comes from the Harvard Business Review of January 1954.

The president of one of our largest oil companies, who was pushing through a program of drastic decentralization of management, stated recently that the last thing he would delegate would be decisions about capital expenditures. This is understandable because capital-expenditure decisions form the framework for a company's future development and are a major determinant of efficiency and competitive power. The wisdom of these corporate investment decisions, therefore, has a profound effect upon a company's future earnings and growth.

From the standpoint of the stockholder and of the consumer, capital expenditures are the principal bulwark against the seemingly endless progression of wage increases. From the standpoint of labor, capital expenditures are the basic economic source of future wage advances since they embody the creative forward strides of advancing technology. Finally, capital expenditures, both by their aggregate size and by their cyclical timing, have a great deal to do with the character of the economy as a whole, and thus with the government's role in maintaining stability.

MANAGEMENT PROGRAM

Farsighted judgment is an essential requisite for wise decisions about capital expenditures. But such judgment, to be sound, must be based on analysis of all the facts, many of them extremely technical and complex. In particular, top management needs an objective means of measuring the economic worth of individual investment proposals in order to have a realistic basis for choosing among them and selecting those which will mean the most to the company's long-run prosperity. The basic measure of economic worth is the productivity of capital, which means its power to produce profits. The purpose of this article is to suggest better ways of making that measurement.

Unfortunately, the problem of managing capital expenditure has not generally been attacked with the kind of thorough and objective analysis that has paid such big dividends in other management areas. I have made a study of the capital-expenditure methods of some fifty large companies. These are all well-managed companies so far as production, engineering, and marketing methods are concerned, and I have a great deal of admiration for their executives. But on capital expenditures they show widespread failure to measure the investment worth of individual proposals directly, lack of defensible objective standards of an acceptable investment, and distorted dedication to procedures and paper work, with inadequate understanding of the economic content of the concepts used. In other words, when it comes to capital expenditures, they are still forced to play by ear to a distressing extent.

The development of an effective system for managing capital expenditures requires a complex combination of disciplines: (*a*) application of economic theory at several vital points; (*b*) knowledge of financial mathematics, which most of us acquired in our apprenticeship days but have inevitably forgotten long since; (*c*) economic forecasting; (*d*) techniques for projecting the amount and timing of outlays and receipts; and (*e*) techniques of control through comparison of actualities with projections. Top management clearly needs technical help. No executive, even if he had the time to analyze each capital proposal personally, could be expected to have all the necessary disciplines at his command; they can only be gathered together in a team of specialists.

This article concentrates on the measurement of the economic worth of individual investment proposals. But we must remember that, though this is likely to be the critical element, it is only one of many components in a well-rounded program of capital management.

ARE PROFITS CONTROLLING?

As we turn, now, to the phase of capital-expenditure management that is our main concern here—measurement of capital productivity—we must face an underlying question: To what degree are investment decisions actually controlled by profit considerations?

Concern with capital productivity of course implies that the company's goal is profits. But actually in many cases money making is a secondary objective. Often the primary goal is strategic—to maintain or increase the company's share of the market, to achieve growth in sales volume or number of employees, or simply to build reputation and status. Often capital expenditures capture and embody this kind of motivation in the form of corporate monuments made "just to become the kind of company we want to be." I am thinking of welfare and prestige investments like gymnasiums, country clubs, and palatial offices.

A corporation is not single-minded. It is composed of groups and individuals whose interests conflict. The concept of management as arbiter among employees, customers, and stockholders can lead to capital-expenditure policies and commitments that stray from the directional beam of capital productivity. Not that this is necessarily wrong. But, at least, when a company does let such goals as welfare or prestige govern, it ought to know the cost of such a policy. The only way to find out this cost is to determine the profitability of capital projects and see how much profit is being passed up in order to build such corporate monuments. The cost of prestige, then, is the amount of earnings foregone by departing from a pattern of investment ruthlessly directed at profit maximization.

Even where money making does dominate, the theory that a company tries to maximize its profits needs some qualification. Much more prevalent is what can be described as the doctrine of *adequate profits.* Of course, when profits performance or outlook is inadequate, the stockholder's power does come into play and capital expenditures are likely to be oriented toward profit maximization. But so long as the company is making adequate profits, the drive to have all capital expenditures selected on the basis of profit maximization is blunted.

Thus, I am well aware that making maximum profits is often not the sole or even the dominant goal in managing capital expenditures. But that does not lessen the importance of being able to measure the productivity of capital (i.e., its power to produce profits). Moreover, my viewpoint here remains that of the missionary rather than the anthropologist. As in other applications of managerial economics, the objective is to help executives improve policies, not simply to report practice (or malpractice).

YARDSTICKS OF INVESTMENT WORTH

The heart of good capital-expenditure management, then, is the measurement of the investment worth of individual proposals. But in order to measure how good a project is, we must have the right kind of yardstick. Just what should a good yardstick do?

The productivity of capital can be indicated in several ways, but the central requirement of a good yardstick is that it should measure what the proposed outlay will do to earnings, and do this in a way that permits realistic comparison of one investment proposal with another. What we seek is a measuring rod which will help decide, for example, whether a $5,000 project that will earn $2,000 a year for three years is more attractive than a $60,000 project that will earn $10,000 a year for ten years.

A good yardstick of investment worth should summarize in a single figure all the information that is relevant to the decision whether or not to make the particular investment, and none that is irrelevant. It should be applicable to all types of proposals and should permit appraisal in terms of a single set of standards. Also, it should provide an index that is relatively simple to compute; once the basic data on the proposal have been assembled, the operating people should be able to measure the project's worth easily and without any need to explain how they do it.

Finally, the yardstick should permit simple adjustments to allow for ranges of uncertainty in the earnings estimates, since one of the facts to be taken into account is man's inability to see very far into the future with any great precision.

How do the three most commonly used yardsticks—(a) degree of necessity, (b) payback period, and (c) rate of return—stack up against those criteria?

Degree of Necessity · The degree of urgency of the proposed project—that is, the extent to which it cannot be postponed to later years—is one kind of yardstick for assigning priority to investment proposals. For example, a railroad might put a power crane replacement proposal ahead of a repair shop modernization request because the old crane had broken down and something had to be done about it immediately, whereas the repair shop project could wait.

Degree of necessity has a place in the capital budgeting scheme. Some investments must be made to meet requirements imposed by a government agency. Grade-crossing eliminations for railroads, sanitary facilities in food-processing plants, and mandatory smoke-control installations are examples. Other investments clearly must be made if the company is to remain in business, e.g., replacement of a washed-out section of a railroad's main line. In these cases the alternative is such that its adoption would have a catastrophic effect on the firm's profits. Projects of this nature seldom bulk large in a company's over-all capital-expenditure program.

A serious defect of degree of urgency is that it fails to measure the capital productivity of a proposal—that is, the effect it will have on the company's earnings. A plant-modernization project may be highly postponable; but if it can produce annual savings which will yield 30 percent on the added capital tied up, it is to be preferred to a less postponable but less profitable project. Or, replacement of a shop destroyed by fire may seem completely unpostponable, whereas actually the company might find its over-all profits enhanced by subcontracting the operations formerly performed in the destroyed facilities.

Moreover, the degree of urgency is not a measurable quantity. Proposed projects cannot be assembled and arranged in a single priority ladder; acceptance standards cannot be set up to choose wisely among projects submitted on a necessity basis.

The most serious result of accepting or rejecting proposals primarily on the basis of how urgent they seem to be is that the capital budgeting program is likely to degenerate into a contest of personalities. The biggest share of the capital-expenditure money will go to the division heads who are the most eloquent or most persistent in presenting their requests, rather than to those who have taken the time and effort necessary to make an objective appraisal of the project's economic worth. The result is that all projects come up for review in an atmosphere of haste and emergency, with full scope allowed for the arts of persuasion and exhortation. Not only will projects whose economic desirability is dubious be pushed through to acceptance, but also a large proportion of investments that would yield big savings and high profits may be put off almost indefinitely.

Payback Period · The yardstick of payback period—that is, the number of years required for the earnings on the project to pay back the original outlay with no allowance for capital wastage—is unquestionably the most widely used measure of investment worth. Payback is superior to postponability since it takes into consideration the projected gross earnings, and it does have certain uses in capital-expenditure management:

Payback can serve as a coarse screen to pick out high-profit projects that are so clearly desirable as to require no refined rate-of-return estimates and to reject quickly those projects which show such poor promise that they do not merit thorough economic analysis. In addition, it may be adequate as a measure of investment worth for companies with a high outside cost of capital and severely limited internal cash-generating ability in comparison with the volume of highly profitable internal investment opportunities. If a shortage of funds forces the company to accept only proposals which promise a payback period after taxes of two years or less, the use of a more refined measure might not affect the list of accepted projects.

It also can be useful for appraising risky investments where the rate of capital wastage is particularly hard to predict. Since payback weights near-year earnings heavily and distant earnings not at all, it contains a sort of built-in hedge against the possibility of a short economic life.

For most corporations, however, payback is an inadequate measure of investment worth. It is a cash concept, designed to answer the single question of how soon the cash outlay can be returned to the company's treasury. As such it fails in three important respects to provide a satisfactory yardstick for appraising all the profit-producing investments of a firm:

1. Payback tends to overweight the importance of liquidity as a goal of the capital-expenditure program. No firm can ignore needed liquidity. But most can achieve it by means that are more direct and less costly than sacrificing profits by allowing payback to govern the selection of capital projects.

2. It ignores capital wastage. By confining analysis to the project's gross earnings (before depreciation) it takes no cognizance of its probable economic life.

3. It fails to consider the earnings of a project after the initial outlay has been paid back. By concentrating on liquidity, it ignores the vital matter of what the life pattern of the earnings will be. Up to the end of the payback period the company has just got its bait back. How much longer the earnings will last is what determines the profitability of the investment. A three-year payback project may yield a 30 percent return on average investment if it has a long life, but only 12 percent if its life is four years, and no return at all if just three years.

In short, because payback does not measure or reflect all the dimensions of profitability which are relevant to capital expenditure decisions, it is neither inclusive enough nor sensitive enough to be used as the company's over-all measure of investment worth.

Rate of Return · Measurement of the economic worth of an investment proposal by means of rate of return relates the project's anticipated earnings to the amount of funds which will be tied up during the investment life of the facility. Rate of return embodies the concept of *net* earnings after allowing for capital wastage. Neither degree of necessity nor payback period uses this concept, since payback is measured in terms of gross earnings, and urgency does not consider earnings at all.

Rate of return has its shortcomings. A sound rate-of-return

system is more complex than most of the methods of rationing a corporation's capital that are in current use. It costs more to install and put into operation. Also it may run into obstacles because it is unfamiliar and possibly because it will block privileged channels from access to capital funds.

But such limitations should not be decisive. Good management of capital expenditures is too vital to be blocked by ignorance, caution, or smugness. Overcoming the old organization's natural resistance to learning new tricks and training it in a new pattern of thought about capital expenditures is a one-shot affair. Once the system is installed, very little effort and cost are needed to keep it going.

The positive superiorities of a rate-of-return measure of investment worth are imposing. It takes account of the full lifetime of a capital-expenditure proposal. Two projects, each of which shows a three-year payback, may differ greatly in the length of time for which they will produce earnings for the company. Take this experience which one company had:

Certain refinery equipment that showed a three-year payback actually became obsolete and was replaced in less than three years. This project's rate of return, therefore, was less than zero, despite what appeared to be a very satisfactory payback. In contrast, a pipeline that had the same three-year payback kept on earning (and promises to continue for twenty years more). Clearly its rate of return was much higher.

Capital wastage—that is, the gradual loss of the economic value of the facility over a period of time—is of vital importance in the appraisal of an investment proposal. Capital productivity should be measured by earnings over the whole life of the investment, even though estimates of the distant future may be subject to wide margins of error.

Because rate of return considers the full life of an investment proposal, correct comparisons of the degree of value of projects can be made. Proposals can therefore be arranged in a ladder of priority even where they seem to be of the same degree of urgency or to have the same payback period. Moreover, the fact that the projects themselves may differ widely in their characteristics does not impede the comparison. New-product investments can thus be compared with cost-reducing projects; or a proposal this year can be compared with one which will not be ready until next year.

Better standards of rejection are made possible by rate of return. A company's combined cost of capital—say, 15 percent—can be used to determine the proper rate of cutoff on the capital-demand ladder just discussed; i.e., the minimum acceptable profitability of a proposal. This not only provides an objective, defensible basis for acceptance or rejection; it also aids top management in delegating authority by providing sound bench marks for personnel down the line to use in killing off the worst propositions before they have gone far up the chain of command.

Finally, rate-of-return rationing is likely to produce more earnings for stockholders, since it directs the flow of funds to their most profitable use by measuring the productivity of capital correctly and comparing it with a relevant standard of acceptable profitability.

MAKING THE ESTIMATES

We have seen that for most companies rate of return is the best yardstick of economic worth. Two problems arise in the practical application of this yardstick. The first concerns the concept for making the empirical projections that are needed to get the three basic determinants of project worth: (a) earnings, (b) economic life, and (c) amount of capital tied up. The second problem (discussed later) is how to combine these determinants in an index of profitability.

Ten Fallacies · The part of this measurement problem which is most often muffed is the job of getting a clear idea of just what needs to be estimated. Why should there be any problem in clarifying the concepts for rate-of-return measurement? The nature of the difficulties and their importance for good measurement can be seen by looking at ten common fallacies.

1. *"No Alternatives."* Perhaps the most common mistake in analyzing a capital proposal is the failure to consider any alternatives. There are always alternatives to an investment proposal, and a systematic analysis of the alternatives is the bench mark for estimating both the investment and the earnings of a capital

project. What will happen if the requested investment is not made measures what the company will get out of it if the investment is made. If, as usual, there are several alternatives differing in the amount of investment required, earnings estimates should logically be built upon the smallest investment alternative which is acceptably profitable. Alternatives which require greater investment are preferable to this one only if the *added* investment over this amount produces enough *added* earnings to yield a satisfactory rate of return.

2. "*'Must' Investment.*" Closely related is the "must" investment fallacy. The common conviction that certain equipment replacements are indispensable for continuing operations implies that top management has no alternatives. True, the alternative is sometimes so catastrophic that it is academic. But even in such a case the reason for making the investment should not be that it is urgent or indispensable, but that its profitability is terrific measured against the catastrophic alternative. Thus the rate of return from replacing a burnt-out pump in an oil pipeline may be astronomical; the investment is small and its earnings are the profits from the whole line, since the only alternative is a complete shutdown.

High-profit investments of this special nature are rarer than realized. Skeptical study of supposed "must" investments will reveal alternatives to many of them and will show that some of them are neither necessary nor even acceptably profitable.

3. "*High Strategy.*" Another fallacy is the notion that some projects are so pivotal for the long-run welfare of the enterprise that they possess high strategic value which overrides mere economic considerations and lifts their evaluation into a mystic realm beyond the ken of economic and financial analysis. For example, the dogma that an integrated oil company should own 75 percent of its crude oil sometimes precludes economic analysis of integration investments.

It is true that some capital expenditures do have benefits which are hard to measure because they are diffused over a wide area of company activity or because they stretch over a protracted time period. And there are some investments which must be made on almost pure faith (e.g., a new research center). Nevertheless, the idea that there is such a thing as strategic value not ultimately rooted in economic worth is demonstrably wrong. If a contemplated investment produces results that do not have any economic value, then directors and stockholders should question its wisdom.

4. *"Routine Replacement."* This fallacy maintains that scheduled periodic replacement of capital facilities is a practical and inexpensive substitute for an investment analysis of the economic desirability of individual replacements. For example, many fleet owners replace motor trucks on a routine basis (i.e., after a certain number of years or a certain number of miles), without determining whether the added net earnings from replacing this or that old truck with a new one will produce an adequate return on the specific added investment. Routine replacement has the virtues of simplicity, orderliness, and predictability. But vintage retirement will not produce as profitable a pattern of investment as will a capital-earnings plan.

5. *"Prediction is Impossible."* Scoffers maintain that since the future cannot be predicted with accuracy, it is futile to try to guess the useful life of a proposed facility or to project its earnings beyond the first year. The consequence of this fallacy is an unwillingness to define concepts in a way that will force explicit projection. People try to duck out by proclaiming that "with a four-year payback, it doesn't matter" or by embracing "unfair" Bureau of Internal Revenue depreciation rates.

The basic mistake is refusing to recognize that forecasting, though difficult and subject to error, is nevertheless necessary in appraising the worth of capital projects. Prediction, whether or not it is done consciously, lies at the heart of any executive judgment about a proposed investment. Usually it is better to *know* what is being done.

6. *"Fair Share of Overhead."* A common error in project analysis is to use allocations of current overhead instead of estimating the added costs that will be caused by the project. This cost-proration fallacy confuses problems of equity with problems of economic consequences. This is illustrated by a question frequently raised: Should a new product line, acquisition of which is being contemplated, carry its full share of the overhead now borne by mature products, or should it get a free ride? Neither of these suggested solutions is correct, at least for estimating project earnings. Old

overheads do not matter—only new overheads. What is needed is not a reallocation of past overheads but a forecast of how future overheads will increase by acceptance as opposed to rejection of the project. This cost increment is wholly unaffected by the conventions of apportionment of common costs.

7. *"Free Ride."* A related fallacy that frequently misguides analysis of capital proposals errs in the opposite direction. It holds that new products or added volume are "plus business" in the sense of incurring negligible additional costs. This "free ride" fallacy leads to the conclusion that earnings from expansion investments are almost equivalent to their revenue. There is something to this notion; long-run incremental costs are often smaller than fully allocated average costs. But they are larger than short-run marginal costs and never negligible.

While short-run marginal costs are relevant for operating decisions, long-run added costs must be used for investment decisions. Herein lies the peril of the "free ride" fallacy. What, for instance, are the earnings from an added gasoline service station when pipeline and bulk plant capacities will just take that added volume? If only the marginal cost of using this bulk-movement capacity is included, rate of return is high. But continued normal growth will soon force expansion of the bulk-movement capacity; the new service station brings this time that much closer. If the full cost of this expansion is included in estimating lifetime earnings, the return of course shows up as much lower.

8. *"Carrying Charge."* The practice of charging the earnings of all projects with an interest cost might be called the "carrying charge" fallacy. Usually this charge is computed by applying the company's short-term borrowing rate to the capitalized portion of the original investment. This approach has the virtue of recognizing that money is not costless, even though no entry is made in the accounts. It has, however, two defects: (*a*) it uses the wrong cost of money, since high-cost equity capital is left out, and (*b*) it introduces cost of money into the capital-management program in the wrong way. Instead of subtracting carrying costs from individual projects, it is better to use cost of capital as a cutoff rate to select acceptably profitable projects.

9. *"Book Value."* Determination of the investment amount looks so easy that it is often done wrong. Bookkeeping is the root

of error here. Accounting conventions that are indispensable for financial reporting give the wrong steer for estimating a project's investment base. The test of what should be included in the investment amount is not how it is handled on the books, which bears only on the tax effects of the proposal, an important but quite separate issue. The test is whether or not the outlay is necessary to produce the stream of earnings contemplated in the proposal.

The "book value" concept would exclude outlays that are expensed (rather than capitalized) from the amount of investment serving as the base for the rate-of-return estimate. Take a proposal to convert an unused portion of a building into a sausage factory requiring $100,000 of capitalizable machinery plus $150,-000 of expensed repairs. The pretax investment amount is the whole $250,000; after deflating the expensed portion for 50 percent income tax rates ($150,000 minus $75,000), the after-tax investment amount is seen to be $175,000. But the book value is only $100,000.

Book value also gives bad investment guidance in propping up, transferring, or abandoning existing assets. The book value of an existing asset is based on recorded historical cost less accumulated depreciation. For investment decisions, its value should be determined by what the company can get for the asset or what the company can do with it in its next best internal use, rather than by the figures that happen to be on the books.

10. *"Taxes Don't Matter."* There is a surprisingly widespread conviction that adjustment for corporate income taxes is academic. This "taxes don't matter" fallacy assumes that the underlying worth of a project is obscured (rather than revealed) by allowing for tax effects, and that the ranking of capital products will be the same whether or not they are deflated for taxes. This beguiling notion is wrong in two respects: (*a*) In order to apply tenable acceptance standards such as the company's outside cost of capital, it is necessary to measure rate of return after taxes, rather than before taxes. (*b*) The impact of taxes differs depending on the time shape of the project; and the after-tax ranking of proposals will differ significantly from their before-tax ranking if taxes are correctly taken into account in computing rate of return. For example, the tax effects of accelerated amortization can con-

vert a border-line project into a highly profitable investment opportunity.

Positive Concepts · Having looked at these ten fallacies, we are in a better position to formulate positive concepts of what needs to be estimated in measuring project earnings and project investment.

A correct estimate of earnings must be based on the simple principle that the earnings from a proposal are measured by the total *added* earnings or savings from making the investment as opposed to not making it. The proper bench mark for computing earnings on a project is the *best alternative* way of doing the job; comparison therewith will indicate the source and amount of the added earnings. Project costs should be unaffected by allocations of existing overheads but should cover all the changes in total overhead (and other) costs that are forecasted to result from the investment, but nothing else—nothing that will be the same regardless of whether the proposal is accepted or rejected.

The value of a proposed investment depends on its future earnings. Hence, the earnings estimate should be based on the best available projections of future volume, wage rates, and price levels. Earnings should be estimated over the economic life of the proposed facilities. Because project earnings vary in time shape, and because this will affect the rate of return, the earnings estimates should reflect the variations in the time trend of earnings.

In estimating economic life of an investment, consideration must be given to (*a*) physical deterioration, (*b*) obsolescence, and (*c*) the possibility that the source of earnings will dry up before either of the first two factors becomes operative.

Interest on investment should not be deducted from project earnings. Charging interest increases the complexity of the rate-of-return computation without adding to the information it provides. Earnings should be stated after corporate income taxes, for only in such form are they relevant for capital attraction and for dividend payment.

The appropriate investment base for calculating rate of return is the added outlay which is occasioned by the adoption of the project as opposed to rejecting it and adopting an alternative which requires less investment. The entire amount of the original added outlay should be included in the investment amount, regardless of how it is treated in the books. Any tax benefit which results from expensing certain items rather than capitalizing them should be reflected. Those repairs which would be made whether or not the proposal is adopted should be excluded from the investment amount, because they are not caused by it.

If the proposal involves a transfer of facilities from another part of the company, the opportunity cost of these facilities (the amount foregone by using them this way rather than another) should be added to the amount of investment. If the opportunity foregone is merely to sell the facilities for scrap, then this will indicate the value to set on the transferred assets.

The amount of the investment should also include the amount of any additional necessary investment in working capital or other auxiliary facilities. Research and promotional expenses to get new products rolling or to develop new methods or to expand business are no less investments than plant and equipment.

CALCULATING RATE OF RETURN

Once the basic estimates of project earnings and investment have been made, there are two major ways of combining them into a rate-of-return measurement. One way—which can be called the "accounting method" because it is closely related to many of the concepts used in conventional accounting procedure—computes rate of return as the ratio of (*a*) the project's earnings averaged over the life of the proposition to (*b*) the average lifetime investment. The other—which can be called "discounted cash flow"—computes rate of return as the maximum interest rate which could be paid on the capital tied up over the life of the investment without dipping into earnings produced elsewhere in the company.

Accounting Method · A characteristic of the accounting method is that it has many variants, each of which produces a different rate-of-return figure for any one investment proposal. One set of variants comes from diverse concepts of the investment amount (e.g., the original outlay, $100,000, versus the average amount tied up in the facility over its life, $50,000). Another source of variants is the diverse concepts of the project earnings. Earnings can be either gross or net of depreciation, either before or after taxes. They can be the average for several years or for the first year only. This variety of alternatives produces a tremendous range of rate-of-return results. But they all fall into the category of accounting method, provided the final result is a ratio of earnings to investment.

This shortcoming can be minimized only by arbitrarily standardizing on one variant of the method and making all computations according to this standard.

A more serious drawback to the use of the accounting method is that it is insensitive to variations in the time pattern of investment outlays and earnings. By taking an annual average of earnings over the life of a project this method ignores the earning trends, which may be quite important.

The economic worth of an investment will be affected by the time shape of its lifetime earnings, because near money has greater economic value than distant money. For example, an oil well has a strikingly different time shape than a service station. A well which comes in as a gusher trails off to a pumper. In contrast, a service station in a new area has a rising curve of earnings and is likely to show post-operative losses in the first year or so. Failure to reflect these time-shape disparities in the index of investment worth leads to unprofitable capital-expenditure decisions.

The effect of time shape on economic worth is especially great when the company's cost of capital is high or when the foregone earnings on projects that are passed up are high. Only a company whose investment projects are roughly similar in time shape and in economic life can ignore this feature. For such a firm the added accuracy of the discounted-cash-flow method probably does not justify the transitional pain and effort required to install the system. But any company which has projects that vary significantly in either time shape or longevity has an important stake in using the most sensitive rate-of-return method available.

Discounted Cash Flow · The mechanics of the cash-flow method consist essentially of finding the interest rate that discounts future

earnings of a project down to a present value equal to the project
cost. This interest rate is the rate of return on that investment.
Exhibit 1 illustrates the way in which rate of return can be determined under the cash-flow method for a cost-reducing machine
which costs $2,200 and has an anticipated life of five years with
no salvage value at the end of that time. In this case, an interest
rate of 20 percent is found to make the present value of the future
earnings stream equal to the present cost of the machine, so this
is the rate of return.

EXHIBIT 1

CASH-FLOW METHOD OF COMPUTING RATE OF RETURN ILLUSTRATED
*(Machine costing $2,200 with anticipated life of five years
and no salvage value at the end of that time)*

Year	Gross earnings before depreciation	Present value of earnings discounted at 18%	20%	22%
1	$ 200	$ 184	$ 182	$ 180
2	600	458	446	432
3	800	510	486	462
4	1,200	640	596	556
5	1,200	534	488	448
Total	$4,000	$2,326	$2,198	$2,078

Conceptually, this method is based on the principle that in
making an investment outlay we are actually buying a series of
future annual incomes—ranging in the example in the exhibit
from $200 the first year to $1,200 by the fourth and fifth years.
We have an investment in each of those incomes, an investment
which compounds in value through time until its own year arrives
and it materializes in cash earnings. Thus, for example, the $596
present value of the fourth year's earnings at 20 percent is the
amount that would have to be invested at 20 percent now to yield
$1,200 gross earnings during the fourth year ($596 compounded
at 20 percent for three and one-half years—since the $1,200 would
begin to come in at the beginning of the fourth year).

The basic simplicity of this method is brought out by this illustration. Earnings are stated as gross cash receipts (not figuring
depreciation). Therefore, it is not necessary to allocate the cost of
the machine over its life before computing return. Depreciation is
allowed for automatically because the interest rate that discounts

the sum of present values to zero is the rate of return on the investment after annual provisions for repaying the principal amount. We are not, as in the accounting method, watching the write-off of original cost; we are watching instead the growth of our investment outlay as we compound it through time.

The method is *simplified* by the fact that there is no need to make a decision as to which earnings base to use (e.g., original outlay, average investment, and so on), nor is there any need to enter interest as a direct cost of the project. Once the data are gathered and set up, there is only one rate-of-return answer possible, and it can be arrived at by straightforward working of charts and interest tables.[1]

Net Superiority of Discounted Cash Flow · The accounting method does have the advantage of familiarity and transparency. Although education would be necessary to get everyone to standardize on one method of averaging earnings and investment, the idea of computing a simple ratio by dividing one number by another is familiar to anyone who went beyond the second grade.

The discounted-cash-flow method admittedly is less familiar. While a method essentially similar to this has been widely used throughout the financial community for computing bond yields, insurance premiums, and rates on leased facilities where accuracy is important and even small errors may cause serious loss, it is new in its application to the measurement of productivity of individual capital-expenditure projects in industry. Hence the job of explaining it to the bookkeeper and the clerk will require time and effort. But its appearance of complexity is deceptive. Once the basic method is understood, it is actually simpler and quicker to use than the accounting method.

Another deterrent to its use is the fact that it does not correspond to accounting concepts about the recording of costs and revenues, so that special analysis is necessary to compute a postmortem on an investment made in the past. But this seems minor in comparison with its imposing superiorities:

1. The discounted-cash-flow method is economically realistic in confining the analysis to cash flows and forgetting about cus-

1. [Cases do arise where the rate of return is not unique. See the references in fn. 2 below. *Editor*]

tomary book allocations. The books, although very valuable for other purposes, are irrelevant for the task of measuring investment worth.

2. The use of this method forces guided thinking about the whole life of the project and concentration on the lifetime earnings.
3. It weights the time pattern of the investment outlay and the cash earnings from that outlay in such a way as to reflect real and important differences in the value of near and distant cash flows.
4. It reflects accurately and without ambiguity the timing of tax savings, either from expensing part of the investment outlay or from writing off capitalized costs over the life of the investment—something quite difficult to do by the accounting method.
5. It permits simple allowances for risks and uncertainties and can be adapted readily to increasing the risk allowance over time.
6. It is strictly comparable to cost-of-capital ratios so that decisions can be made quickly and safely on the basis of the relationship between indicated rate of return and the value of money to the company.

CONCLUSION

Examination of the capital-expenditure policies and procedures of some fifty well-managed companies shows that top management is forced to a distressing degree to rely on intuition and authority. Management lacks the skilled analysis and the scientific control needed for sound judgment on these intricate, vital capital decisions. The pivotal problem of capital-expenditure management is the measurement of the investment worth of individual proposals.

Systematic exploration to assure that investment opportunities are ferreted out and objectively analyzed is a prerequisite for the measurement of investment worth. Long-range capital plans and projections enable management to appraise projects in better perspective and to fit them into broader patterns. The comprehensive short-range capital budget which forecasts the timing of probable cash outlays for investment and the timing of cash inflows is essential for determining cut-off points by cash-generation criteria.

For orderly operation of rate-of-return rationing, management needs not only good management of capital productivity but also objective and defensible standards of minimum acceptability. These should generally be based on the company's cost of capital. Candid and economically realistic post-completion audits are indispensable incentives for measuring project profitability accurately; they also provide the systematized experience for improving project measurement in the future.

Special forms and procedures to implement these capital-expenditure management principles also need to be tailored to the particular conditions of the individual company. Above all, good capital-expenditure management must operate in an enlightened intellectual environment throughout the company; all the personnel concerned should understand the economics of capital expenditures and of the measurements and controls which a sound program entails.

For most companies, productivity of capital should be measured by rate of return, rather than by payback or degree of necessity. Estimates of a project's rate of return should be based on concepts of capital investment and projects earnings, which are indicated by what would happen if the company were to go ahead on the project instead of selecting some alternative which requires a smaller investment.

Prediction is essential; project worth depends solely on future earnings—the added earnings that will result from the added investment. These future earnings need to be forecasted over the whole economic life of the facility. Project costs should be unaffected by allocations of existing overhead, but should include all increases in overhead (and in other costs) that will be caused by the project. Earnings should be deflated for taxes. The investment base should be the entire added outlay regardless of bookkeeping—adjusted for corporate income taxes.

The discounted-cash-flow method of computing rate of return is demonstrably superior to existing alternatives in accuracy, realism, relevance, and sensitivity. Acceptance of rate-of-return capital budgeting should not hinge on willingness or reluctance to go this far in breaking with traditional methods.[2]

2. [For further discussion of criteria for choosing investments, see J. Lorie and L. Savage, "Three Problems in Rationing Capital" (1955), E. Solomon, "The Arithmetic of Capital Budgeting Decisions" (1956), and E. Renshaw, "A Note on the Arithmetic of Capital Budgeting Decisions" (1957), all in the *Journal of Business. Editor*]

Business and Economic Forecasting

Business Week

*The following selection is an abridgement of
an article which appeared in the September
24, 1955 issue of* Business Week.

Many economists—among them some who have physically left
the academic cloisters—still regard economic forecasting as a low
and disreputable pursuit for learned men. "We don't know
enough about the past to know anything much about the future,"
they say. So, they suggest, business must wait another hundred
years or so before it can expect the savants to say anything meaningful about the future. Meanwhile, they maintain, it is proper
that they should qualify all statements about the future to the
point of meaninglessness.

But the number of economists who hold to this pure patient
view of their calling is shrinking. More and more of them feel that
if economics is to have any pretense of being a useful study its
claim must rest on its ability to predict developments, and to provide solid foundations for policymakers to build on.

One of the chief reasons for the fact that more of them are overcoming their inhibitions about forecasting, and are concentrating
on improving its techniques, is that they are being immersed
deeper and deeper in government and business, where eyes are
always on the future.

It would take volumes to explain all the forecasting techniques used these days. It is possible, though, to take up the chief techniques that economists use when they are working with any of the three basic strategies of forecasting.

TREND EXTRAPOLATION

Extrapolation is a six-bit word borrowed from the mathematicians. In this case it means predicting the future movements of an economic factor by projecting into the future the trends you know it has taken in the past. On a chart, an extrapolation looks like this:

CHART A

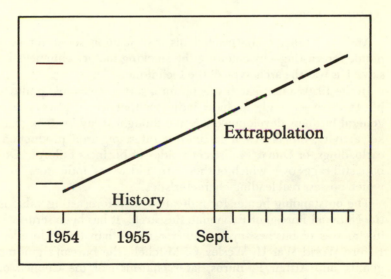

What makes an extrapolation useful to a forecaster is the statistical fact that a trend that is advancing will keep advancing—at least until something else happens. Unfortunately, the technique won't tell you when the "something else" will come. For instance, a wage series that is pushing upward will tend to push prices upward, and that will tend to push wages up again—only not ad infinitum. Eventually, some other series, like a falling sales volume, may halt or reverse the upward wage-price spiral.

But if, in your business, you don't need to care much about cyclical swings around a trend—if, for instance, you are figuring out the number of telephones or kilowatt hours the American people will want to use in the next ten years—trend extrapolation is a useful technique.

Of course, you can put trend extrapolation to work in a more sophisticated way than simply by laying a ruler over the past direction of a business indicator and projecting it on into the future. If you sell books or whiskey you may find your sales correlate nicely with the trend of disposable personal income, or if you sell oil or copper your sales may link up well with the Federal Reserve Index of Production.

"LEADING" SERIES

Andrew Carnegie constructed his own leading series for economic forecasting—by counting the smoking factory chimneys he saw. His was the archetype of the technique.

In the 1920s a hot search was on for a sort of economic philosopher's stone—a single business indicator that would always lead general business development. Some thought it lay in stock market activity; others saw it in interest rates, pig iron production, carloadings, or Dun & Bradstreet's index of business failures. Debate still rages over which of these are "old wives' indicators" and which possess real leading characteristics.

The outstanding hunter for indicators with forecasting value is the National Bureau of Economic Research. It has been scrutinizing masses of business-cycle data for more than three decades. Before World War II, Wesley C. Mitchell, the bureau's guiding genius, and Arthur F. Burns, later chairman of the Council of Economic Advisers under President Eisenhower, examined hundreds of series and picked a set of twenty-one leading, coincident, and lagging indicators, whose movements had regularly traced the course of the business cycle.

After the war, the bureau's Geoffrey H. Moore set to work updating Mitchell's and Burns's work. Moore examined 801 monthly and quarterly indicators and selected twenty-one, some of which were the same as those chosen by Mitchell and Burns. Of the twenty-one, Moore's eight leading series are: residential building contracts, commercial and industrial building contracts, new orders for durable goods, prices of industrial common stocks, wholesale prices of basic commodities, average work week in manufacturing, new incorporations, and business failures.

These indicators do regularly lead the business cycle's turns—though there is argument over just why this happens. But the chief trouble with them is that they are all extremely sensitive. They oscillate a great deal from month to month. So it is hard to know, when making a forecast, whether an up or downturn in one or another of the leading series means the real McCoy, or whether it is only a temporary wiggle.

DIFFUSION INDEXES

To find the meaning of those upturns and downturns, the bureau has invented the diffusion index. The bureau developed the index after it discovered that business cycle movements "have invariably been preceded by a remarkably regular cycle in the proportion of industrial activities undergoing expansion or contraction."

Forecasters make the index by counting the number of indicators in a given group that are rising at a given time. They convert this into a percentage of the number of indicators in the group. The bureau labels this percentage as a diffusion index because it believes it shows how widely diffused economic movements are. The bureau's diffusion indexes generally reach their peaks and troughs six months to twelve months ahead of the peaks and troughs of general business activity.

Not all economists think the diffusion index is much of a step forward. Arthur L. Broida, a Federal Reserve Board economist, maintains that it isolates cyclical turning points from all other changes in the economy's direction some time after the event. He holds that the index shows nothing different from what statisticians have long achieved by noting rates of growth and decline of a series of indicators. Their notes have already shown that a slower rate of increase in an index generally precedes its downturn.

SYSTEMATIC FORECASTING

Test-tube or systematic forecasting is the classic strategy of economic analysis. The technique here is to discover enduring relationships among economic factors and apply them to situations in the past, present, or future.

Analyzing the general business picture and making quantitative estimates of what conditions may be like a year or more ahead requires all the theoretical training, knowledge of institutional and statistical facts, technical skill, and political insight that an economist can command.

In dealing with comprehensive forecasting problems, economists today have two tremendous advantages over those who worked twenty years ago.

The first is economics' own "unified field theory." It is the product of the Keynesian revolution. Before John M. Keynes wrote his *General Theory of Employment, Interest, and Money*, economic theory tended to be fragmented into separate theories of wages, money, foreign trade, and so on. None of these separate principles had much relationship to each other. Economists may argue how much of the Keynesian revolution is attributable to Keynes himself. But there can be little doubt that general comprehension of how all the parts of an economy mesh together has advanced greatly since the mid–1930s.

The second advantage is the system of national income accounts developed since the early 1930s by the Commerce Department and the National Bureau of Economic Research. These give the economist a detailed and comprehensive picture of the national economy.

From unified economic theory and national income accounting stem the two most important techniques for systematic economic forecasting.

The "lost horse" technique is the first. That, anyway, is how it was christened by Sidney Alexander. He took the name from the old gag about how to find a lost horse. You do it by going to where the horse was last seen and asking yourself where you would go from there if you were a horse.

When you take that theory off the farm and put it to work in general business forecasting, each component of the gross national product (consumption, expenditures, gross private domestic investment, net foreign investment, government purchases of goods and services) plays the part of the lost horse. The analyst first finds out where each of these was when last reported by the Commerce Department's National Income Division.

But how he answers the question of where each section of GNP is going depends on his skill, patience, insight, and information

An economist who wants to fake impressively can simply guess figures for each part of the coming year's GNP. (Projecting gross private domestic investment at $49.6 billion is obviously more impressive than projecting it at $50 billion.) If there were state licensing boards for economists, a forecaster caught doing this would be convicted of malpractice and sentenced to run a checkout register in a supermarket for the rest of his days.

But the honest economist will go deeply behind each component of GNP when he prepares his forecast. He will study government plans and policies, analyze budget estimates, weigh the likelihood of the passage of important legislation and attempt to estimate the price tags the various bills will bear.

He will look behind private investment at the factors affecting the capital goods industries, study ratios of inventories to sales and of production to capacity. He will look at the factors that affect building construction, such as credit terms, availability of mortgage money, vacancy rates, rents, and price movements. He will measure his analysis against the findings of capital spending surveys.

He will try to gauge the effect of government fiscal policies on private investment and consumption, estimate the relationship between the growth of investment and consumption. Then he will see how money credit conditions may affect people's spending or saving, their liquid assets, their supplies of durable goods. And he will measure this against the finding of consumer intention surveys.

He must put all these parts together to make a whole—but he must also carry in his mind an image of how the whole will affect the parts. He will also have to sense how non-economic factors— like international relations and national elections—will affect the picture.

Since the task of preparing a forecast of the national economy can be almost endless, the economist must figure out the point at which he has all the information he can handle. But, at best, the time he has for these analyses is always pretty short, since he must base his forecasts on the most current information. If he takes too long, his facts grow cold. The best course for the forecaster is to stay at his task continuously, constantly modifying his forecast on the basis of new information.

The only way to judge whether an economist has done a thoroughly sensitive forecast—or blooped his way through one—is to examine carefully the details of his analysis. Of course, a lost horse analysis depends a lot on the economist's subjective judgments about the data he receives and on his somewhat "artistic" perception of relations. So all of his analysis may not show on paper.

A more rigorous way of tackling the problem of what will happen to the millions of factors and relations that make up the national economy is to build an econometric model of the economy. The method here is related to the lost-horse technique, but it is a lot more elegant, for the practice of econometrics is one of blending economics, mathematics, and statistics.

An economist starts to build a model by first selecting an economic theory, or set of theories, that he believes will take into account all the significant factors likely to affect the general business or particular industry situation that he is forecasting.

He translates the theory into a set of mathematical equations that make up his econometric model. The equations relate the factors he wants to discover (the dependent variables) to the factors he already knows, or can estimate easily (the independent variables). These independent variables can be of two types: first, those that are historic facts, such as last year's profits or inventory spending; and second, future elements, such as government spending, that can be estimated from advance information.

The econometrician bases his forecast on the past relations between the dependent and independent variables. He assumes that relations that were stable in the past will remain stable in the future. Of course, the relation between large economic aggregates, like consumption and income, won't be perfectly stable. So the question the forecaster must first answer is: "Will they be stable enough, within some estimated range of probability, to be used for forecasting?" If it turns out that they aren't stable enough for the job they are supposed to perform, the forecaster can assume that the theory behind his equations is not valid. Even then he has achieved something—and, in this way, econometrics can be a useful technique for junking false economic theories.

Econometric models come in for plenty of criticism from forecasters who stick to other techniques.

One of the chief complaints against them is that they make complex mathematical operations on data that is too rough to permit such manipulation. Stephen M. DuBrul, a General Motors economist, says that to apply intricate econometric techniques to the rough data that is available is "gold-plating crowbars."

But econometricians keep building their models and trying to improve them. They try to fit more factors into their figuring to overcome the complaints that their models are mechanically unsound and insensitive to social movements.

There are plenty of econometric model-builders at work to handle this task of improvement.

At Michigan University's Research Seminar in Quantitative Economics, three econometricians, Lawrence Klein, Daniel Suits, and Arthur S. Goldberger, have built a 25-equation model of the U.S. economy.[1]

They do not look on their model as a once-and-for-all job, but are continuously testing and strengthening it. When a forecast turns out to be off the mark, the Michigan group probes into the machinery of the model to find out just where the fault lies, changes the model to try to correct the mistake next time. And to make the model more realistic, the group is also making intensive studies of particular sectors of the economy, including the construction industry, foreign trade, agriculture, and the money market.

Industry's own economists are beginning to get into the model-building field. For industry's purposes the models have been simplified. Management has found them useful for doing one of the principal jobs for which business is turning to economists:

1. [For a more recent model, see J. Duesenberry, G. Fromm, L. Klein, and E. Kuh, *The Brookings Quarterly Econometric Model of the U.S. Economy* (North Holland, 1965). *Editor*]

helping guide planning for capital spending and expansion programs by producing long-range projections of specific industries' places in the national economy.

Some industry economists say the models provide the best technique yet developed for organizing massive and complex statistical data, for cumulating knowledge and profiting from past errors and successes, and for systematizing the whole forecasting process.

Forecasting in Industry

NATIONAL INDUSTRIAL CONFERENCE BOARD

This article comes from the National Industrial Conference Board's Forecasting in Industry (*Studies in Business Policy*)

1. KELLOGG COMPANY

A typical example of a forecast built up from the grass roots of the sales force is given in the following account of the methods of the Kellogg Company, a large food manufacturer. The company makes two principal types of forecasts. The first, for one year, is used as a basis for planning advertising, promotion and selling expenditures, setting salesmen's quotas, and controlling raw material purchases. The second is a long-range forecast covering three to five years, and is used for planning factory expansion.

Annual Forecast · The annual sales forecast originates in the company's twenty-one sales territories under the direction of the branch sales managers. Each territory is broken up into subdistricts, which are covered by one to five salesmen under the leadership of a subdistrict salesman. In the fall of each year, the branch managers, who head the sales organization of the territories, call in the subdistrict salesmen one by one to discuss the sales outlook. General business conditions in the district, population changes, and other factors which might influence sales are all considered. Sales records for past years, together with A. C. Nielsen Company information on competitive activities, contribute to the development of estimated sales for subdistricts. Assisting the branch manager in this process is a staff of a half dozen or more who handle all of the statistical work. Special forms are printed each year to record data.

Adjustment for Advertising. After the branch manager has completed these meetings, members of the home office sales departments, the advertising department, and representatives of the company's advertising agency meet with each branch office manager to discuss the tentative sales forecast for his territory. In arriving at his estimates, the branch manager does not know the amount of advertising and promotion effort that will be expended in his area. The purpose of these meetings is to determine how much advertising and promotion will be necessary to achieve the forecast. The forecast is revised in the light of probable promotional expenditures.

Production and Purchasing. After these meetings are completed, a recapitulation of the branch sales forecasts is made at the home office and a tentative advertising and promotion budget is set. These are submitted to the production and purchasing departments who determine if it is possible to procure and produce the volume of goods represented by the forecasts. When production and purchase facilities are strained, as in recent years, this review may have an important bearing on the ultimate goal established.

Final Review. The next step is the preparation of a preliminary operating statement for consideration by top management. Members of the sales and advertising departments meet with the top officers of the company and give the sales forecast and the advertising and promotion budget a final review. The president, sales manager, advertising manager, and comptroller are among those who participate in this balancing operation.

Throughout the entire process, previous sales experience, the general business outlook, and changes in the competitive situation are given serious consideration.

The forecast is finally approved by the president and the vice-president in charge of sales. When the year's operating budget comes up for review, the board of directors also adds its approval.

Responsibility. Responsibility for organizing and directing the forecasting procedure rests with the sales supervisor, who is chief assistant to the vice-president in charge of marketing and has charge of the home office sales department and general control over all branch offices.

Revisions · The annual forecast is revised only when some radical change has taken place, such as an important fluctuation in prices, a serious shortage of raw materials, or, as during World War II, when the government sets up restrictions on the use of some items used by the company.

Period Forecasts · Three times a year, however, period forecasts are made. The period forecast is, in a sense, a refinement and revision of the annual forecast. The basic purpose is to estimate sales for each of the ensuing four months. These period forecasts are used for setting production schedules, scheduling shipments of incoming materials, and planning purchases of materials that do not have to be contracted for long in advance.

In making the period forecasts, the subdistrict salesmen are not consulted. Instead, the home office sales staff makes the forecasts on the basis of information obtained during the formulation of the annual forecast plus a study of current sales trends.

Accuracy · To encourage the development of accurate forecasting by the sales force, the branch manager receives each month a comparison of the actual sales with the forecast previously made for each subdistrict of his territory. He can thus observe whether he is meeting his quota. While the normal tendency under such an arrangement would be to make low forecasts so that quotas would be easy to attain, the fact that the advertising and promotion expenditure in his territory is allocated somewhat on the basis of his forecast of sales makes it undesirable for the branch manager to underestimate sales. He knows that if his forecast is low, his allocation for advertising and sales promotion will also be low.

Long-range Forecast · The long-range forecast is largely based upon an averaging of opinions of the sales staff, the market research department, and the comptroller's office. Other things are taken into consideration—the sales trend of the industry for several years past, the economic condition of the country, the sales trend of the company's own brands, new-product development outlook, and competitors' activities.

2. ELI LILLY AND COMPANY

Eli Lilly and Company, manufacturers of drugs and pharmaceuticals, have long made use of correlation analysis between sales and a well-known income series. Study and investigation by company specialists had revealed a very definite relation between the sales of pharmaceuticals and disposable personal income.[1] The company followed this lead and developed a whole system of forecasting based on the relation of sales to movements in disposable personal income.

Industry Forecast · It is usually easier to forecast the sales of an entire industry than those of a particular company. The reason for this is that the foundation of forecasting, the facts and figures, are most generally available on an industry-wide basis. Eli Lilly was most fortunate in having at its disposal reliable data on total industry sales of ethical drugs.

After adjusting both industry sales and the income figures for price changes, the company found through correlation analysis that this relation existed: for every 10-percent growth or decline in disposable personal income, the industry's sales show a corresponding increase or decrease of about 5 percent. Aside from this influence, analysis of the record revealed a steady rate of growth in pharmaceutical sales, which the company attributes to constantly increasing expenditures for research and the resulting new major product developments (see Chart 1). As long as research expenditures continue to increase and new products are evolved the company believes that this trend will continue.

Knowing this trend, and the relationship to personal disposable income, industry sales can be forecast by use of this formula:

$$\text{Industry Volume} = \text{Income (weighted)} \times \text{Growth Trend}$$

From the visual evidence in Chart 2, it is apparent that the company is in a position to derive a forecast of total industry sales when forecasts of income are made available.

1. Disposable personal income is the income remaining to persons after deduction of personal taxes and other payments to general government.

CHART 1

GROWTH TREND FOR DOMESTIC SALES OF ETHICAL DRUGS, AFTER ALLOWING FOR CHANGES IN DISPOSABLE PERSONAL INCOME

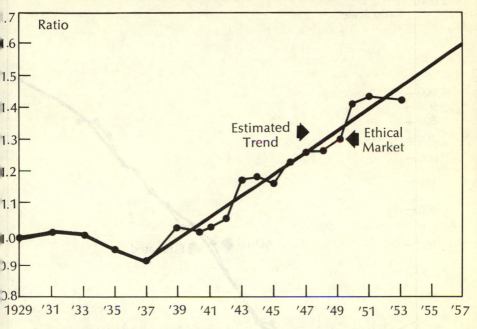

Company Forecast · There still remained the problem of estimating what portion of the forecasted sales of the industry would be obtained by the company. This estimate is obtained by studying the share of the national market the company obtained in past years and projecting the trend of company participation into the future. In order to do a good job, management feels that the reasons underlying the pattern of past performance must be understood if future trends are to be evaluated properly. In this connection, consideration is given to such pertinent details as relative manufacturing capacity, general customer acceptance of the company's products, company research expenditures, and the estimated effect of each of these on past and prospective sales performance.

District and Product Forecasts · Essentially the same technique was used to break down the over-all company sales forecast into

CHART 2

U.S. Domestic Sales of Drugs

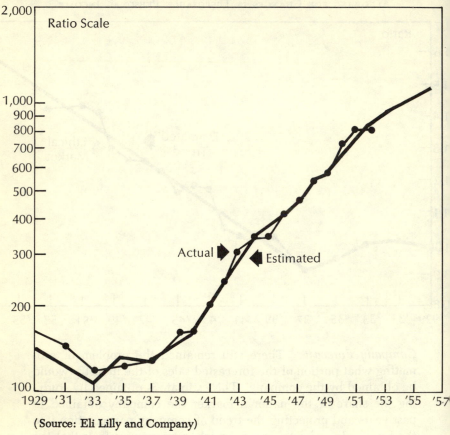

(Source: Eli Lilly and Company)
(Millions of Dollars)

detailed district and product sales forecasts. To obtain district
sales forecasts, past sales were related to the levels of income
for the particular sales district. After allowance was made for
this relationship, the district's rate of sales growth was compared
with the over-all company growth trend. As in the case of the
correlation studies mentioned earlier, the first step was the
preparation of a scatter diagram. In constructing it (Chart 3), the
company plotted district sales volume against company sales

volume, both excluding the estimated effect of income levels. The dot at the lower left-hand corner, for example, indicates that in one year adjusted company sales volume was $15 million and adjusted district sales volume was $300,000.

Judging by the closeness of this relationship, the company was able to draw a line on the scatter diagram which represents the average relationship between total company sales and the sales district under study. The closeness of the various dots to this line is an indication of the reliability of the correlation.

CHART 3

DISTRICT SALES VOLUME ADJUSTED FOR INCOME, RELATED TO COMPANY SALES VOLUME ADJUSTED FOR INCOME

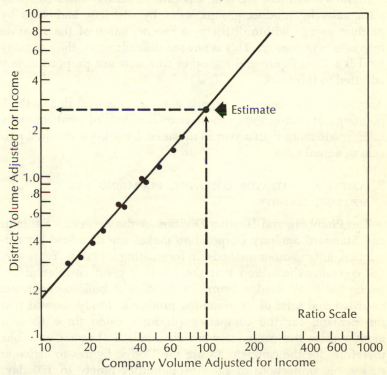

(Source: Company data)

(Millions of Dollars)

On this basis, if company sales are forecast at $100 million on growth factors alone, then this district's figure would be $2.5 million. The sales forecast for the district is then arrived at by adjusting this $2.5 million amount upward or downward, depending upon the forecast of personal disposable income for the district.

Forecasts of sales by product groups are derived by using basically the same methods as for total company sales, but in this case the correlation analysis deals with the single product group and its relation to income instead of the total company operation. Product group sales estimates at the district sales level are likewise obtained by using the basic approach outlined above.

Inasmuch as there are four separate forecasts—total company sales, sales by product groups, sales by districts, and sales by product groups within districts—a reconciliation of the separate forecasts is necessary. This is not too difficult, since the company total is a fixed figure and the other forecasts are proportionately adjusted to this total.

Accuracy · The company reports good success with this method, pointing out that in some recent years forecasts of total company sales, made more than a year in advance, have been within 2 percent of actual sales.

3. AMERICAN RADIATOR COMPANY, PLUMBING AND HEATING DIVISION

The Plumbing and Heating Division of the American Radiator and Standard Sanitary Corporation makes use of a lead-lag correlation, among other methods, in forecasting its sales. Years ago, the company discovered that there was a good correlation between the F. W. Dodge figures on residential building contracts awarded and sales of its plumbing products. Study showed that the demand for the company's products came three to four months after the contracts were awarded. It became possible, therefore, for the company to use the Dodge figures to arrive at reasonable projections of sales probabilities ninety to 120 days in advance, together with some evidence of the sales trend in the following six to nine months. Chart 4 shows the closeness of the relationship.

Application · The company uses this correlation in the following manner. Contract award figures by individual counties are tabulated into sales territory totals. Dodge contract award figures covering thirty-seven Eastern states are compared with sales within the area of the division's twelve sales districts and twenty-nine sales offices that are covered by such data. A "factor" is computed for each sales district and sales office within a district expressing the relationship between contract award figures in that territory and the past records of company sales. This comparison is aided by the fact that the company's territories are

CHART 4

AMERICAN-STANDARD PLUMBING SALES AND RESIDENTIAL CONTRACTS AWARDED

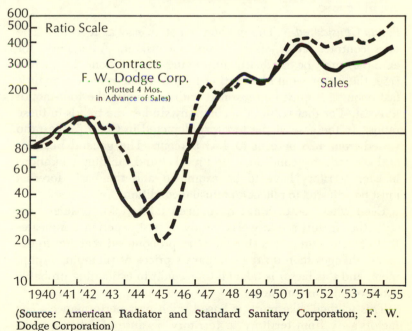

(Source: American Radiator and Standard Sanitary Corporation; F. W. Dodge Corporation)

(Index numbers: 12-mos. moving averages)

bounded by county lines, and contract award data can be obtained on a county basis.

The factor for each territory is obtained by computing the ratio of sales to contracts, using a twelve-month moving total for comparison. Since contracts lead sales by about four months, sales are recorded with a 120-day lag for the purpose of comparison.

For example, Chart 5 shows the trend of contract awards in a typical territory, plotted four months ahead of sales. The company's latest twelve months sales at the time this chart was drawn averaged 4.63 percent of total contract awards. This factor is first applied to the latest twelve-month figures on contract awards (which precede company's sales by four months), thereby deriving an estimate of sales for the twelve months ending 120 days ahead. From this total, the company then subtracts the actual sales for the preceding eight months, thus deriving an estimate of sales for the following four months, one of which has almost elapsed because of the time required to compile the contract award figures.

Points Considered · The method is not as easy as it seems. The sales contract factor, itself, is not a constant. A territory, for example, may be gradually improving its position. In such a case, the factor would be getting larger. If the rate of growth is fast enough, it must be reckoned with in making the four-month forecast. For that reason the company studies the trends in these ratios. In the case of the territory depicted in Chart 5, the ratio varied from 4.28 percent to 4.63 percent. The general business outlook, industry conditions, and market and building conditions in each territory have to be examined and the basic forecast must be adjusted to reflect an unusual condition.

Even when these things have been taken into consideration, still other factors are at work. Study of past experience indicates that construction prices show a more pronounced reaction to demand changes than do the company's prices of plumbing equipment, and this factor is taken into account in estimating probable ratios of sales to contracts.

This method, like most, is based upon past performance. The factors vary from territory to territory because of differences in the ability of salesmen, the acceptance of the company's products, or the strength of competition. In an effort to bring a low-

CHART 5

AMERICAN-STANDARD PLUMBING SALES IN ONE TERRITORY, COMPARED WITH RESIDENTIAL BUILDING CONTRACTS AWARDED *

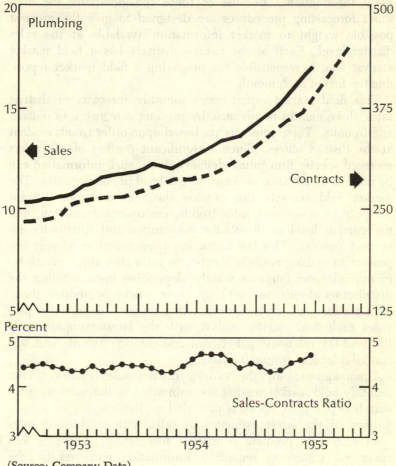

(Source: Company Data)

* Building contracts plotted ahead four months.

producing territory up to par, the company may be prepared to exert greater sales effort or to make a larger promotional expenditure. The forecaster must take these possible influences into consideration before setting the final figure. In short, after applying this method, the forecaster must exercise considerable sound judgment in order to obtain a final figure that reflects current conditions.

Field Information · Because of these considerations, the division's forecasting procedures are designed to give the greatest possible weight to market information available at the sales district level. Each of the twelve districts has a field market analyst who is responsible for preparing a field market report, due the first of each month.

This field market report gives monthly forecasts of district sales, three months in advance, by product categories, in dollars, and in units. These forecasts are based upon order trends evident at the district offices. Since a significant portion of all orders received specify firm future delivery dates, such information can be used as an advance indicator of the level of coming sales. The market field analysts also canvass the sales force on current competitive conditions, sales trends, customer information, and the current level of distributor inventories and distributor inventory policies. This last factor has been found to be very important in making realistic short-term estimates, since month-to-month sales can fluctuate widely, depending upon whether the distributors decide to build up their stocks or reduce them.

In addition, the division's marketing research department provides each field market analyst with the latest comparison of the lead-lag relationship between construction awards and territorial sales on a continuing basis.

Upon approval by the various district sales managers, the monthly field market reports are submitted to the marketing research department. Space is provided on these forms for a comparison of the latest estimates of sales with established sales quotas to help promote consistent forecasting. There is also space for comments regarding information gathered by the market analyst on the following subjects: district construction activity, general business conditions, price levels, corrective action indicated, color trends, product design, sales promotional activity, sales training, and competition.

These comments form the basis for a monthly report distributed by the marketing research department to general management that highlights specific conditions in the various sales territories.

The district sales forecasts are combined and totaled by the marketing research department and are used as a guide in preparing over-all divisional sales forecasts.

Home Office Forecast · The sales forecasting procedure at the home office is as follows. Once a month a forecast preparations committee, which consists of the technical assistant to the general marketing manager and the supervisor of sales analysis, who represents the marketing research department, meet with each of the seven product managers. In this way a unit forecast is arrived at by product, month-by-month, for the succeeding twelve-month period. In progressing to its forecasts, the committee takes into consideration the forecasts from the district sales offices, the latest estimates based on the lead-lag correlation, the record of previous sales estimates, and the current rate of sales, as well as the special knowledge its members bring to bear on the situation. For example, the product managers provide information regarding various sales campaigns and promotions, as well as new product developments in their particular lines and estimate their possible effect on sales.

Once a quarter the forecast review committee meets to consider the recommendations of the forecast preparations committee. Membership consists of the general marketing manager, the general sales manager, the product line managers, the manager of marketing research, and the manager of order handling. Based upon the combined opinion of this committee the forecasts of the forecast preparation committee are accepted or modified as seen fit. This projection is the principal factor in the establishment of the annual sales budget as well as the basis for establishing production schedules and inventory levels.

4. LONG ISLAND LIGHTING COMPANY

The Long Island Lighting Company's forecasts of sales and revenue are the basis of its economic planning. In most businesses, managerial action can guide the course of future events. In the case of public utility companies such control is not so easy.

Must Supply Demand · Houses are built, industries are established, appliances are sold, new equipment is installed, and the local gas and electric company must, by law, supply the new demand. It can promote and encourage use but it cannot refuse or even limit service without serious consequences.

The need for sound sales forecasting is made apparent by the fact that it may take five years to plan and build a new power plant. A transmission line can be constructed more rapidly, but it may take two years to secure the necessary right-of-way, and the design cannot be drawn until the rights-of-way are known. Even small lines and gas mains require considerable time to design and build.

In many utility companies, it is therefore customary to forecast sales at least five years ahead. The Long Island Lighting Company forecasts sales eighteen months ahead by months and five years ahead by years. These forecasts show the probable trend of new customers, of sales, and of revenues, both by classes of business and by location.

Judgment Essential · Although heavy reliance is placed upon statistical methods involving the study and extension of trends, cycles, and seasonal patterns, the company feels that the application of statistical techniques alone will not necessarily produce a reasonable forecast. All company forecasting is therefore centralized in a planning committee which consists of the heads of the following departments: budget, commercial, engineering, operating, rate, research, and sales. Through this committee, independent estimates which encompass all phases of the business are collectively analyzed to produce a mutually acceptable forecast. One of the principal values the company derives from the planning committee is the opportunity to collect independent judgments about the future from the various department heads representing different points of view.

Methods Used · This company's method of forecasting sales evolves about the study of four basic related factors: (1) population; (2) meters or customers; (3) consumption; (4) revenue. Each is studied separately and also in relation to the other three. These interrelationships or "links" serve as cross-checks. They are: (1) the meter ratio (number of people per meter); (2) sales per meter; (3) revenue per meter; and (4) revenue per unit of power sold vs. consumption per meter. With the aid of information from the field, mathematical formulas and sound judgment, the trends of these link factors can be extended into the future.

Population Studies · Changing population is the prime factor affecting company sales, so much time is naturally spent in analyzing and forecasting population trends. Careful and continuous population studies are made of the areas served by the company. These studies take into account the birth and death rates, the migration of people, new construction, and other similar factors. From these studies estimates of current population are made (Chart 6) and a trend of population is established and forecast.

CHART 6

POPULATION OF NASSAU AND SUFFOLK COUNTIES, LONG ISLAND

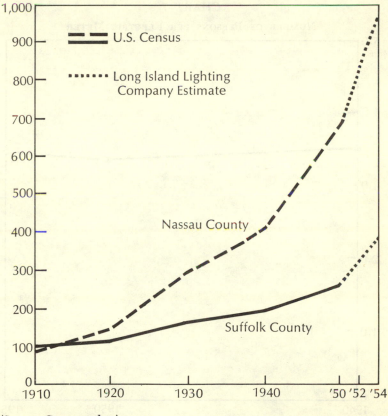

(Source: Company data)

(In thousands)

The company also maintains correlation studies between population and active meters. Regular reports based on field surveys are made by local managers on new construction and new industrial developments in their territories. Each field survey is checked against applications for service on file and against building-permit records in local government offices. The relation between new construction and new meters is generally quite close so that short-range predictions can be made with great accuracy.

These reports are studied also for possible effect on population-meter ratios (Chart 7). By applying the forecast population-meter ratio to estimates of future population, the number of meters in use can be forecast.

CHART 7

NUMBER OF PERSONS PER ELECTRIC METER

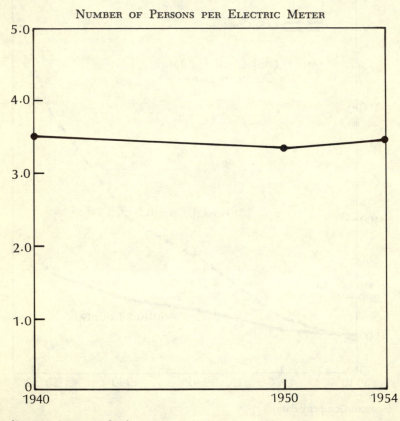

(Source: Company data)

Consumption and Revenue · The next step is to forecast the estimated power consumption per customer. For residential customers, a twelve-month moving average of energy use per customer (or meter) shows a gradual rise, which can be projected into the future by means of a trend line.

The forecast of energy sales is obtained from the combination of the forecast of meters in use and the forecast of estimated use per customer. This forecast is tested in the planning committee against information available to the sales department of electrical appliances in use and of the probable effect of the company's promotional activities.

To obtain a forecast of revenue, the company makes use of the known relation between energy sales per billed meter and revenue per billed meter, both on a billing day basis (Chart 8). From the line of average relation, accurate average revenue rates can be determined for any given level of consumption. Information provided by the rate department regarding prospective rate adjustments can be used to temper the forecast of revenue per kilowatt hour, and then, by applying it to the forecast of energy sales, a revenue forecast is obtained.

The forecast of industrial sales and revenue is handled separately. Most of the short-range information on future demand is obtained from the customers themselves. Any contemplated plant expansions, work-shift changes or installation of new equipment is reported to the company and is taken into account in the forecast of industrial revenue. This technique is confined to large industrial customers who consume about half of the energy sold in this rate classification. The balance is assumed to match proportionately the trend indicated by these large consumers, because much of the small business is subsidiary to the large business in this territory.

The sum of the individual estimates of residential, commercial, and industrial sales when added to estimates of other sales such as street lighting, sales to other utilities and the like, produce a total sales estimate. This estimate is compared with independent estimates of energy demand forecast by the operating and engineering departments and differences are reconciled.

Engineering and Operating Departments' Forecast · The engineering and operating departments' procedure is entirely differ-

CHART 8

RESIDENTIAL CLASS OF BUSINESS—KWH PER BILLED METER PER
BILLING DAY RELATED TO REVENUE PER BILLED METER
PER BILLING DAY, 1953

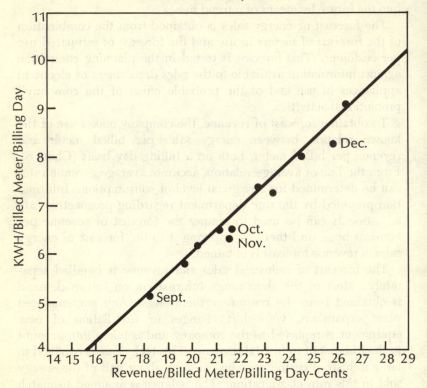

(Source: Company data)

ent, and is based on the relationship between peak demand and average energy requirements. First, the peak demand in the previous year is corrected for the estimated effect on demand of actual versus "normal" weather conditions and is then further adjusted for any unusual operating conditions in existence at the time of the actual peak. For instance, a big industrial plant may have been on strike.

To this corrected peak is added an increment representing demand expected from all new customers. This gives an estimate of the peak demand for the following years, assuming normal weather and normal operating conditions. The process is then repeated for each of the succeeding four years.

Finally, the trend in the ratio of average kilowatt demand to peak demand (the load factor) is examined and projected for the five-year forecast. This is feasible because this ratio moves slowly and a trend projection is reasonably accurate. Annual forecasts of kilowatt hours generated are then derived as the product of peak demand and average load factor, multiplied by a factor of 8,760 (the number of hours in a year).

From the power generation derived as above, estimates of the amount of energy lost and used by the company itself are subtracted. The resultant figures now represent energy sales and can be compared with the sales projection based on trends in population, customers, and energy consumption. Any differences are then reconciled by applying the consensus judgment of the planning committee.

Revisions · The process of gathering background information for the forecasts is continuous, but new forecasts are issued officially twice a year, on June 1 and October 1. On June 1 the revision for the current year and preliminary estimates for the five succeeding years, by years, are issued. On October 1 final estimates for the next budget year, by months, plus a revision of the five-year forecast are issued. The timing coincides with the dates of budget revision.

Accuracy · The company reports that the present method of forecasting has been in use for about three years. During that time the margin of error has been slightly above 1 percent for forecasts made one year in advance, and between 5 percent and 10 percent for the most distant years. Perhaps as important as accuracy is the ease with which new developments in the use of electricity can be incorporated in the forecast. Also, the establishment of the planning committee has made available more information upon which to base estimates.

Responsibility for Forecasts · Many departments are involved in the company's sales forecasting activities. The budget department, with technical assistance from the commercial research department on statistical techniques, prepares the revenue forecasts from the planning committee's sales forecasts. The sales department supplies information and keeps records on merchandising activity by the company and local dealers. The commercial department keeps records on new customers added. The rate department is responsible for all information dealing with customer bill distributions and rate changes. The system engineering department keeps weather data and makes estimates of its effect on sales. This department also coordinates the work of the engineering, electric operating, and gas operating departments in the forecasts of peak demand.

5. THE B. F. GOODRICH COMPANY

The methods used are well-illustrated by the practices of the B. F. Goodrich Company in forecasting passenger-car tire demand.

Passenger-car tire sales are of two types: Those made to automobile manufacturers, to be used as part of the original equipment, and those sold to car owners to replace worn-out tires.

To estimate sales for original equipment, all a company needs to know is: (1) how many vehicles will be produced; (2) how many and what types and sizes of tires will they be equipped with; and (3) what share of the total sales will the company obtain.

The long-term forecast of passenger-car production involves several steps. In the first step, the number of cars already in use is considered in relation to the nation's level of income. The company's business research department compared the number of passenger cars in operation at the end of each year, for a period of years back to 1930, with the corresponding year's level of disposable personal income, adjusted for changes in purchasing power. It was found that the following relationship existed: for every million dollars of income there were approximately 200 passenger cars in use (see Table 1).

The second step involves the preparation of an estimate of the future trend of disposable personal income based on certain assumptions as to the nation's potential economic growth. The business research department starts by making an economic fore-

TABLE 1

Passenger Cars in Operation and Disposable
Personal Income

Year	Passenger Cars in Operation at End of Year (In Thousands)	Disposable Personal Income (Billions of Constant 1947 Dollars)	Cars per $1 Million Disposable Income
1930	20,533	105.8	194.0
1940	25,939	129.6	200.2
1950	37,619	194.1	193.8
1951	39,638	199.2	199.0
1952	40,475	205.1	197.4
1953	42,945	213.8	200.9

Source: U. S. Department of Commerce and B. F. Goodrich Business
Research Department.

cast of gross national product (GNP), which measures the sum
total of goods produced by the nation's economy. Analysis has
shown that once the effect of changing price levels is removed
the rate at which the economy's output grows depends on four
factors: population, the proportion of the population employed
in the labor force, the length of the average work week, and
productivity as measured by gross national product per man-hour
of work (see Table 2).

For some components of these factors long-term trends may be
calculated and extended into the future. One such factor is output per man-hour of work, which examination of the record
has shown to increase over the years at a more or less regular,
and predictable rate. For other factors, however, such as the size
of the armed forces, flat assumptions must be made, based on the
best-informed opinion at the time.

Future levels of gross national product are estimated from
the resulting projections of man-hours worked and of gross
national product per man-hour (productivity). The forecasts
of gross national product are used in turn to estimate the future
levels of personal income. This is made possible because of the
close connection between GNP and personal income (see Chart 9).
Deducting estimated personal tax payments from the estimates of
personal income results in a forecast of disposable personal
income.

TABLE 2

EMPLOYMENT, MAN-HOURS, AND GROSS NATIONAL PRODUCT

Year	Population Age 15 and Over (Millions)	Civilian Labor Force (Millions)	Unemployment (Millions)	Employed (Including Armed Forces) (Millions)	Average Hours Per Week	Annual* Man-hours (Billions)	Gross National Product in 1947 Dollars (Billions)	Gross National Product per Man-hour (1947$)
1930	87.1	49.8	4.3	45.8	49.0	116.7	135.2	1.159
1940	99.0	55.6	8.1	47.9	44.6	111.1	171.6	1.545
1950	110.0	63.1	3.1	61.5	41.7	133.4	264.7	1.984
1951	112.1	62.9	1.9	63.9	42.2	140.2	282.9	2.018
1952	113.1	63.0	1.7	64.7	42.4	142.7	294.2	2.062
1953	114.2	63.4	1.5	65.8	41.9	143.4	306.6	2.138

* Annual man-hours equals total employed (including armed forces) multiplied by average hours per week, times fifty-two weeks.

Source: U. S. Department of Commerce and B. F. Goodrich Business Research Department.

CHART 9

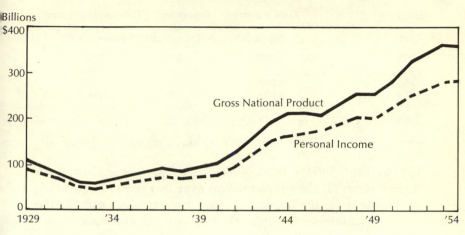

After these estimates have been made, the company is in a position to project the trend of automobile production in future years. Knowing the probable number of cars that will be in use and allowing for anticipated scrappage (which depends upon production in prior years, the average life of cars currently in operation, and economic factors which lead to a rate of scrappage above or below average) the company knows how many cars will probably have been produced in order to replace cars scrapped and to make net additions to the nation's stock of cars.

As this provides only an estimate of new-car production for domestic use, the export demand and the production of military vehicles using passenger-car tires must be estimated and added to get the total.

From these estimates of vehicle production, industry sales forecasts of original equipment tires are derived by applying a factor of about 5.5. The company explains that although new passenger cars are equipped at the factory with five passenger-car tires, original equipment shipments generally exceed this figure somewhat for the reason that these shipments also include passenger-car tires used on light trucks and the like (see Table 3).

TABLE 3

ORIGINAL EQUIPMENT PASSENGER-CAR TIRE SHIPMENTS

Year	Passenger Car Total Factory Sales (In Thousands)	Original Equipment Tires Shipped (In Thousands)	Original Equipment Tire Shipments per Passenger Car
1933..........	1,573	9,031	5.74
1940..........	3,717	19,560	5.26
1950..........	6,666	36,678	5.50
1951..........	5,338	26,422	4.95
1952..........	4,321	24,034	5.56
1953..........	6,117	33,082	5.41

Source: B. F. Goodrich Research Department.

Replacement Sales · Replacement sales are dependent upon three factors: (1) the number of cars over two years of age which are in use; [2] (2) the amount of wear tires receive; and (3) the wearing qualities of the tires. Data on past sales of replacement-car tires are collected by the Rubber Manufacturers' Association. The average number of cars over two years of age which are in use is obtained by subtracting from the total number in operation half of the current year's new car sales, all of the first preceding year and half of the second preceding year.

A "replacement tire factor" is obtained by dividing the total number of tire units sold by the total number of passenger cars over two years of age in operation. The company has found that the average automobile user continues to buy tires and keep his automobile in operation despite significant changes in income. A convenient method of allowing for the longer service and higher quality built into tires is to extend into the future the long-run trend of replacement tire shipments per passenger car over two years of age in operation. The annual decline in this ratio from 1933 to 1953 averages out at about 1 percent each year (see Table 4).

The final step in the preparation of the sales forecast is to check carefully all assumptions and extensions of trends and mathematical relationships used in building up the forecast. In

---

2. Experience has shown that original equipment tires last approximately two years and therefore demand for new tires does not begin until cars reach this age.

TABLE 4

REPLACEMENT PASSENGER-CAR TIRE SHIPMENTS

Year	Average Number of Passenger Cars Over 2 Years of Age in Operation (In Thousands)	Civilian Replacement Tire Shipments (In Thousands)	Replacement Tire Shipments Per Vehicle
1933.........	16,636	29,138	1.75
1940.........	19,487	30,903	1.59
1950.........	25,615	47,103	1.84
1951.........	27,075	34,121	1.26
1952.........	29,639	45,315	1.53
1953.........	32,013	45,787	1.43

Source: Rubber Manufacturers' Association and B. F. Goodrich Business Research Department.

some instances, sound judgment may indicate modifications in the statistical results. The forecast is also checked against other projections of general business and the outlook for the industry. All sales forecasts, whether long-run or short-run, are revised periodically in the light of more recent experience.

Economics and Business Planning

Sidney S. Alexander

Sidney Alexander is Professor of Industrial Management at the Massachusetts Institute of Technology. This article is taken from his contribution to Economics and the Policy Maker, *published in 1959.*

While the most obvious task of the economist in the large corporation is short-run forecasting, his most valuable contribution, it seems to me, is in long-run planning. To some extent, this is a consequence of the greater amenability of long-run developments to economic forecasting techniques. While it is often quite hard to estimate whether the fourth quarter of next year will have a gross national product higher or lower than the fourth quarter of this year, it can quite reliably be estimated that the gross national product ten years from now will be some 35 percent higher than it was this year. More precisely, it can be estimated that the long-term trend value that economic historians will come to assign to 1969 will be some 35 percent greater than the long-term trend value they will come to assign to 1959.

The major contribution that an economic mode of thought in particular, or a scientific mode of thought in general, can make to the analysis of business problems, and those of government too, is the reduction of the problems to rational study, the transfer of as much as possible out of the field of the intuitively and implicitly appraised to that of the rationally and explicitly appraised.

The best consultants I know are uniform in their agreement that they contribute to their clients little more than applied common sense. But why can applied common sense be a contribution? Essentially because in attacking the problem the first task is to recognize the problem explicitly, and this is not habitually done by an active type. No discredit is implied here; the contemplative type is probably not very good at making and executing decisions. We should not be surprised that in this activity as in others, productivity can be increased by the division of labor, provided, as always, the extent of the market will support the division of labor. One man can profitably specialize in running a business and meeting its day-to-day problems and another in studying those factors that are likely to affect the business in the long run. Different skills and temperaments are suited to each of these activities.

Many of the critical decisions of long-run planning are once-in-a-decade decisions, some are once in a lifetime. It can hardly be expected that anyone could handle such problems on the basis of his own personal experience. There should be no wonder that this sort of analysis is a field for specialization. Those skills most important for the businessman—skills in negotiation, in execution, and in administration—are not usually associated with the sort of introspective analysis appropriate for the projection into an "as if" world of the future. But the economist is a specialist in the analysis of the "as if." As one Brookings author has stated, "Economic analysis is a substitute for the sixth sense of businessmen." The sixth sense probably does better in sensing the short-run situation, but not as well in sensing the long-run. Even when the businessman himself would be highly skilled at making such a study, the doctrine of comparative advantage suggests that it may be more advantageous to turn the study over to a specialist in analysis while the businessman concentrates on problems of administration and execution.

The characteristic long-run problem of the business enterprise is what business should it be in and on what scale. This is the principal content of business planning, and it centers on capital budgeting.

Long-range planning, or LRP, as it is frequently referred to, is now a big word in business. The devotees of LRP speak of its advantages much as the old line socialists spoke of society under socialism—when everything will be better. "Fuzzy management disappears when LRP is applied." "Crisis management becomes less pronounced." "Short-term dips assume less significance." "New markets are entered as soon as possible." "Money and men come easier." "Long-range planning . . . is a mark of industrial leadership by which good management is made more effective and good companies retain or attain recognition in their industry." These statements, taken out of their context of a discussion of long-range planning in a management journal, possibly give an oversimplified picture of the enthusiasm for long-range planning on the part of its advocates, but they do not exaggerate the intensity of that enthusiasm.

Clearly, planning can confer such benefits only if it is good planning. Most of the literature on planning in business is aimed at the form rather than the substance of planning. Implicit in this is the idea that even a poor plan is better than none at all, since the planning process is unlikely to result in a worse outcome than unplanned behavior. And there is probably some truth in this. Because the very act of planning does require explicit consideration of the relevant factors, it is less likely that an important consideration will be ignored. But most of the literature stops short of the substantive problem of how, in fact, the future is to be projected as the basic assumption for the long-range plans. That is the great opportunity for the economist.

The economist can make a valuable contribution to the solution of long-run business problems because his mode of thought, based on microeconomics and descriptive economics, is particularly attuned to the analysis of the long run, and because his role of outsider affords a broader perspective and leads to explicit examination of practices that would otherwise be taken for granted. Any scientifically trained person would share many of these characteristics, but the economist has the further advantage of familiarity with the class of problems encountered in business and with the data and the techniques of empirical research appropriate to this class of problems.

Part Four

Linear Programming and Related Techniques

THE essays in Part Four provide an introduction to the nature, purpose, and usefulness of various concepts and techniques in operations research. They do not delve into technical details but concentrate instead on those aspects of operations research which a general manager would find useful.

The first two papers are concerned with the nature of operations research. Cyril Herrmann and John Magee attempt to define operations research and to describe the ways in which it has been applied to business problems. They identify and discuss four concepts of fundamental importance to the practice of operations research: the model, the measure of effectiveness, the necessity for decision, and the role of experimentation. The second article, from *Fortune*, describes some of the techniques used by operations researchers: mathematical programming, game theory, statistical decision theory, scheduling techniques, and dynamic programming.

The next three papers are concerned with mathematical programming, one of the most important of these techniques. Alexander Henderson and Robert Schlaifer describe how the H. J. Heinz Company used mathematical programming to determine the level of production in various plants as well as the pattern of shipments from plants to warehouses. George Dantzig discusses the basic concepts involved in linear programming and describes the sort of problems that this technique can handle. To be a linear programming model, Dantzig explains, a system must satisfy certain assumptions of proportionality, nonnegativity, and additivity. Using graphical techniques, Robert Dorfman presents a very simple example of mathematical programming. The final article, by Garvin and his associates, describes in somewhat more detail how linear programming has been used to help solve specific problems in the oil industry. This article is rather more difficult than the others in this book, and is for readers with some familiarity with algebra.

Operations Research

CYRIL HERRMANN AND JOHN MAGEE

This article appeared in the Harvard Business Review, *August 1953. At that time Cyril Herrmann was a faculty member at Massachusetts Institute of Technology and John Magee was on the staff of Arthur D. Little, Inc.*

Operations research has helped companies to solve such diverse business problems as directing salesmen to the right accounts at the right time, dividing the advertising budget in the most effective way, establishing equitable bonus systems, improving inventory and reordering policies, planning minimum-cost production schedules, and estimating the amount of clerical help needed for a new operation.

Operations research makes possible accomplishments like these and many others because (*a*) it helps to single out the critical issues which require executive appraisal and analysis, and (*b*) it provides factual bases to support and guide executive judgment. Thus, it eases the burden of effort and time on executives but intensifies the potential of their decision-making role. In this sense operations research contributes toward better management.

ESSENTIAL FEATURES OF OPERATIONS RESEARCH

Operations research apparently means different things to different people. To some businessmen and scientists it means only the application of statistics and common sense to business problems. Indeed, one vice president of a leading company remarked that if his division heads did not practice it every day, they would not last long. To others it is just another and perhaps more comprehensive term for existing activities like market research, quality control, or industrial engineering. Some businessmen consider it a new sales or production gimmick; some, a product of academic people interfering in the practical world. In truth, operations research is none of these things.

It should not be surprising that there has been this confusion. Operations research is not an explicit, easily identifiable concept that developed to meet the specific needs of industry. It was first applied in World War II by groups of scientists who were engaged by the government to help frame recommendations for the improvement of military activities. After the war a few soundly managed companies experimented with it and found that it worked successfully in business operations as well; and it has since gained a secure foothold in industry.

Early attempts by operations analysts to describe their activities, based on the objective of arriving at a precise and comprehensive definition of operations research, tended to be overly generalized, broad, and self-conscious, and suffered from emphasis on military applications. Some of the confusion surrounding the meaning of the term "operations research" has resulted from attempts at identification with special techniques or unnecessarily rigid distinctions between operations research and other management service activities.

Now, let us see if we can cut through some of this confusion.

The first point to grasp is that operations research is what its name implies, research on operations. However, it involves a particular view of operations and, even more important, a particular kind of research.

Operations are considered as an entity. The subject matter studied is not the equipment used, nor the morale of the participants, nor the physical properties of the output; it is the combination of these in total, as an economic process. And operations so conceived are subject to analysis by the mental processes and the methodologies which we have come to associate with the research work of the physicist, the chemist, and the biologist—what has come to be called "the scientific method."

The basic premise underlying the scientific method is a simple and abiding faith in the rationality of nature, leading to the belief that phenomena have a cause. If phenomena do have a cause, it is the scientists' contention that by hard work the mechanism or system underlying the observed facts can be discovered. Once the mechanism is known, nature's secrets are known and can be used to the investigator's own best advantage.

The scientist knows that his analogue to nature will never be perfect. But it must be sufficiently accurate to suit the particular purposes at hand; and, until it is, he must repeat the processes of observation, induction, and theory construction—again and again. Note that a satisfactory solution must be in quantitative terms in order that it can be predictive—the only accepted fundamental test of being physically meaningful.

The scientific method, in its ideal form, calls for a rather special mental attitude, foremost in which is a reverence for facts. Of course all modern executives are accustomed to using figures to control their operations. But they are primarily concerned with results and only secondarily with causes; they interpret their facts in the light of company objectives. This is a much different attitude from seeking out the relationships underlying the facts.

Thus, when an executive looks at sales figures, he looks at them primarily in terms of the success of his sales campaign and its effect on profits. By contrast, when the scientist looks at these same figures, he seeks in them a clue to the fundamental behavior pattern of the customers. By the process of induction he tentatively formulates a theoretical system or mechanism; then by the inverse process of deduction he determines what phenomena should take place and checks these against the observed facts. His test is simple: Does the assumed mechanism act enough like nature—or, more specifically in this case, does it produce quantitative data such as can be used for predicting how the customers will in fact behave?

Through the years mathematical and experimental techniques have been developed to implement this attitude. The application of the scientific attitude and the associated techniques to the study of operations, whether business, governmental, or military, is what is meant by operations research.

Newton was able to explain the apparently totally unrelated phenomena of planetary motion and objects falling on the earth by the simple unifying concept of gravity. This represented a tremendous step forward in helping men to understand and control the world about them. Again, more recently, the power of the scientific method was demonstrated by the ability of the nuclear physicists to predict the tremendous energy potential lying within the atom.

Here are a few summary examples of the way this same kind of approach has been applied to down-to-earth business problems.

A company with a number of products made at three different locations was concerned about the items to be produced at each location and the points at which the items would be warehoused. Freight costs constituted a substantial part of the delivered cost of the material. Operations research showed that what appeared to be a complex and involved problem could be broken into a series of rather simple components. Adaptations of linear programing methods were used to find the warehousing schedule which would minimize freight costs. The study is now being extended to determine the best distribution of products among manufacturing plants and warehouse locations in order to minimize net delivered cost in relation to return on investment.

A manufacturer of chemical products, with a wide and varied line, sought more rational or logical bases than the customary percentage of sales for distributing his limited advertising budget among products, some of which were growing, some stable, and others declining. An operations research study showed that advertising effectiveness was related to three simple characteristics, each of which could be estimated from existing sales data with satisfactory reliability: (*a*) the total market potential; (*b*) the rate of growth of sales; (*c*) the customer loss rate. A mathematical formulation of these three characteristics provided a rational basis for distributing advertising and promotional effort.

In a company making a line of light machines, the executive board questioned the amount of money spent for missionary salesmen calling on customers. Studies yielded explicit mathematical statements of (*a*) the relation between the number of accounts called on and resulting sales volume and (*b*) the relation between sales costs and manufacturing and distribution costs. These were combined by the methods of differential calculus to set up simple tables for picking the level of promotion in each area which would maximize company net profits. The results showed that nearly a 50 per cent increase in promotional activity was economically feasible and would yield substantial profits.

An industrial products manufacturer wanted to set time standards as a basis for costs and labor efficiency controls. The operations research group studied several complex operations; expressed the effect of the physical characteristics of products and equipment and the time required to produce a given amount of output in the form of mathematical equations; and then, without further extensive time study or special data collection, set up tables of production time standards according to product characteristics, equipment used, and worker efficiency, which could be applied to any or all of the production operations.

A company carrying an inventory of a large number of finished items had trouble maintaining sound and balanced stock levels. Despite careful attention and continued modification of reorder points in the light of experience, the stock of many individual items turned out to be either too high for sales or inadequate to meet demand. The problem was solved by a physical chemist who first collected data on the variables, such as size and frequency of order, length of production and delivery time, etc.; then set up an assumed system, which he tried out against extreme sales situations, continually changing its characteristics slightly until it met the necessary conditions—all on paper (a technique well known to physical scientists); and thus was able to determine a workable system without cost of installation and risk of possible failure.

These examples should serve to give some idea of how the scientific method can be applied. But they represent only a few of the many scientific techniques available (as we shall see when we examine further cases in more detail). Some practitioners even take the rather broad point of view that operations research should include the rather indefinite and qualitative methods of the social science fields. Most professional opinion, however, favors the view that operations research is more restricted in meaning, limited to the quantitative methods and experimentally verifiable results of the physical sciences.

BASIC CONCEPTS OF OPERATIONS RESEARCH

There are four concepts of fundamental importance to the practice of operations research: (*a*) the model, (*b*) the measure of effectiveness, (*c*) the necessity for decision, and (*d*) the role of experimentation.

The most frequently encountered concept in operations research is that of the model—the simplified representation of an operation, containing only those aspects which are of primary importance to the problem under study. It has been of great use in facilitating the investigation of operations. To illustrate with some familiar types of "models" from other fields:

(1) In aeronautical engineering the model of an aeroplane is used to investigate its aerodynamic properties in a wind tunnel. While perfectly adequate for this purpose, it would hardly do for practical use. It has no seats; it may not even be hollow. It is, however, a satisfactory physical model for studying the flight characteristics of the ship.

(2) Another, quite different kind of model is the accounting model. This is essentially a simplified representation on paper, in the form of accounts and ledgers, of the flow of goods and services through a business enterprise. It provides measures of the rate of flow, the values produced, and the performances achieved, and to that extent is useful (though it is hardly a realistic representation of operations).

(3) Many models are used in physics. Three-dimensional models of complex molecules are probably most familiar to laymen, but the most powerful models in this field are sets of mathematical equations.

There are several different types of operations research models. Most of them are mathematical in form, being a set of equations relating significant variables in the operation to the outcome.

Related to the concept of a model or theory of operation is the measure of effectiveness, whereby the extent to which the operation is attaining its goal can be explicitly determined. One common over-all measure of effectiveness in industrial operations is return on investment; another is net dollar profit. Measures of effectiveness down the scale might be the number of customers serviced per hour, the ratio of productive to total hours of a machine operation, etc.

A consistent statement of the fundamental goals of the operation is essential to the mathematical logic of the model. (It does not matter if the goals are complex.) Just as the model cannot make two and two add up to five, so it is impossible to relate fundamentally inconsistent objectives and produce consistent and meaningful results.

Operations research has frequently brought to light inconsistencies in company goals. Take production scheduling, for instance. Very often its object has been stated as scheduling production to meet sales forecasts with minimum production costs, with minimum inventory investment, and without customer-service failure. Yet minimizing inventory investment typically requires the use of start-and-stop or at best uneven production plans, resulting in excessive production costs; and eliminating the risk of not being able to ship every customer order immediately requires huge inventories, in the face of fluctuating and at least partially unpredictable demand. The solution is to combine and sublimate such otherwise inconsistent goals to a higher unified and consistent goal.

The statement of a complete and wholly consistent goal of company operations must be recognized as an ideal. Business goals are very complex, and to catch the full flavor of the objectives of an intricate business operation in any simple, explicit statement is difficult. Many business goals remain, and probably ever will remain, at least in part intangible—e.g., efforts to improve employee morale or contribute to the public welfare. To that extent, the objective of operations research must be more modest than the construction of a complete model and the measurement of the extent to which the operation is attaining the complete set of goals established for it. But it still can serve to clarify the interdependency of those intangibles with the company goals which in fact are measurable, thus providing a guide to executive decision.

The third concept inherent in operations research is that of decision and decision making. An essential element in all true operations research problems is the existence of alternative courses of action, with a choice to be made among them; otherwise the study of an operation becomes academic or theoretical. This should be clear from the cases already cited.

In sum, the objective of operations research is to clarify the relation between the several courses of action, determine their outcomes, and indicate which measures up best in terms of the company goal. But note that, while this should be of assistance to the executive in making his decision intelligently, in every case the ultimate responsibility still lies with him.

The fourth significant concept concerns the role of experimentation. Operations research is the application of experimental science to the study of operations. The theory, or model, is generally built up from observed data or experience, although in some cases the model development may depend heavily on external or a priori information. In any event, the theory describing the operation must always be verifiable experimentally. Two kinds of experiments are important in this connection:

(1) The first kind is designed simply to get information. Thus, it often takes the form of an apparently rather impractical test. In one case the operations analysts directed advertising toward potential customers the company knew were not worth addressing, and refrained from addressing customers the company typically sought—and for a very simple reason. There was plenty of evidence indicating what happened when advertising was directed toward those normally addressed but not enough about its effects upon those not normally addressed. To evaluate the effectiveness of the advertising, therefore, it was necessary to find out what happened to those normally promoted when they were not promoted, and what happened to those normally not promoted when they were.

(2) The other type of experiment is the critical type; it is designed to test the validity of conclusions. Again, what appear to be rather impractical forms of experimentation are sometimes used. Thus, in the most sensitive experiments of this type, the validity of the theory or model can often be tested most revealingly in terms of the results of extreme policies rather than in terms of the more normal policy likely to be put into practice.

Decision Theory and Program Scheduling

Fortune MAGAZINE

The author, George A. W. Boehm, is an associate editor of Fortune; this article appeared in the April 1962 issue.

Throughout history men have employed elaborate rituals for making up their minds. They have poured libations and sacrificed oxen in hopes of persuading a capricious and possibly hostile Nature to reward their decisions. They have consulted sibyls and watched the flight of birds to discover what the future holds in store. They have put their faith in proverbs and rules of thumb devised to take some of the guesswork out of living. They have sought divine guidance, as did George Romney, former president of American Motors, when he fasted and meditated before deciding to seek the Republican nomination for governor of Michigan.

In managing the affairs of modern business and government more scientific decision methods are needed. Unaided, the human mind cannot possibly weigh the manifold complexities involved in the development of a missile, the erection of a forty-story office building, the operation of an enterprise producing hundreds of products for millions of customers. Thousands of decisions go into scheduling jobs, ordering supplies, managing inventories, negotiating with contractors, hiring labor, pricing goods, and planning production facilities. The executive is further harassed by such uncertainties as the unpredictable tastes of consumers and the speculative nature of economic forecasts and research and development programs. Thus all too often he must act largely on hunch and intuition—and go home with the gnawing suspicion that he might have decided more wisely.

In recent years scientists have been showing the executive how to avoid some of the perplexity that attends decision making. They have been putting together a voluminous bundle of mathematical techniques for evaluating possible courses of action. In attempting to rationalize the process of deciding, they have developed "decision theory." This is not really a single theory of how to make decisions, but rather a collection of techniques for weighing many factors in logical fashion. Some of the techniques are best suited to situations in which, though all the factors are known or predictable, the complexity is so confusing that the human mind cannot arrive at a wholly rational decision. Other techniques cope with "risks"—chances that can be accurately measured or calculated, such as the probability that a given number of insurance policyholders will die within a year. Still others deal with "uncertainties" (which scientists carefully distinguish from "risks")—chances that can be estimated only roughly at best, because, for example, they depend on future developments or the behavior of a competitor. All decision theory, however, has a common purpose: to show decision makers surer ways to attain their goals.

Decision theorists use some tools that were developed several decades ago, notably statistical sampling, and some that are less familiar, such as linear programing, a short-cut method of finding the best way to allocate scarce resources. In addition, some brand-new techniques are being perfected. Two of the most successful, PERT and CPM (which will be explained later), are now used to schedule most United States space programs and many large construction jobs. To date, the various kinds of mathematical decision aids have been effectively applied to controlling inventory levels, arranging bus schedules, planning preventive maintenance, determining the best operating conditions for oil refineries, and scheduling many other industrial and military logistic operations that depend on the making of many routine but intricately related decisions.

Decision theory caught on first in the petroleum industry, which has a tradition of exploiting scientific techniques to control its production and marketing procedures. Other research-minded enterprises, including most of the big chemical and electrical firms, are now also making wide use of decision theory, and a few other industries are beginning to adopt it.

The techniques are too complicated to be applied by amateurs; the executive must call upon a specialist. Many big companies have staffs of decision experts, who are usually designated by some other name—e.g., planning, applied mathematics, or operations research. The executive without such a staff can turn to any of more than a score of consultants, many of whom specialize in industrial production, economic planning, or some other field of decision making. The Air Force has its own group of decision-theory consultants—the Rand Corporation. Serving private industry are a number of consulting firms that are capable of inventing new decision techniques for special applications.

Any group of decision experts is likely to include men with varied backgrounds, for the theoretical ideas stem from a wide range of scientific disciplines: mathematics, physics, systems engineering, econometrics, statistics, and servomechanism theory, which originally applied to automatic controls. But whatever his approach, the decision theorist must understand how to use computers. The techniques usually demand a prodigious amount of calculation. To apply them on large-scale problems without a computer would be as unthinkable as to work out a complex engineering design with Roman numerals.

The new scientific approach might suggest the possibility that even the most far-reaching business decisions could be turned over entirely to computers. But executives have no reason to fear that they will be replaced by machines producing decisions "untouched by human brains." Hunch and intuition are still invaluable. Indeed, most decision theorists today are looking for ways to incorporate expert judgment with their mathematics. They want to take full advantage of the comprehensiveness of the human mind to augment the precision of computers. For his part, the executive of the future will depend on the tools of decision theory much as an airplane pilot relies on his instruments. If he can learn to understand the theory well enough to appraise its applications, he can free himself from many routine responsibilities and broaden the scope of his thinking.

This inclusion of judgment is making decision theory more realistic, but at the same time it may cost the theory some of its mathematical incisiveness. Some leaders in the field used to cherish the somewhat arrogant hope that pure mathematics might produce perfectly precise and automatic decisions. Now they are aware that decision theory will be used less to dictate optimal courses of action, more to present the human decision maker with a choice of feasible actions and help him choose a good one.

The marriage of judgment to mathematics requires considerable ingenuity. Not infrequently the decision theorist must be a virtuoso psychologist in order to translate intuition and opinions into the numbers and mathematical functions that a computer can process. People tend to think about their jobs in one way, describe them in another, and actually perform them in a third way. For example, the warehouse manager who claims he has never been late on a promised delivery date may be talking quite frankly; but perhaps he has achieved his remarkable record by setting back the date whenever he has foreseen a jam. He may also find it difficult to assess the value of some quite ordinary factors—e.g., how much an inventory shortage might cost his company in lost sales and irate customers. He might be able, however, to estimate the cost indirectly in different terms, such as the amount he would be willing to spend for air freight in an emergency.

Far knottier problems arise because people are often erratic and inarticulate when they try to explain what they want to accomplish. Theoretical economists conceive of a marvelously rational being whom they call "economic man": he has a clear idea of what ends he wants to attain, and, given alternatives, he has the wisdom to calculate which one will be most rewarding in terms of his personal scale of values. But the very fact that personal values are part of the equation casts doubt on whether there can ever be an authentic "economic man." One of the most valuable services a decision theorist can perform is to list alternative courses of action and spell out the risks and payoffs associated with each. But if he is actually going to recommend an acceptable decision, he may first have to determine his client's attitude toward taking chances, which is an element in the client's personal scale of values. Several gambling strategies have been formulated mathematically so that they can be incorporated in some decision methods. For the pessimist who regards himself as an underdog faced by hostile Nature, there is the "minimax" strategy. This guides him to choose the course of action that entails the minimum risk of disaster, although it may also reduce his chance of winning. Against a wise and powerful adversary, "minimax" is clearly the prudent policy. For the unbridled optimist who likes to plunge on long shots, this is "maximax." This enables him to shoot for big gains although he runs a big risk of large loss. And for the patient man who regards life as an unending series of gambles and expects his luck to average out, there is the "maximum expected value" strategy. Given about an even number of good and bad breaks, this will maximize his chances of profiting in the long run.

Interest in decision theory is now booming, thanks largely to the striking success of two new scheduling procedures: Critical Path Method (CPM) and Program Evaluation and Review Technique (PERT), which differ from each other only in a few details. They enable managers to keep tight control of the timing and budgets of even the most complex and widely scattered projects. Scheduling of such programs actually consists of a multitude of interrelated decisions—e.g., when to promise delivery, how many electricians to hire for a given week, when to order materials and how to ship them, which contractor to employ. The new procedures are relatively simple to apply and interpret. Yet they produce many decisions almost automatically, while giving the manager wide scope to use his judgment and without burdening him with mathematical details.

In both CPM and PERT, the first step is to analyze all the work that must be done, break it down into individual tasks, and then estimate how long each will probably take and how much it will cost. This information is then diagramed as a network showing what activities must await the completion of other jobs and what work can be carried on in parallel with other phases of the project.

The scheduling network is based on the obvious logic that people commonly apply to any number of everyday activities. For example, a methodical hostess planning a party might make a list including all that will have to be done: order meat and vegetables, bake a cake, polish the silver, hire a maid, buy liquor, buy a new dress, get a permanent, set up a bar, set the table, etc. And she will have a good idea of the timing of every item on the list. Similarly, most able industrial managers presumably have kept in the backs of their minds at least a vague idea of a job network. But until the advent of electronic computers, it would have been futile actually to draw detailed networks. Projects large enough to require elaborate planning are usually represented by networks that are far too complicated for the unaided human mind to analyze and adjust—over 1,000 steps for the construction of a modest industrial plant, up to perhaps 30,000 for the development of a large missile.

A modern computer, however, can derive all sorts of useful information from the network. All the time and cost estimates and the relation of every job to all the others are reduced to a numerically coded program. Then, in a matter of minutes, the computer can calculate how long the project will take and how much it will cost. The over-all time estimate depends on a key concept: the "critical path." This is a sequence of jobs in which any slowdown will delay the completion of the entire project. Conversely, if these jobs are rushed, the whole project will be completed earlier. Generally, most jobs do not lie along the critical path; if they take a little longer than expected, the project will still finish on time. In principle, a human being could apply this concept just as a computer does, and take steps to shorten the time along the critical path. But it might take him days, even weeks, to find just which path is critical. The computer also does what no human mind could possibly accomplish: it shows continually how plans should be changed to keep the project on schedule and within the budget. Users of network scheduling avoid costly over-all crash programs; they have found that even in emergencies they seldom have to expedite more than ten per cent of the work. Besides, they don't have to waste time in tedious coordinating conferences.

The inventors of CPM and PERT started with somewhat different objectives but wound up with the same basic concepts. Early in 1957 a group of operations-research specialists from E. I. du Pont de Nemours got together with computer-applications experts at the Remington Rand division of Sperry Rand to design a procedure for scheduling chemical-plant construction. CPM was the result, and much of the credit for it belongs to James E. Kelley Jr., then with Remington Rand. Kelley not only exploited the critical-path concept but also introduced ways of "crashing" a project in an economical fashion. CPM caught on almost immediately in the construction industry.

CHART 1

How a Computer Decides the Cheapest Schedule for a Project

Job	Normal days	Normal cost	Crash days	Crash cost	Cost of crashing dollars per day
A	3	$140	2	$210	$70
B	6	215	5	275	60
C	2	160	1	240	80
D	4	130	3	180	50
E	2	170	1	250	80
F	7	165	4	285	40
G	4	210	3	290	80
H	3	110	2	160	50
Total		$1300		$1890	

Major industrial projects, such as the building of a ship or a factory or the development of a missile, involve so many activities that no human mind can keep close track of all that is going on, much less schedule every detail in the most efficient way. New mathematical techniques, however, are giving project managers a clearer view of their work and a better opportunity to use their judgment effectively. The essential steps in one of these new techniques, Critical Path Method, are demonstrated by the analysis of a tiny hypothetical project. The manager begins the scheduling by listing all the jobs that must be done (see chart above) together with estimates of normal time and cost for each. Next he estimates how much it would cost to rush each job to completion by a crash program. All this information is fed into a computer. As the totals show, the manager could get each job done as fast as possible by spending an extra $590. But he may be able to shorten the time of completing the whole project without "crashing" every job. This is what the computer will investigate.

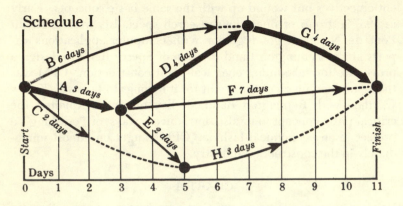

Schedule I

The manager diagrams the order in which the jobs must be done. This shows, for example, that C can be done in parallel with A but that D cannot be started until A is finished. The computer calculates the "critical path" (heavy black line) from this information. The jobs on this path determine the time (eleven days) needed to complete the whole project; the rest can be delayed somewhat (broken lines) without affecting the over-all schedule.

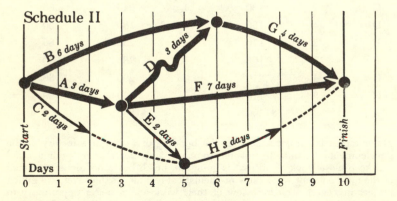

Schedule II

Next the computer calculates ways to shorten the over-all schedule by crashing some of the jobs. There may be several ways, but the computer selects the cheapest. The diagram above shows that if D is accelerated to three days instead of four, the over-all schedule can be reduced to ten days. Two more jobs, B and F, become part of a critical path, but there is still some leeway in C, E, and H. The cost of crashing D is an extra $50.

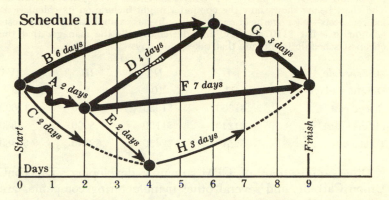

Again rescheduling the project so that it can be finished in nine days, the computer finds that it is best to crash both A and G by one day. Surprisingly, the extra effort put on these jobs makes it possible to relax a bit on D and allot the normal four days for its completion. Crashing A and G will cost a total of $150, but the relaxation of D saves $50, so the acceleration of the whole project from ten to nine days costs only $100 more.

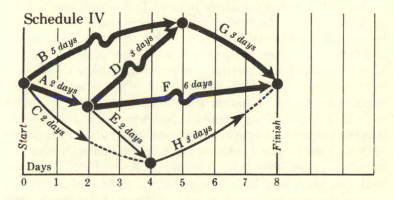

If the manager wants to lop another day from the schedule, he can do so most economically by crashing three jobs: B, D, and F. Although the chart shows that F could be shortened by as much as three days, the extra hurry would have no effect on the over-all schedule, so F is shortened by only one day. The manager has now spent $300 on the crash program, compared with the $590 he might have spent to crash all the jobs.

To decide which schedule is actually best from all viewpoints, the manager can instruct the computer to take other factors into account. There may be a penalty for failing to complete the project on schedule. Sometimes in actual practice contractors have found that they can make more profit by proceeding slowly and paying a penalty rather than paying heavy overtime. The chart below shows how the computer might include on its calculations indirect costs—e.g., overhead or penalties. In this example the indirect costs amount to a flat $110 per day, and the chart tells the manager that the cheapest schedule is the one that takes nine days.

Schedule	I	II	III	IV
Duration (days)	11	10	9	8
Direct cost	$1300	$1350	$1450	$1600
Indirect cost	$1210	$1100	$990	$880
Total cost	$2510	$2450	$2440	$2480

Other applications of CPM are now developing. Du Pont, Union Carbide, and several other manufacturing companies are using it to schedule maintenance on large plants. Most production lines have to be shut down and overhauled from time to time. By scheduling hundreds of maintenance steps in an optimal way CPM can often shorten the shutdown period and save thousands of dollars of production that would otherwise be lost.

PERT (Program Evaluation Review Technique) was born of sheer desperation. In 1956, during the early stages of the Navy's Polaris submarine-missile development program, a Special Projects Office was set up to manage this immense project. The men in charge found that all the conventional managerial methods were hopelessly inadequate to keep track of the schedule. Superimposed on the job of coordinating the efforts of 11,000 contractors was a degree of uncertainty as to when crucial research and development stages might be completed. So, Willard Fazar of the SPO, with the help of Lockheed's Missile and Space Division and consultants from Booz, Allen & Hamilton, devised PERT as a network flow chart with built-in uncertainty. Instead of assigning a single time estimate to each task, as Kelley had done with CPM, Fazar called for three estimates: optimistic, normal, and pessimistic. Such multiple estimating made the computations somewhat more difficult but they were still well within the capability of a high-speed computer.

PERT worked well from the time it was put into operation in 1958. Polaris chief Vice Admiral W. F. Raborn, Jr. has given the technique much credit for the fact that the development of the first Polaris missile required two years' less time than originally estimated. PERT is also beginning to find uses outside government projects. The most noteworthy to date was a schedule for the production of a Broadway play. PERT kept track of some 200 steps the producers had to take before the play opened—e.g., rent the theatre, sign the stars, hire a scenery designer, buy props, dispense publicity, and set a date for the dress rehearsal.

Both CPM and PERT are still in the evolutionary stage. Kelley has worked out a way to schedule a number of simultaneous projects that must share available resources, such as labor, machines, space, or money.

Most executive decisions hinge on the question of **how to make** the most of whatever is available—time, money, raw materials, manpower, production facilities, storage space, shipping. A manager may have to decide how many of each of three items he should produce. For example, the first item must be painstakingly assembled by hand; the second needs a great deal of machining; the third is bulky. If he were to concentrate on any one item, he would run short of labor, machines, or warehouse space. The decision technique called linear programing, a method older than and somewhat different from CPM or PERT, can tell him precisely the most profitable combination of the three items.

Some linear programs, such as those that portray the entire distribution system of a large company, involve several hundred interrelated variables. The programer starts by putting down in mathematical terms all the relations among the variables. Some are in the form of equations, others in the form of "inequalities"— e.g., mathematical statements that say a machine can produce *no more than* so many items per hour. By a mathematical stratagem the inequalities are then converted to equations. The variables outnumber the equations, so there is no unique algebraic solution. But such a system of equations can be made to yield optimum solutions—i.e., solutions that maximize profits, minimize costs, or make some other element in the business as small or large as possible. This is the purpose of linear programing.

The mathematical procedure generally used to find optimal solutions is the "simplex" method, invented in 1947 by George Dantzig. The method belies its name; it is extremely complicated. It is essentially a trial-and-error approach. But the groping for a solution is entirely methodical. It guarantees finding a better solution at each step and an optimal solution in a finite number of steps. Most practical linear-programming problems would take months, even years, to solve by hand, but a fast computer usually handles them in a few minutes.

Linear programing has been so thoroughly studied and so widely applied that experts usually classify problems into a number of standard types. They schedule truck and airline fleets with the transportation type. Another linear program, sometimes called the nutrition problem, decides how to mix animal feed so as to meet nutritional specifications at minimum cost; it is also used for blending gasoline to meet octane-number specifications. Paper and sheet-steel mills rely on the trim-loss reduction program to minimize waste when small orders are cut from large rolls.

Linear programing is especially valuable to the petroleum industry. There it is used more or less routinely for scheduling the distribution of products, balancing availability of raw crude with refinery operations so as to produce the most profitable assortment of products, blending gasoline, and even deciding where new refineries are needed.

In recent years linear programing has gained an important new dimension. In 1949, Albert W. Tucker, Harold W. Kuhn, and David Gale, following up a conjecture by the late John von Neumann, proved that every linear program has a shadow, called its "dual program." When a mathematician sets up a linear program to achieve one objective, he can in an easy step solve the dual program and thereby achieve a different objective. For example, the original program might find a production scheme that minimized costs for a fixed labor force and consumption of raw materials; the dual program would determine a system of internal pricing that would maximize the value of net output while balancing the direct costs of labor and raw materials. Looking at the solutions of both the original program and its dual gives the manager another degree of flexibility in making decisions. In addition to learning how to make the most profit with the machines at hand, he may be able to tell how to increase profits by installing more or different machines. Related mathematical techniques indicate what would happen if some of the variables were to change slightly. The same procedures also reveal how critical an error in the data might be; thus the manager knows when he can get away with an offhand estimate and when he has to make a careful study. The significance of all this additional information is that it enables the non-mathematical executive to ask questions he would naturally want to ask, even those that may not have occurred to him when the programing was begun. The decision theorist is able to use this kind of analysis also to increase the realism of his technique by blending hunches and judgments with the mathematics.

New mathematical inventions are beginning to break through some of the limitations of linear programing. Many programs are unwieldy; even the fastest computer takes several hours to perform the 200 million calculations needed to solve a program with 400 equations. Recently, however, Dantzig and Philip Wolfe worked out a computational shortcut, which they call the "decomposition" principle. It seems particularly applicable to situations that are not very tightly knit—e.g., the production scheduling of a company with many plants, each specializing in a few products that it feeds into a centralized marketing system. Decomposition is a mathematical way of chopping a huge program into many smaller ones and then solving each and coordinating the results in succession. As yet there have been no industrial applications, but several computer-service groups are coding the decomposition principle so that it can be fed into computers.

Another limitation of linear programing stems from the fact that it fails to distinguish between fractions and whole numbers. In some real problems only whole numbers are feasible. A program for scheduling a fleet of planes might, for example, tell an airline that 8.26 planes should be assigned to one particular route and 3.74 to another. The obvious step would be to round off the numbers to eight and four. But actually this is not safe; oddly enough, it might well prove more economical to assign six planes to each route. For such linear-programing problems Ralph E. Gomory, a young I.B.M. mathematician, has invented a brand-new technique called "integer programing." It usually requires a good deal more computation than the conventional simplex method, but it produces the best solution that can be expressed in whole numbers. Its greatest potential application appears to be in such problems as determining the overall costs of a new production plant where there is a major initial cost of building the plant as well as the continuing variable costs of its operation.

Elements of uncertainty complicate the decision process, often to such an extent that linear programing cannot produce a realistic solution in a reasonable time. In extreme cases a decision maker starts with almost total ignorance as to what decisions are possible, what the consequences might be, how long the situation will last, or even what goals he should seek. He gropes along, committing himself when he has to and changing his mind as his view becomes clearer. A new decision technique called "dynamic programing" formulates this groping in a logical way so that the decision maker behaves optimally at every stage—optimally, at least, within the limits of his knowledge at each stage.

The basic logic and the mathematics of dynamic programing are directly related to the theory of servomechanisms, the feedback controls that, for example, enable an autopilot to sense variations in an airplane's flight and bring it back on course. Richard Bellman, a Rand mathematician who is the leading exponent of dynamic programing, aims at a more sophisticated kind of control. Whereas an autopilot is designed for a specific goal—to keep the plane steady in flight—Bellman would like to design controls that would learn from experience what their goals should be and how best to attain them.

Bellman's theory is comprehensive enough to embrace decision making in business, economics, biology, and statistics, as well as engineering. The computational difficulties are formidable in many applications, but in the long run, dynamic programing promises to solve many hitherto intractable decision problems. It may, for example, help solve the dilemma of a physician who is testing a drug to determine whether it will cure a lethal disease. He is confronted with partly conflicting goals. As a scientist, he wants to prove conclusively whether the drug is effective, and he resolves to give it to only half his patients. But by following this plan he will almost surely doom the rest of the patients and so, as a practitioner, he is tempted to give the drug to all. Ordinarily, he must decide either to carry out a scientifically impeccable experiment or to do everything possible to cure patients. In principle, dynamic programing offers the physician a partial escape from this burdensome decision. He may be able to alter the testing procedure as he accumulates experimental results. If in the early stages of testing the drug seems to be effective, dynamic programing should tell him better than previous techniques how to administer it to a larger proportion of patients without casting doubts on the scientific validity of the test.

Dynamic programing is actually an extension of some concepts that have brought statistics into the realm of decision theory. During World War II a Columbia University statistician, Abraham Wald, devised a new way to decide how much statistical evidence was needed to support a conclusion.

Wald's "sequential" decision theory was based on earlier ideas that had been developed in the early thirties by Egon S. Pearson and Jerzy Neyman in England. Pearson and Neyman had included in their statistical methods the risks and consequences of drawing wrong conclusions. To these Wald had added another variable: the cost of sampling and testing. His methods had obvious practical appeal. Testing—indeed, acquiring knowledge of any sort—costs something, and the faster a statistician can make up his mind, the more money he saves.

As a consequence of Wald's theory, human judgment had to be embodied in statistical analysis. The statistician had to invent some formal procedure for deciding when to stop testing, and this procedure inevitably depended on expert opinion as to the consequences of drawing a wrong conclusion.

Some further attempts to extend the use of human judgment in statistics have aroused a major controversy. One group of statisticians advocates using expert opinion as if it were experimental evidence; this group is called the "neo-Bayesian" school after the Reverend Thomas Bayes, an eighteenth-century British contributor to the mathematics of probability theory. The neo-Bayesians use judgment to determine a priori probabilities—i.e., assumptions of likelihood—which can then be used mathematically to help calculate the probability that a given hypothesis is true. Neyman and most other conventional statisticians go along with this idea, but only up to a point. They employ a priori probabilities only when they are derived from repetitive observations of relevant data. In such cases there is a clear relationship between probability and frequency. They balk at the notion of applying a priori probabilities and judgment to analysis of once-in-a-lifetime situations.

These, significantly, are the situations that are involved in most major executive decisions—e.g., whether to merge with a company in another field, whether to bid on a missile contract, whether to open a plant in Europe. The neo-Bayesians would ask the executive for an opinion of his chances of success and they would use this "expert" opinion as if it were the result of an actual experiment.

The use of judgmental probability makes it possible to reinforce the subjective beliefs of a business executive—or a military commander—with a good deal of objectivity in the form of decision theory. Nevertheless, over-reliance on opinion can lead to bad decisions. Samuel S. Wilks cautions: "The danger is that you may be accepting a bad guess when you really should be buying more experimental knowledge."

Sir Solly Zuckerman, a British scientist who is one of the fathers of operations research, is greatly concerned because military analysts are applying probability laws that pertain to repetitive situations to once-in-a-lifetime situations. Writing in *Foreign Affairs*, Zuckerman warns: "If one decides wrongly about the use of nuclear weapons, we shall be in a situation which may never repeat itself. . . ."

Mathematical Programing

ALEXANDER HENDERSON AND
ROBERT SCHLAIFER

Alexander Henderson was Professor of Economics at the Graduate School of Industrial Administration at Carnegie Institute of Technology. Robert Schlaifer is Professor of Business Administration at Harvard University. This paper comes from the Harvard Business Review *of May 1954.*

In recent years mathematicians have worked out a number of new procedures which make it possible for management to solve a wide variety of important company problems much faster, more easily, and more accurately than ever before. These procedures have sometimes been called "linear programing." Actually, linear programing describes only one group of them; "mathematical programing" is a more suitable title.

Mathematical programing is not just an improved way of getting certain jobs done. It is in every sense a new way. It is new in the sense that double-entry bookkeeping was new in the Middle Ages, or that mechanization in the office was new earlier in this century, or that automation in the plant is new today. Because mathematical programing is still new, the gap between the scientist and the businessman—between the researcher and the user—has not yet been bridged. Mathematical programing has made the news, but few businessmen really understand how it can be of use in their own companies.

Where to Ship · Let us look at a case where the technique was put to use as a routine operating procedure in an actual company.

The H. J. Heinz Company manufactures ketchup in half a dozen plants scattered across the United States from New Jersey to California and distributes this ketchup from about seventy warehouses located in all parts of the country.

In 1953 the company was in the fortunate position of being able to sell all it could produce, and supplies were allocated to warehouses in a total amount exactly equal to the total capacity of the plants. Management wished to supply these requirements at the lowest possible cost of freight; speed of shipment was not important. However, capacity in the West exceeded requirements in that part of the country, while the reverse was true in the East; for this reason a considerable tonnage had to be shipped from western plants to the East. In other words, the cost of freight could not be minimized by simply supplying each warehouse from the nearest plant.

This problem can immediately be recognized as a problem of programing because its essence is the minimization of cost subject to a fixed set of plant capacities and warehouse requirements. It can be handled by linear programing because the freight bill for shipments between any two points will be proportional to the quantity shipped. (The quantities involved are large enough so that virtually everything will move at carload rates under any shipping program which might be chosen.)

This is, in fact, the simplest possible kind of problem that can be solved by this method. Certain complexities which make solution by trial and error considerably more difficult than usual—in particular, the existence of water-competitive rates, which make it practical to send California ketchup all the way to the East Coast—add no real difficulty to the solution by linear programing. Given the list of plant capacities and warehouse requirements, plus a table of freight rates from every plant to every warehouse, one man with no equipment other than pencil and paper solved this problem for the first time in about twelve hours. After H. J. Heinz had adopted the method for regular use and clerks had been trained to become thoroughly familiar with the routine for this particular problem, the time required to develop a shipping program was considerably reduced.

The actual data of this problem have not been released by the company, but a fair representation of its magnitude is given by the similar but hypothetical examples of Exhibits 1 and 2, which show the data and solution of a problem of supplying twenty warehouses from twelve plants.

Exhibit 1 shows the basic data: the body of the table gives the freight rates, while the daily capacities of the plants and daily requirements of the warehouses are in the margins. For example, factory III, with a capacity of 3,000 cwt. per day, can supply warehouse G, with requirements of 940 cwt. per day, at a freight cost of seven cents per cwt.

Any reader who wishes to try his hand will quickly find that without a systematic procedure a great deal of work would be required to find a shipping program which would come reasonably close to satisfying these requirements and capacities at the lowest possible cost. But with the use of linear programing the problem is even easier than the Heinz problem.

Exhibit 2 gives the lowest-cost distribution program. For example, warehouse K is to get 700 cwt per day from factory I and 3,000 cwt. per day from factory III. On the other hand, factory III ships nothing to warehouse A, although Exhibit 1 shows that factory III could ship at less expense to this warehouse than to any other.

One of the most important advantages gained by the H. J. Heinz Company from the introduction of linear programing was relief of the senior members of the distribution department from the burden of preparing shipping programs. Previously the quarterly preparation of the program took a substantial amount of their time; now they pay only as much attention to this problem as they believe necessary to keep the feel of the situation, while the detailed development of the program has been handed over to clerks. Freed from the burden of working out what is after all only glorified arithmetic, they have this much more time to devote to matters which really require their experience and judgment.

An equally important gain, in the opinion of these officials themselves, is the peace of mind which results from being sure that the program is the lowest-cost program possible.

The direct dollars-and-cents saving in the company's freight bill was large enough by itself to make the use of this technique very

EXHIBIT 1

TABLE OF RATES, REQUIREMENTS, AND CAPACITIES

Factory	I	II	III	IV	V	VI	VII	VIII	IX	X	XI	XII	Daily requirements (cwt.)
					Freight rates (cents per cwt.)								
Warehouse A	16	16	6	13	24	13	6	31	37	34	37	40	1,820
B	20	18	8	10	22	11	8	29	33	25	35	38	1,530
C	30	23	8	9	14	7	9	22	29	20	38	35	2,360
D	10	15	10	8	10	15	13	19	19	15	28	34	100
E	31	23	16	10	13	16	20	14	17	17	25	28	280
F	24	14	19	13	23	14	18	9	14	13	29	25	730
G	27	23	7	11	27	8	16	6	10	11	16	28	940
H	34	25	15	4	16	15	11	9	16	17	13	16	1,130
J	38	29	17	11	16	27	17	19	8	18	19	11	4,150
K	42	43	21	22	18	10	21	18	24	16	17	15	3,700
L	44	49	25	23	10	6	13	19	15	12	10	13	2,560
M	49	40	29	21	6	15	14	21	12	29	14	20	1,710
N	56	58	36	37	5	25	8	19	9	21	15	26	580
P	59	57	44	33	8	21	6	10	8	33	15	18	30
Q	68	54	40	38	16	24	7	19	10	23	23	23	2,840
R	66	71	47	43	20	33	12	26	19	20	25	31	1,510
S	72	58	50	51	26	42	22	16	15	13	20	21	970
T	74	54	57	55	30	53	26	19	14	7	15	6	5,110
U	71	75	57	60	37	44	30	30	41	8	23	37	3,540
Y	73	72	63	56		49	40	31	31	10	8	25	4,410
Daily capacity (cwt.)	10,000	9,000	3,000	2,700	500	1,200	700	300	500	1,200	2,000	8,900	40,000

EXHIBIT 2

LOWEST-COST DISTRIBUTION PROGRAM

(DAILY SHIPMENTS FROM FACTORY TO WAREHOUSE IN CWT.)

Factory	I	II	III	IV	V	VI	VII	VIII	IX	X	XI	XII	Total	Row value
Warehouse A	1,820												1,820	16
B	1,530												1,530	20
C		2,360											2,360	28
D	100												100	10
E		280											280	28
F		730											730	19
G	940												940	27
H				1,130									1,130	28
J		4,150											4,150	34
K	700		3,000										3,700	42
L	1,360					1,200							2,560	44
M		140		1,570									1,710	45
N	580												580	56
P								30					30	51
Q		1,340			500				500			500	2,840	59
R	810						700						1,510	66
S								90				880	970	57
T												5,110	5,110	42
U	2,160							180		1,200			3,540	71
Y											2,000	2,410	4,410	61
Total	10,000	9,000	3,000	2,700	500	1,200	700	300	500	1,200	2,000	8,900	40,000	
Column value	0	−5	−21	−24	−51	−38	−54	−41	−49	−63	−53	−36		

much worth while. The first shipping program produced by linear programing gave a projected semiannual freight cost several thousand dollars less than did a program prepared by the company's previous methods, and this comparison is far from giving a full measure of the actual freight savings to be anticipated.

Shipping schedules rest on estimates which are continuously subject to revision. The capacity figures in part represent actual stocks on hand at the plants, but in part they are based on estimates of future tomato crops; and the figures for requirements depend almost wholly on estimates of future sales. The fact that schedules are now quickly and accurately prepared by clerks has enabled the company to reschedule monthly rather than quarterly, thus making much better use of new information on crops and sales as it becomes available.

Furthermore, the risk of backhauling is very much reduced under the new system. It had always been company practice early in the season to hold "reserves" in regions of surplus production, in order to avoid the danger of shipping so much out of these regions that it became necessary to ship back into them when production and sales estimates were revised. In fact, these reserves were largely accidental leftovers: when it became really difficult to assign the last part of a factory's production, this remainder was called the reserve. Now the company can look at past history and decide in advance what reserve should be held at each factory and can set up its program to suit this estimate exactly. Since the schedule is revised each month, these reserves can be altered in the light of current information until they are finally reduced to nothing just before the new pack starts at the factory in question.

Many important problems of this same character unquestionably are prevalent in business. One such case, for instance, would be that of a newsprint producer who supplies about 220 customers all over the United States from six factories scattered over the width of Canada.

Similar problems arise where the cost of transportation is measured in time rather than in money. In fact, the first efforts to solve problems of this sort systematically were made during World War II in order to minimize the time spent by ships in ballast. Specified cargo had to be moved from specified origins to specified destinations; there was usually no return cargo, and the problem was to decide to which port the ship should be sent in ballast to pick up its next cargo. An obviously similar problem is the routing of empty freight cars, and a trucker operating on a nationwide scale might face the same problem with empty trucks.

Where to Produce · When ketchup shipments were programed for the H. J. Heinz Company, factory capacities and warehouse requirements were fixed before the shipping program was worked out, and the only cost which could be reduced by programing was the cost of freight. Since management had decided in advance how much to produce at each plant, all production costs were "fixed" so far as the programing problem was concerned.

The same company faces a different problem in connection with another product, which is also produced in a number of plants and shipped to a number of warehouses. In this case, the capacity of the plants exceeds the requirements of the warehouses. The cost of production varies from one plant to another, and the problem is thus one of satisfying the requirements at the least *total* cost. It is as important to reduce the cost of production (by producing in the right place) as it is to reduce the cost of freight (by supplying from the right place). In other words, management must now decide two questions instead of one: (*a*) How much is each factory to produce? (*b*) Which warehouses should be supplied by which factories?

It is tempting to try to solve these two problems one at a time and thus simplify the job, but in general it will not be possible to get the lowest total cost by first deciding where to produce and then deciding where to ship. It is obviously better to produce in a high-cost plant if the additional cost can be more than recovered through savings in freight.

This double problem can be handled by linear programing if we may assume (as businessmen usually do) that the cost of production at any one plant is the sum of a "fixed" cost independent of volume and a "variable" cost proportional to volume in total but fixed per unit, and if these costs are known. The variable cost is handled directly by the linear programing procedure, while the fixed part is handled by a method which will be explained later.

Actually, the problem can be much more complicated and still

lend itself to solution by linear programing. For example, we can
bring in the possibility of using overtime, or of buying raw materials at one price up to a certain quantity and at another price
beyond that quantity.

Exhibit 3 shows the cost information needed to solve a hypothetical example of this sort. It is assumed that there are only
four plants and four warehouses, but any number could be
brought into the problem.

In our first approximation (which we shall modify later) we
shall assume that no plant will be closed down entirely and,
therefore, that "fixed costs" are really fixed and can be left out of
the picture. Like Exhibit 1, Exhibit 3 shows the freight rates
from each plant to each warehouse, the available daily capacity
at each plant, and the daily requirements of each warehouse; it
also shows the "variable" (fixed-per-unit) cost of normal production at each plant and the additional per-unit cost of overtime
production. The total capacity is greater than the total requirements even if the factories work only normal time.

EXHIBIT 3

COST INFORMATION FOR DOUBLE PROBLEM

A. *Warehouse requirements (tons per day)*

Warehouse	A	B	C	D	Total
Requirements	90	140	75	100	405

B. *Factory capacities (tons per day)*

Factory	I	II	III	IV	Total
Normal capacity	70	130	180	110	490
Additional capacity on overtime	25	40	60	30	155

C. *Variable costs (per ton)*

Factory	I	II	III	IV
Normal production cost	$30	$36	$24	$30
Overtime premium	15	18	12	15
Freight rates to:				
Warehouse A	$14	$ 9	$21	$18
B	20	14	27	24
C	18	12	29	20
D	19	15	27	23

On the basis of these data, the lowest-cost solution is given by part *A* of Exhibit 4. It is scarcely surprising that this solution calls for no use of overtime. So long as fixed costs are taken as really fixed, it turns out that it is best to use the entire normal capacity of factories I, II, and III, and to use 25 tons of factory IV's normal capacity of 110 tons per day. The remaining 85 tons of normal capacity at IV are left unused. The total variable cost under this schedule (freight cost plus variable production cost) will be $19,720 per day.

Presented with this result, management would certainly ask whether it is sensible to keep all four factories open when one of

EXHIBIT 4

LOWEST-COST DISTRIBUTION PROGRAM
(DAILY SHIPMENTS IN TONS FROM FACTORY TO WAREHOUSE)

A. With all four factories open

Factory	I	II	III	IV	Total
Warehouse A			90		90
B		80	60		140
C		50		25	75
D	70		30		100
Idle normal capacity				85	85
Total	70	130	180	110	490

B. With factory I closed

Factory	II	III	IV	Total
Warehouse A		90		90
B	130	10		140
C			75	75
D		80	20	100
Idle normal capacity			15	15
Total	130	180	110	420

C. With factory IV closed

Factory	I	II	III	Total
Warehouse A			90	90
B		55	85	140
C		75		75
D	70		30	100
Total	70	130	205	405

them is being left about 80 per cent idle. Even without incurring overtime, factory I, the smallest plant, could be closed and the load redistributed among the other plants. If this is done, the lowest-cost distribution of the requirements among factories II, III, and IV is that given by part *B* of Exhibit 4. Under this program the total variable cost would be $19,950 per day, or $230 per day more than under the program of Exhibit 4A, which depended on the use of all four plants. If more than $230 per day of fixed costs can be saved by closing down factory I completely, it will pay to do so; otherwise it will not.

It might be still better, however, to close down some plant other than factory I even at the cost of a certain amount of overtime. In particular, a very little overtime production (25 tons per day) would make it possible to close factory IV. A person asked to look into this possibility might reason as follows: Under the shipping schedule of Exhibit 4A, the only use of factory IV's capacity is to supply 25 tons per day to warehouse *C*. Looking at Exhibit 3 for a replacement for this supply, he would get the following information on costs per ton:

Factory	Normal cost of production	Overtime premium	Freight to warehouse C	Total
I	$30	$15	$18	$63
II	36	18	12	66
III	24	12	29	65

Apparently the cheapest way of using overtime, if it is to be used at all, would be to produce the needed 25 tons per day at factory I and ship them to warehouse *C* at a total variable cost of $63 per ton. Under the program of Exhibit 4A, with all plants in use, warehouse *C* was supplied from factory IV at a total variable cost of $30 for production plus $20 for freight, or a total of $50 per ton. The change would thus seem to add a total of $325 per day (25 tons times $13 per ton which is the difference between $63 and $50 per ton).

But, in fact, closing factory IV need not add this much to the cost of the program. If we take factory IV out of the picture and then program to find the best possible distribution of the output of the remaining plants, we discover that the program of part *C* of Exhibit 4 satisfies all requirements at a total variable cost of $19,-

995 per day, or only $275 per day more than with all plants in use. The overtime is performed by factory III, which does not supply warehouse *C* at all.

This last result deserves the reader's attention. *Once a change was made in a single part of the program, the best adjustment was a general readjustment of the entire program.* But such a general readjustment is impractical unless complete programs can be developed quickly and at a reasonable cost. It is rarely clear in advance whether the work will prove profitable, and management does not want to throw a heavy burden of recalculation on senior personnel every time a minor change is made. Mathematical programing avoids these difficulties. Even minor changes in the data can be made freely despite the fact that complete recalculations of the program are required, because the work can be done quickly and accurately by clerks or machines.

We can proceed to compute the lowest possible cost of supplying the requirements with factory II or factory III closed down completely. We can then summarize the results for all alternatives like this:

Total freight plus variable production cost

All four factories in use	$19,720
Factory I closed, no overtime	19,950
Factory II closed, overtime at factory III	20,515
Factory III closed, overtime at factories I, II, and IV	21,445
Factory IV closed, overtime at factory III	19,995

Management now has the information on variable costs which it needs in order to choose rationally among three alternatives: (1) operating all four plants with a large amount of idle normal capacity; (2) shutting down factory I and still having a little idle normal capacity; (3) shutting down factory II, III, or IV and incurring overtime. Its choice will depend in part on the extent to which fixed costs can be eliminated when a particular plant is completely closed; it may depend even more on company policies regarding community relations or some other nonfinancial consideration. Mathematical programing cannot replace judgment, but it can supply some of the factual information which management needs in order to make judgments.

Problems of this general type are met in purchasing as well as in producing and selling. A company which buys a standard raw material at many different geographical locations and ships it to a number of scattered plants for processing will wish to minimize the total cost of purchase plus freight; here the solution can be obtained in exactly the same way as just discussed. The Department of Defense is reported to have made substantial savings by using linear programing to decide where to buy and where to send certain standard articles which it obtains from a large number of suppliers for direct shipment to military installations.

Linear Programming:
Examples and Concepts

GEORGE DANTZIG

George Dantzig is head of the Operations Research Center at the University of California, Berkeley. This article comes from his book, Linear Programming and Extensions, *published in 1963.*

THE PROGRAMMING PROBLEM

Industrial production, the flow of resources in the economy, the exertion of military effort in a war theater—all are complexes of numerous interrelated activities. Differences may exist in the goals to be achieved, the particular processes involved, and the magnitude of effort. Nevertheless, it is possible to abstract the underlying essential similarities in the management of these seemingly disparate systems. To do this entails a look at the structure and state of the system, and at the objective to be fulfilled, in order to *construct a statement of the actions to be performed, their timing, and their quantity (called a "program" or "schedule"), which will permit the system to move from a given status toward the defined objective.*

If the system exhibits a structure which can be represented by a mathematical equivalent, called a mathematical model, and if the objective can also be so quantified, then some computational method may be evolved for choosing the best schedule of actions

191

among alternatives. Such use of mathematical models is termed mathematical programming. The observation that a number of military, economic, and industrial problems can be expressed (or reasonably approximated) by mathematical systems of linear inequalities and equations[1] has helped give rise to the development of linear programming.

The following three examples are typical programming problems which can be formulated linearly; they are analogous to the ones which originated research in this area. It is well to have them in mind before we discuss the general characteristics of linear programming problems.

The objective of the system in each of the three examples to be considered happens to be the minimization of total costs measured in monetary units. In other applications, however, it could be to minimize direct labor costs or to maximize the number of assembled parts or to maximize the number of trained students with a specified percentage distribution of skills, etc.

1. *A cannery example.* Suppose that the three canneries of a distributor are located in Portland (Maine), Seattle, and San Diego. The canneries can fill 250, 500, and 750 cases of tins per day, respectively. The distributor operates five warehouses around the country, in New York, Chicago, Kansas City, Dallas, and San Francisco. Each of the warehouses can sell 300 cases per day. The distributor wishes to determine the number of cases to be shipped from the three canneries to the five warehouses so that each warehouse should obtain as many cases as it can sell daily at the minimum total transportation cost.

The problem is characterized by the fifteen possible *activities* of shipping cases from each of the canneries to each of the warehouses (Fig. 1). There are fifteen *unknown activity levels* (to be determined) which are the *amounts* to be shipped along the fifteen routes. This *shipping schedule* is generally referred to as the *program*. There are a number of constraints that a shipping schedule must satisfy to be feasible: namely, the schedule must

1. The reader should especially note we have used the word *inequalities*. Systems of linear inequalities are quite general; linear inequality relations such as $x \geqq 0$, $x + y \leqq 7$ can be used to express a variety of common restrictions, such as quantities purchased, x, must not be negative or the total amount of purchases, $x + y$, must not exceed 7, etc.

FIGURE 1

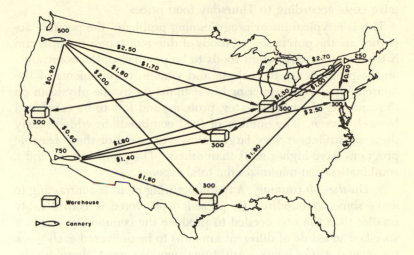

The problem: find a least cost plan of shipping from canneries to warehouses (the costs per case, availabilities and requirements are as indicated).

show that each warehouse will receive the required number of cases and that no cannery will ship more cases than it can produce daily. (Note there is one constraint for each warehouse and one for each cannery.) Several *feasible shipping schedules* may exist which would satisfy these constraints, but some will involve larger shipping costs than others. The problem then is to determine an *optimal shipping schedule*—one that has least costs.

2. *The housewife's problem.* A family of five lives on the modest salary of the head of the household. A constant problem is to determine the weekly menu after due consideration of the needs and tastes of the family and the prices of foods. The husband must have 3,000 calories per day, the wife is on a 1,500-calorie reducing diet, and the children require 3,000, 2,700, and 2,500 calories per day, respectively. According to the prescription of the family doctor, these calories must be obtained for each member by eating not more than a certain amount of fats and carbohydrates and not less than a certain amount of proteins. The diet, in fact, places emphasis on proteins. In addition, each member of

the household must satisfy his or her daily vitamin needs. The problem is to assemble menus, one for each week, that will minimize costs according to Thursday food prices.

This is a typical linear programming problem: the possible activities are the purchasing of foods of different types; the program is the amounts of different foods to be purchased; the constraints on the problem are the calorie and vitamin requirements of the household, and the upper or lower limits set by the physician on the amounts of carbohydrates, proteins, and fats to be consumed by each person. The number of food combinations which satisfy these constraints is very large. However, some of these feasible programs have higher costs than others. The problem is to find a combination that minimizes the total expense.

3. *On-the-job training.* A manufacturing plant is contracting to make some commodity. Its present work force is considerably smaller than the one needed to produce the commodity within a specified schedule of different amounts to be delivered each week for several weeks hence. Additional workers must, therefore, be hired, trained, and put to work. The present force can either work and produce at some rate of output, or it can train some fixed number of new workers, or it can do both at the same time according to some fixed rate of exchange between output and the number of new workers trained. Even were the crew to spend one entire week training new workers, it would be unable to train the required number. The next week, the old crew *and* the newly trained workers may either work or train new workers, or may both work and train, and so on. The commodity is semi-perishable so that amounts produced before they are needed will have to be stored at a specified cost. The problem is to determine the hiring, production, and storage program that will minimize total costs.

This, too, is a linear programming problem, although with the special property, not shared with the previous two examples, of *scheduling activities through time.* The activities in this problem are the assignment of old workers to either of two jobs, production or training, and the hiring of new workers each week. The quantities of these activities are restricted by the number of workers available at the beginning of each week and by the instructor-student ratio. The cumulative output produced by all workers through the number of weeks in the contractual period has to equal or exceed the required output. A possible production-training program is shown in Fig. 2. The problem can now be stated

FIGURE 2

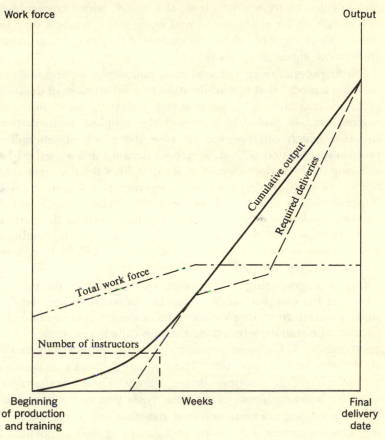

The problem: determine a least-cost hiring, production and storage program to meet required deliveries.

more precisely: determine the proper balance between hiring and training of workers, between teaching and production, and between over- and under-production in order to minimize total costs.

LINEAR PROGRAMMING DEFINED

We shall use the term *model building* to express the process of putting together of symbols representing objects according to certain rules, to form a structure, *the model,* which corresponds to a system under study in the real world. The symbols may be small-scale replicas of bricks and girders or they may be, as in our application, algebraic symbols.

Linear programming has a certain philosophy or approach to building a model that has application to a broad class of decision problems encountered in government, industry, economics, and engineering. It probably possesses the simplest mathematical structure which can be used to solve the practical scheduling problems associated with these areas. Because it is a method for studying the behavior of systems, it exemplifies the distinguishing feature of management science, or operations research, to wit: "Operations are considered as an entity. The subject matter studied is not the equipment used, nor the morale of the participants, nor the physical properties of the output, it is the combination of these in total as an economic process." (Cyril Herrmann and John Magee, 1953).

Linear programming[2] is concerned with describing the interrelations of the components of a system. As we shall see, the first step consists in regarding a system under design as composed of a number of elementary functions that are called "activities."[3] As a consequence, T. C. Koopmans introduced the term *activity analysis* to describe this approach. The different activities in which a system can engage constitute its technology. These are the representative building blocks of different types that might be recombined in varying amounts to rear a structure that is self-supporting, satisfies certain restrictions, and attains as well as possible a stated objective. Representing this structure in mathematical terms often results in a system of linear inequalities and equations; when this is so, it is called a linear programming model. Like

2. The term "linear programming" was suggested to the author by T. C. Koopmans in 1951 as an alternative to the earlier form, "programming in a linear structure."

3. The term "activity" in this connection is military in origin. It has been adopted in preference to the term "process," used by von Neumann in "A Model of General Economic Equilibrium."

architects, people who use linear programming models manipulate "on paper" the symbolic representations of the building blocks (activities) until a satisfactory design is obtained. The theory of linear programming is concerned with scientific procedures for arriving at the best design, given the technology, the required specifications, and the stated objective.

To be a linear programming model, the system must satisfy certain assumptions of proportionality, nonnegativity, and additivity. How this comes about will be discussed below. It is important to realize in trying to construct models of real-life situations, that life seldom, if ever, presents a clearly defined linear programming problem, and that simplification and neglect of certain characteristics of reality are as necessary in the application of linear programming as they are in the use of any scientific tool in problem solving.

The rule is to *neglect the negligible*. In the cannery example, for instance, the number of cases shipped and the number received may well differ because of accidental shipping losses. This difference is not known in advance and may be unimportant. In the optimum diet example the true nutritional value of each type of food differs from unit to unit, from season to season, from one source of food to another. Likewise, production rates and teaching quality will vary from one worker to another and from one hour to another. In some applications it may be necessary to give considerable thought to the differences between reality and its representation as a mathematical model to be sure that the differences are reasonably small and to assure ourselves that the computational results will be operationally useful.

What constitutes the proper simplification, however, is subject to individual judgment and experience. People often disagree on the adequacy of a certain model to describe the situation.

BASIC CONCEPTS

Suppose that the system under study (which may be one actually in existence, or one which we wish to design) is a complex of machines, people, facilities, and supplies. It has certain over-all reasons for its existence. For the military it may be to provide a striking force, or for industry it may be to produce certain types of products.

The linear programming approach is to consider a system as decomposable into a number of elementary functions, the *activities*. An activity is thought of as a kind of "black box"[4] into which flow tangible inputs, such as men, material, and equipment, and out of which may flow the products of manufacture, or the trained crews of the military. What happens to the inputs inside the "box" is the concern of the engineer or of the educator; to the programmer, only the rates of flow into and out of the activity are of interest. The various kinds of flow are called *items*.

The quantity of each activity is called the *activity level*. To change the activity level it is necessary to change the flows into and out of the activity.

Assumption 1: Proportionality · In the linear programming model the quantities of flow of various items into and out of the activity are always proportional to the activity level. If we wish to double the activity level, we simply double all the corresponding flows for the unit activity level. For instance, in Example 3, if we wish to double the number of workers trained in a period, we would have to double the number of instructors for that period and the number of workers hired. This characteristic of the linear programming model is known as the proportionality assumption.

Assumption 2: Nonnegativity · While any positive multiple of an activity is possible, negative quantities of activities are not possible. For instance, in Example 1, a negative number of cases cannot be shipped. Another example occurs in a well-known classic: the Mad Hatter, you may recall, in *Alice's Adventures in Wonderland*, was urging Alice to have some more tea, and Alice was objecting that she couldn't see how she could take more when she hadn't had any. "You mean, you don't see how you can take *less* tea," said the Hatter, "it is very easy to take more than nothing." Lewis Carroll's point was probably lost on his pre-linear-programming audience, for why should one emphasize the obvious fact that the activity of "taking tea" cannot be done in negative quantity? Perhaps it was Carroll's way of saying that mathemati-

4. Black box: Any system whose detailed internal nature one willfully ignores.

cians had been so busy for centuries extending the number system from integers, to fractions, to negative, to imaginary numbers, that they had given little thought on how to keep the variables of their problems in their original nonnegative range. This characteristic of the variables of the linear programming model is known as the nonnegativity assumption.

Assumption 3: Additivity · The next step in building a model is to specify that the system of activities be complete in the sense that a complete accounting by activity can be made of each item. To be precise, for each item it is required that the total amount specified by the system as a whole equals the sum of the amounts flowing into the various activities minus the sum of the amounts flowing out. Thus, each item, in our abstract system, is characterized by a *material balance equation*, the various terms of which represent the flows into or out of the various activities. In the cannery example, the number of cases sent into a warehouse must be completely accounted for by the amounts flowing out of the shipping activities from various canneries including possible storage or disposal of any excess. This characteristic of the linear programming model is known as the additivity assumption.

Assumption 4: Linear Objective Function · One of the items in our system is regarded as "precious" in the sense that the total quantity of it produced by the system measures the payoff. The precious item could be skilled labor, completed assemblies, an input resource that is in scarce supply like a limited monetary budget. The contribution of each activity to the total payoff is the amount of the precious item that flows into or out of each activity. Thus, if the objective is to maximize profits, activities that require money contribute negatively and those that produce money contribute positively to total profits. The housewife's expenditures for each type of food, in Example 2, is a negative contribution to total "profits" of the household; there are no activities in this example that contribute positively. This characteristic of the linear programming model is known as the linear objective assumption.

The Standard Linear Programming Problem · The determination of values for the *levels* of activities, which are positive or zero, such that flows of each item (for these activity levels) satisfy the material balance equations and such that the value of the payoff is a maximum is called the standard linear programming problem. The representation of a real system, as in any one of the three examples above, as a mathematical system which exhibits the above characteristics, is called a linear programming model. The problem of programming the activities of the real system is thus transformed into the problem of finding the solution of the linear programming model.

Linear Programming:
A Graphical Illustration

ROBERT DORFMAN

Robert Dorfman is Professor of Economics at Harvard University. This selection is from his article "Mathematical or Linear Programming," which appeared in the 1953 American Economic Review.

Let us consider an hypothetical automobile company equipped for the production of both automobiles and trucks. This company, then, can perform two economic tasks, and we assume that it has a single process for accomplishing each. These two tasks, the manufacture of automobiles and that of trucks, compete for the use of the firm's facilities. Let us assume that the company's plant is organized into four departments: (1) sheet metal stamping, (2) engine assembly, (3) automobile final assembly, and (4) truck final assembly—raw materials, labor, and all other components being available in virtually unlimited amounts at constant prices in the open market.

The capacity of each department of the plant is, of course, limited. We assume that the metal stamping department can turn out sufficient stampings for 25,000 automobiles or 35,000 trucks per month. We can then calculate the combinations of automobile and truck stampings which this department can produce. Since the department can accommodate 25,000 auto-

mobiles per month, each automobile requires 1/25,000 or 0.004
per cent of monthly capacity. Similarly each truck requires
0.00286 per cent of monthly capacity. If, for example, 15,000 automobiles were manufactured they would require 60 per cent of
metal stamping capacity and the remaining 40 per cent would be
sufficient to produce stampings for 14,000 trucks. Then 15,000
automobiles and 14,000 trucks could be produced by this department at full operation. This is, of course, not the only combination of automobiles and trucks which could be produced by the
stamping department at full operation. In Figure 1, the line
labeled "Metal Stamping" represents all such combinations.

Similarly we assume that the engine assembly department has
monthly capacity for 33,333 automobile engines or 16,667
truck engines or, again, some combination of fewer automobile
and truck engines. The combinations which would absorb the
full capacity of the engine assembly department are shown by
the "Engine Assembly" line in Figure 1. We assume also that
the automobile assembly department can accommodate 22,500
automobiles per month and the truck assembly department 15,000
trucks. These limitations are also represented in Figure 1.

We regard this set of assumptions as defining two processes:
the production of automobiles and the production of trucks. The
process of producing an automobile yields, as an output, one automobile and absorbs, as inputs, 0.004 per cent of metal stamping
capacity, 0.003 per cent of engine assembly capacity, and 0.00444
per cent of automobile assembly capacity. Similarly the process
of producing a truck yields, as an output, one truck and absorbs,
as inputs, 0.00286 per cent of metal stamping capacity, 0.006 per
cent of engine assembly capacity, and 0.00667 per cent of truck
assembly capacity.

The economic choice facing this firm is the selection of the
numbers of automobiles and trucks to be produced each month,
subject to the restriction that no more than 100 per cent of the
capacity of any department can be used. Or, in more technical
phraseology, the choice consists in deciding at what level to employ each of the two available processes. Clearly, if automobiles
alone are produced, at most 22,500 units per month can be made,
automobile assembly being the effective limitation. If only trucks
are produced, a maximum of 15,000 units per month can be made

FIGURE 1

CHOICES OPEN TO AN AUTOMOBILE FIRM

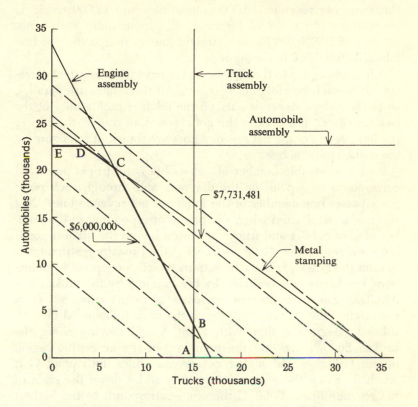

because of the limitation on truck assembly. Which of these alternatives should be adopted, or whether some combination of trucks and automobiles should be produced depends on the relative profitability of manufacturing trucks and automobiles. Let us assume, to be concrete, that the sales value of an automobile is $300 greater than the total cost of purchased materials, labor, and other direct costs attributable to its manufacture. And, similarly, that the sale value of a truck is $250 more than the direct cost of manufacturing it. Then the net revenue of the plant for any month is 300 times the number of automobiles produced plus 250

times the number of trucks. For example, 15,000 automobiles and
6,000 trucks would yield a net revenue of $6,000,000. There are
many combinations of automobiles and trucks which would yield
this same net revenue; 10,000 automobiles and 12,000 trucks is
another one. In terms of Figure 1, all combinations with a net
revenue of $6,000,000 lie on a straight line, to be specific, the line
labelled $6,000,000 in the figure.

A line analogous to the one which we have just described corresponds to each possible net revenue. All these lines are parallel,
since their slope depends only on the relative profitability of the
two activities. The greater the net revenue, of course, the higher
the line. A few of the net revenue lines are shown in the figure by
the dashed parallel lines.

Each conceivable number of automobiles and trucks produced
corresponds to a point on the diagram, and through each point
there passes one member of the family of net revenue lines. Net
revenue is maximized when the point corresponding to the number of automobiles and trucks produced lies on the highest possible net revenue line. Now the effect of the capacity restrictions is
to limit the range of choice to outputs which correspond to points
lying inside the area bounded by the axes and by the broken line
ABCDE. Since net revenue increases as points move out from
the origin, only points which lie on the broken line need be considered. Beginning then with Point A and moving along the
broken line we see that the boundary of the accessible region
intersects higher and higher net revenue lines until point C is
reached. From there on, the boundary slides down the scale of
net revenue lines. Point C therefore corresponds to the highest
attainable net revenue. At point C the output is 20,370 automobiles and 6,481 trucks, yielding a net revenue of $7,731,481 per
month.

Applications of Linear Programming in the Oil Industry

W. W. Garvin, H. W. Crandall, J. B. John, and R. A. Spellman

The authors of this article, which appeared in Management Science *in 1957, are officials of Standard Oil of California and California Research Corporation.*

As technology advances and improves, problems become more interwoven and complex. The problems of the oil industry are no exception. They can logically be grouped into categories according to the different phases of our business as shown in Figure 1. An integrated oil company must first of all carry out exploration activities to determine the spots where oil is most likely to be found. The land must then be acquired or leased and an exploratory well or "wildcat" as it is called is drilled. If luck is with us, we hit oil. Additional wells are drilled to develop the field and production gets under way. The oil is transported by various means to the refinery, where a variety of products are manufactured from it. The products in turn leave the refinery, enter the distribution system, and are marketed.

Needless to say, each of the areas shown in Figure 1 is full of unanswered questions and problems. Different methods exist for exploring the oil potentialities of a region. How should they be combined for maximum effectiveness? An oil field can be produced in many different ways. Which is best? The complexity of a modern refinery is staggering. What is the best operating plan? And what precisely do we mean by "best"? Of course, not all the problems in these areas lend themselves to linear programming but some of them do. What we would like to do is to pick out a few representative *LP* type problems from each area, show how they were formulated, and, in some cases, discuss the results that were obtained.

FIGURE 1

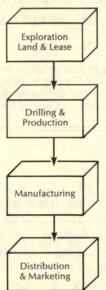

We had hoped to find applications [of linear programming] in all four of the areas shown in Figure 1. Unfortunately, we were successful only in three. We did not find any nonconfidential applications in the field of exploration. Exploration is one of the most confidential phases of our business and it is for that reason that oil companies are not very explicit about their studies in this field. We can state, however, from personal experience, that a number of applications to exploration are under investigation.

Let us therefore turn our attention to the remaining three areas of Drilling and Production, Manufacturing, and Distribution and Marketing. Out of the Drilling and Production area the problem of devising a model for a producing complex was selected. In the case of Manufacturing, the selection was difficult because historically this was the first area of application and much work has been done in this field. The problem of incremental product costs illustrates the technique of parametric programming and also shows what can happen if too many simplifications are introduced.

FIGURE 2

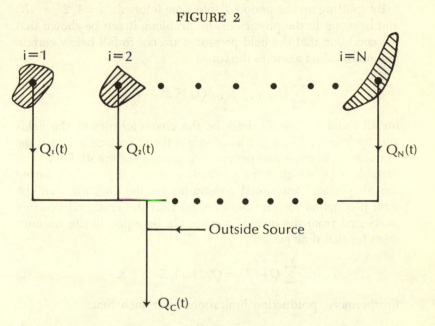

MODEL OF A PRODUCING COMPLEX

Let us now turn our attention to the model of a producing complex. We are indebted to the Field Research Laboratory of Magnolia Petroleum Company and to Arabian American Oil Company for contributing this application. Consider N oil fields or reservoirs $(i = 1, 2 \cdots N)$, as shown in Figure 2, which are producing at rates $Q_i(t)$ where t is the time. The total production of the N reservoirs is to be adjusted to meet a commitment $Q_c(t)$ (such as keeping a pipe line full or a refinery supplied). An outside source of crude oil is also available. Let the profit realizable per barrel be $c_i(t)$ and consider that the operation is to be run on this basis for a period of T years. Production limitations exist which require that the $Q_i(t)$ do not exceed certain values and that the pressures in the reservoirs do not fall below certain values. These limits may be functions of time. We shall consider the case where these fields are relatively young so that development drilling activity will occur during the time period under consideration. The problem is to determine a schedule of $Q_i(t)$ such that the profit over T years is a maximum.

By splitting up the period T into time intervals ($k = 1, 2 \cdots K$) and bringing in the physics of the problem, it can be shown that the condition that the field pressures are not to fall below certain minimum values assumes the form:

$$\sum_{j=1}^{k} (f_{i,k-j+1} - f_{i,k-j})Q_{ij} \leqq P_{io} - P_{i \min} \tag{1}$$

for all i and k. The f's describe the characteristics of the fields and are known. The right-hand side is the difference between the initial and the minimum permissible pressure of the ith field. The variable is Q_{ij} which is the production rate of the ith field during the jth period. Additional constraints on the Q_{ij}'s are that the total production for any time period plus the crude oil possibly purchased from the outside source, Q_j, be equal to the commitment for that time period:

$$\sum_{i=1}^{N} Q_{ij} + Q_j = Q_{cj}, j = 1, 2 \cdots K \tag{2}$$

Furthermore, production limitations exist such that:

$$Q_{ij} \leqq Q_{ij \max} \tag{3}$$

which are simple under bound constraints. The objective function expressing profit over the time period considered is:

$$\sum_{j=1}^{K} \sum_{i=1}^{N} c_{ij}Q_{ij} + \sum_{j=1}^{K} c_jQ_j = \max \tag{4}$$

which completes the formulation of the linear programming problem. The coefficients c_{ij} and c_j are the profit per barrel of the ith reservoir at time j and correspondingly for purchased crude oil.

Thus far, everything has been rather straightforward. But now, the time has come to clutter up the theory with facts. Let us take a closer look at the coefficients c_{ij}. If we plot revenue versus a particular production rate Q_{ij}, we get a straight line passing through the origin as shown in Figure 3. Cost versus Q_{ij} is also more or less a straight line which, however, does not pass through the origin. The cost function is discontinuous at the origin, corresponding to a set-up charge such as building a road, a pipeline, or harbor facilities, or installing a gas-oil separator.

FIGURE 3

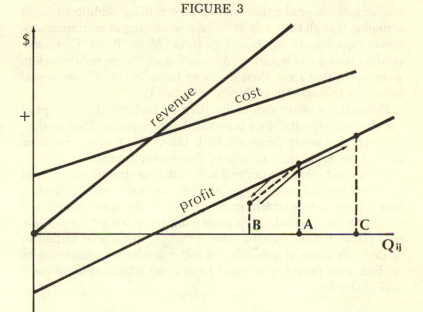

It drops to zero when $Q_{ij}=0$ because this corresponds to not yet developing the field. Also shown in Figure 3 is profit versus Q_{ij} which is the difference between revenue and cost. The profit function thus is the straight line shown plus the origin. Hence, we can say that profit from Q_{ij} production is $c_{ij}Q_{ij}-s_{ij}$ where s_{ij} is zero if Q_{ij} is zero and s_{ij} is a constant if $Q_{ij}>0$. This is a particularly difficult constraint. No general methods are available for handling this except a cut-and-try approach. This type of fixed set-up charge constraint occurs in many practical problems and we shall meet it again later on.

One other complicating feature should be mentioned. Consider that during a certain time period, Q_{ij} was at level "A" as shown in Figure 3 and that in the succeeding time period $Q_{i,\ j+1}$ has dropped to level "B." The profit at level "B" is not obtained by following the profit line to operating level "B" but rather by following a line as shown which is parallel to the revenue line. The reduction in level from "A" to "B" involves merely turning a few valves and essentially does not entail any reduction in operating costs. If, on the other hand, we go from "A" to "C" in succeeding time periods, then we do follow the profit line because an increase in production necessitates drilling additional wells assuming that all the wells at "A" are producing at maximum economic capacity. If we should go from "A" to "B" to "C" in succeeding time periods and if "A" was the maximum field development up to that time, then in going from "B" to "C" we would follow the broken path as shown in Figure 3.

This state of affairs can be handled by building the concept of "production capacity" into the model and requiring that production capacity never decreases with time. But this can be done only at the expense of enlarging the system appreciably.

There exist other factors and additional constraints which must be taken into account. As is so often the case, we are dealing here with a system which on the surface looks rather simple but which becomes considerably more complex as we get deeper into it to make it more realistic. Nevertheless, the simple system or modest extensions of it enables an entire producing complex to be studied, thus providing a good basis upon which to build more realistic models.

INCREMENTAL PRODUCT COSTS

Let us now leave the problems of petroleum production behind us and venture into the petroleum refinery. As was indicated before, a great deal of work has been done in this area. The few problems we shall discuss will be illustrative of what is going on in this field.

We shall consider at first a simple but nevertheless instructive example. A refinery produces gasoline, furnace oil and other products as shown in Figure 4. The refinery can be supplied with a fairly large number of crude oils. The available crude oils have different properties and yield different volumes of finished products. Some of these crudes must be refined because of long-term minimum volume commitments or because of requirements for specialty products. These crudes are considered fixed and yield

FIGURE 4

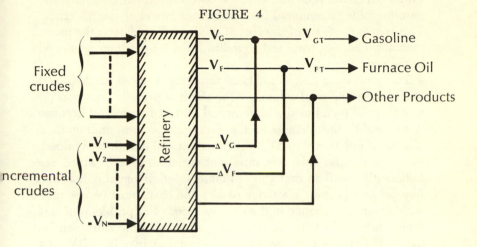

gasoline and furnace oil volumes V_G and V_F respectively. From the remaining crudes and from those crudes which are available in volumes greater than their minimum volume commitment must be selected those which can supply the required products most economically. These are the incremental crudes. Denote the gasoline and furnace oil volumes which result from the incremental crudes by ΔV_G and ΔV_F and the total volumes (fixed plus incremental) by V_{GT} and V_{FT}. The problem is to determine the minimum incremental cost of furnace oil as a function of incremental furnace oil production keeping gasoline production and general refinery operations fixed.

The formulation of this problem is straightforward:

$$\sum_1^N a_{Gi} V_i = V_{GT} - V_G = \Delta V_G \tag{5}$$

$$\sum_1^N a_{Fi} V_i = V_{FT} - V_F = \Delta V_F \tag{6}$$

$$V_i \leqq V_{i\,max} \tag{7}$$

$$\sum_1^N c_i V_i = \min \tag{8}$$

where a_{Gi} and a_{Fi} are the gasoline and furnace oil yields of the ith crude, V_i and $V_{i \, max}$ are the volume and availability of the ith incremental crude and c_i is the cost of producing incremental gasoline plus incremental furnace oil per barrel of the ith crude. This cost is made up of the cost of crude at the refinery, the incremental processing costs and a credit for the by-products produced at the same time.

The procedure now consists of assuming a value for ΔV_F and obtaining an optimal solution. The shadow price of equation (6) will then be equal to the incremental cost of furnace oil because it represents the change in the functional corresponding to a change of one barrel in ΔV_F. The incremental cost thus obtained, however, is valid only over ranges of variation of ΔV_F which are sufficiently small so that the optimum solution remains feasible. Beyond that permissible range of ΔV_F the basis must be changed with a resulting change in the shadow price. For problems of this type, the so-called "parametric programming" procedure can be used. This procedure has been incorporated into the IBM 704 LP code. It starts with an optimal solution and then varies in an arbitrary but preassigned manner the constants on the right-hand side until one of the basic variables becomes zero. The computer then prints out the optimal solution which exists at that time, changes the basis to an adjacent extreme point which is also optimum, and repeats this process until a termination is reached.

An actual problem was run with the model shown in Figure 4. Thirteen incremental crudes were available and incremental gasoline production was fixed at 14,600 barrels daily. The results are shown in Figure 5 which shows the minimum total incremental cost as a function of incremental furnace oil production. Ignore the dashed line for the moment. The circles represent points at which the optimum basis had to be changed. The functional is a straight line between these points. It turned out that incremental furnace-oil production was possible only in the range from about 7,100 bpd to about 11,200 bpd. Between the two extremes, the functional exhibits a minimum at about 8,000 bpd. The reason for the minimum is to be found in the fact that near the two extremes of furnace oil production, little choice exists in the composition of the crude slate. Volume is the limitation and economics plays a secondary part. Away from the two

FIGURE 5

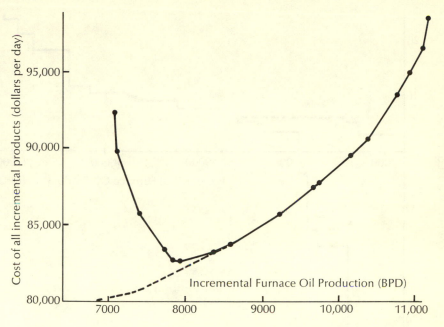

extremes, however, we have greater flexibility in crudes run and thus have the freedom to pick the cheapest crude combination. Figure 6 shows the incremental cost of furnace oil as a function of furnace oil production. It is a staircase type function because the shadow price remains unchanged as long as the optimum basis remains feasible and jumps discontinuously whenever the basis is changed. At low levels of incremental furnace oil production, the incremental cost becomes negative because in that region it is *more* expensive to make *less* furnace oil.

If we now were to show our model and our results to the refiner, he would immediately detect a fly in the ointment. The negative incremental cost at low furnace oil production runs counter to his intuitive feeling for the problem. He would point out, and rightly so, that the formulation of our model is not complete. Common sense would dictate the making of the larger volumes of furnace oil at lower cost and disposing of the excess furnace oil in some manner. For example, this excess can be mixed into heavy fuel production. If all the heavy fuel that is made can be sold, the net cost of the furnace oil overproduction

FIGURE 6

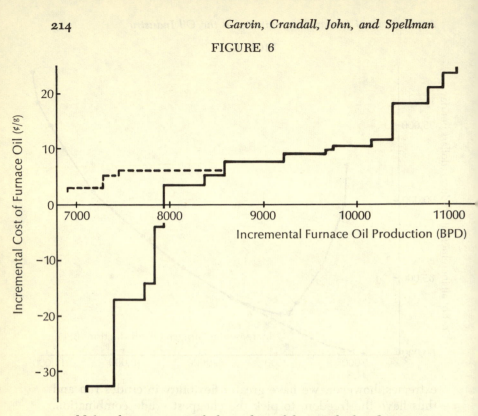

would be the negative of the value of heavy fuel indicating a credit we receive for increasing heavy fuel production.

We are tempted, therefore, to try the formulation shown in Figure 7 where we permit the diversion of some furnace oil to heavy fuel. The equation for gasoline production remains unchanged but the furnace oil equation now reads:

$$\sum_1^N a_{iF} V_i - s_1 = \Delta V_F \tag{9}$$

and the objective form is:

$$\sum_1^N c_i V_i - v_{HF} s_1 = \min \tag{10}$$

where s_1 is a slack variable indicating the volume of furnace oil diverted to heavy fuel and v_{HF} is the value per barrel of heavy fuel. It is not possible, however, to divert unlimited amounts of furnace oil into heavy fuel without violating heavy fuel's speci-

FIGURE 7

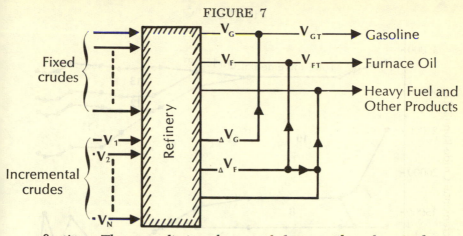

fications. The upper limit on how much furnace oil can be mixed into heavy fuel depends on the volume of heavy fuel produced which in turn is related to the crude slate, and would depend also on the specifications of heavy fuel. Furthermore, if we bring heavy fuel into the picture explicitly, the cost coefficients used before must be modified. The problem is beginning to become more complex. To take these effects into account would form the basis of an entirely new study. For purposes of the present illustration, however, the situation can be handled roughly as follows. It turns out from experience and by considering the volumes involved that the excess furnace oil production should be less than or at most equal to about 15 percent of the incremental furnace oil production if all the excess is to go to heavy fuel and specifications on heavy fuel are to be met. Therefore, the additional constraint

$$\sum_1^N a_{iF} V_i + s_2 = 1.15\Delta V_F \qquad (11)$$

was added to the system where s_2 is a slack variable. This constraint insures that no undue advantage is taken of the freedom introduced by excess furnace oil production.

The results for this second formulation of the problem are shown by the dashed lines in Figures 5 and 6. The abscissa now refers to that part of incremental furnace oil production which leaves the refinery as furnace oil. Excess furnace oil is produced below incremental furnace oil production of about 8,600 bpd.

FIGURE 8

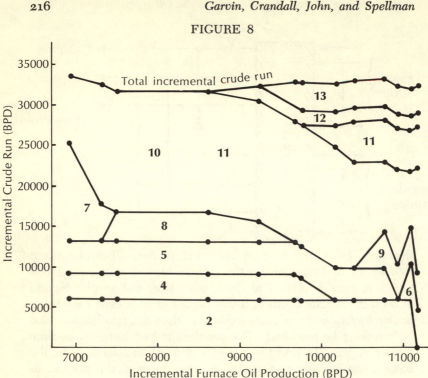

Above that level, it is not economic to produce more furnace oil than required and, consequently, there is no difference between the two formulations of the problem. Constraint (11) is limiting for incremental furnace oil production below about 7,500 bpd. Figure 8 shows the composition of the optimum crude slate for the second formulation as a function of incremental furnace oil production. This is useful information to have on hand. Note that no changes occur in the range of incremental furnace oil production from 7,500 to 8,600 bpd. In this range, actual incremental furnace oil production remains fixed at 8,600 bpd with any excess going into heavy fuel.

The modern refinery is a complicated system with strong interdependence among the activities within it. The example just described illustrates this point and shows the importance of the refiner's experience in correctly isolating portions of the refinery which can be separately considered.

Part Five

Decision Theory, Game Theory, and
Other Techniques

THE papers in Part Five deal with decision-making under uncertainty, the theory of games, and inventory and queuing theory. To begin with, John Pratt, Howard Raiffa, and Robert Schlaifer present elements of modern statistical decision theory, including a description of decision trees. In a brief note, Martin Shubik discusses some alternative theories of decision-making under uncertainty. A. A. Walters then presents a detailed application of decision theory to a specific example, the problem being to determine whether or not a tax should be imposed on a particular commodity and whether a survey should be carried out to obtain relevant information.

The next two papers are concerned with the theory of games. John McDonald discusses one-person, two-person, and three-person games, using the liquor industry to illustrate games with more than two persons. J. D. Williams shows how conflict situations must be described in order to be amenable to game-theory analyses; the basic elements are the number of persons, the pay-off, the strategy, and the game matrix.

The last two papers in this part are an introduction to inventory and queuing theory. The short piece by Thomson M. Whitin introduces the reader to the lot-size formula used to calculate economical purchase quantities. As Whitin points out, this formula is by no means new. William Baumol describes the salient characteristics of queuing problems, which have received a great deal of attention from operations researchers, and shows how Monte Carlo techniques can be used to solve them.

Introduction to Statistical
Decision Theory

John Pratt, Howard Raiffa,
and Robert Schlaifer

John Pratt, Howard Raiffa, and Robert Schlaifer are professors in the Graduate School of Business Administration at Harvard University. This article is taken from their book, Introduction to Statistical Decision Theory, *published in 1965.*

THE PROBLEM OF DECISION UNDER UNCERTAINTY

When all of the facts bearing on a business decision are accurately known—when the decision is made "under certainty"—careless thinking or excessive computational difficulty are the only reasons why the decision should turn out, after the fact, to have been wrong. But when the relevant facts are not all known—when the decision is made "under uncertainty"—it is impossible to make sure that every decision will turn out to have been right in this same sense. Under uncertainty, the businessman is forced, in effect, to gamble. His previous actions have put him in a position where he must place bets, hoping that he will win but knowing that he may lose. Under such circumstances, a right decision consists in the choice of the best possible bet, whether it is won or lost after the fact. A businessman who buys fire insurance does not censure himself if his plant has not burned down by the time the insurance expires, and the following example is typical of other decisions which must be made and judged in this way.

An oil wildcatter who holds an option on a plot of land in an oil-producing region must decide whether to drill on the site before the option expires or to abandon his rights. The profitability of drilling will depend on a large number of unknowns— the cost of drilling, the amount of oil or gas discovered, the price at which the oil or gas can be sold, and so forth—none of which can be predicted with certainty. His problem is further complicated by the fact that it is possible to perform various tests or experiments that will yield a certain amount of information on the geophysical structure below the land on which he has an option. Since some structures are more favorable to the existence of oil than others, this information would be of considerable help in deciding whether or not to drill; but the various tests cost a substantial amount of money, and hence it is not at all obvious that any of the available tests should be performed. The wildcatter must nevertheless decide which if any of the tests are to be performed, and ultimately, if not now, he must decide whether or not to drill.

Decision Trees · The essential characteristics of this example are two in number:

1. A *choice* or in some cases a sequence of choices must be made among various possible courses of action.
2. This choice or sequence of choices will ultimately lead to some *consequence*, but the decision maker cannot be sure in advance what this consequence will be because it depends not only on his choice or choices but on an unpredictable *event* or sequence of events.

The essence of any such problem can be brought out very clearly by a type of diagram known as a *decision tree*.

As an example that will illustrate all the essential points involved in the construction of a decision tree without useless complexities, we shall take a somewhat simplified version of the oil-drilling problem described just above. For our present purpose we shall assume that:

1. If the well is drilled at all, it will be drilled on a fixed-price contract for $100,000;

2. If oil is struck, the wildcatter will immediately sell out to a major producer for $450,000;

3. Only one type of test or experiment, namely a seismic sounding, can be performed before deciding whether or not to drill. This experiment costs $10,000; if it is performed, it will reveal with certainty whether the structure is of Type *A* (very favorable to the existence of oil), Type *B* (less favorable), or Type *C* (very unfavorable).

On these assumptions the wildcatter's decision problem can be represented by the tree shown as Figure 1. We imagine the decision-maker as standing at the base of the tree (the left side of the diagram) and as being obliged to choose first between having the seismic sounding made and not having it made. If the wildcatter's choice is to have the sounding made, one of three events will occur: the subsurface structure will be revealed to be of Type *A*, *B*, or *C*. If the wildcatter's choice is not to have the sounding made, then only one event can occur: no information.

Whatever the wildcatter's first-stage choice may be and whatever the first-stage event, the wildcatter must now enter a second stage by making a choice between drilling and abandoning the option. If he drills, then one or the other of two events will occur: oil or dry hole; if he chooses to abandon the option, the only possible "event" is "option rights lost."

Finally, at the end (right) of the tree we write down a description of the consequence of each possible sequence of choices and events. If the wildcatter chooses not to have the sounding made and to abandon his option, the consequence is simply $0—we neglect whatever he may originally have paid for the option because this is a sunk cost that cannot be affected by any present decision and therefore is irrelevant to the decision problem. Suppose, on the contrary, he decides to drill even though he has learned nothing about the subsurface structure; if he strikes a dry hole, he loses the $100,000 drilling cost, whereas if he strikes oil, his profit is the $450,000 for which he sells the rights less the $100,000 cost of drilling. If in the first stage he decides to have the sounding made, then the consequences of abandoning the option, drilling a dry hole, or striking oil are all reduced by the $10,000 cost of the sounding.

FIGURE 1

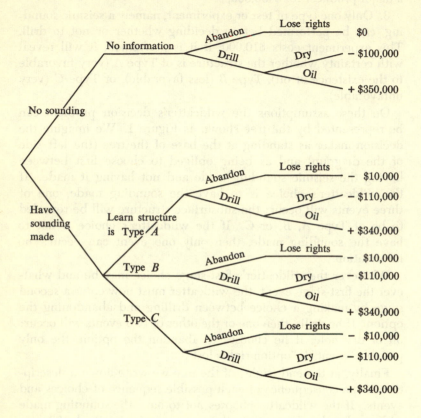

THE PROBLEM OF ANALYSIS

Analysis of the Simplest Problems · Before we even try to say what we mean by a "reasoned solution" of a complex decision problem of the kind we have just described, let us try to get a start by seeing what a sensible businessman might do when he solves a much simpler problem.

We consider an example. A manufacturer, Mr. L. K. Jones, has recently experienced a serious decline in demand for his product and as a result will be forced to lay off a substantial portion of his work force, spend money for protective treatment of idle machinery, and so forth, unless he can obtain a large order which the XYZ Company is about to place with some supplier. To have a chance at obtaining this order, Jones will have to incur considerable expense both for the making of samples and for sending a team of sales engineers to visit the XYZ Company; he must now decide whether or not to incur this expense. Formally, his problem can be described by the tree shown in Figure 2, where the three possible consequences of the two possible acts are represented by symbols:

C_1 = layoff of substantial part of work force, cost of protecting machinery;

C_2 = same as C_1, and in addition the cost of unsuccessful attempt to obtain order;

C_3 = substantial monetary profit on order, less cost of obtaining it.

FIGURE 2

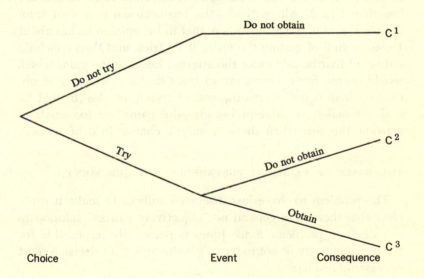

Do not obtain — C^1

Do not try

Try

Do not obtain — C^2

Obtain — C^3

Choice   Event   Consequence

The structure of *this* problem is simple enough to make quite clear to anyone the issues that are involved in its solution. Jones (or any other sensible businessman faced with a problem of this sort) will feel that his decision will depend on two separate considerations: (1) his judgment concerning his chances of getting the order if he tries, and (2) a comparison of the cost of trying with the advantages which will accrue to him if he succeeds. If the cost is quite small relative to the advantages which would accompany success, he will make the attempt even if he thinks the chances of success are quite small; if, on the other hand, the cost of trying to get the order is so large that it would eat up most of the profits, he will not make the attempt unless he feels virtually sure that the attempt will succeed.

Sometimes a businessman who is thinking about a problem of this kind will go even further and *quantify* some if not all of his reasoning. He may say, for example, that there is so much to be gained by obtaining the order that he would try to obtain it even if there were only 1 chance in 3 of success; he may then conclude either (*a*) that he *will* make the attempt because in his opinion the chances are at least as good as 1 in 3, or else (*b*) that he *will not* make the effort because in his opinion the chances of success are less than 1 in 3. Alternatively, the businessman may start from the other side of the problem, say that in his opinion he has about 1 chance in 3 of getting the order if he tries, and then conclude either (*a*) that he *will* make the attempt because the gains which would accrue from success are so great that a 1/3 chance of obtaining them is well worth the cost of trying, or else (*b*) that he *will not* make the attempt because the gains are too small to warrant the cost when there is only 1 chance in 3 of success.

THE BASES OF DECISION: PREFERENCE AND JUDGMENT

The problem we have just discussed suffices to make it quite clear that there is in general no "objectively correct" solution to *any* decision problem. Since Jones is personally responsible for the decision to try or not to try to get the order, his decision must *necessarily* rest on:

1. How good *he feels* the chances of obtaining the order would have to be to make it worth his while to try;

2. How good *in his opinion* the chances of obtaining the order actually are.

What the businessman actually does when he answers questions of type 1 is quantify his *personal preference* for C_1 relative to C_2 and C_3; what he does when he answers questions of type 2 is quantify his *personal judgment* concerning the relative strengths of the factors that favor and oppose certain events. If he behaves reasonably, he then chooses the solution of the problem which is *consistent* with this personal preference and this personal judgment.

ANALYSIS OF COMPLEX PROBLEMS; THE ROLE OF FORMAL ANALYSIS

Since reasonable decisions in even the simplest problems must rest necessarily on the responsible decision maker's personal judgments and personal preferences, it is intuitively quite clear that these same elements must be involved in the solution of complex problems represented by decision trees with many levels and many branches at each level. It would be folly, in other words, to look for a method of analysis that will lead to an "objectively correct" solution of the oil-drilling problem we have used. A reasonable decision-maker wants his decision to agree with his preferences and his best judgments, and he will have (and should have) no use for any proposal that purports to solve his problem by some "formula" that does *not* incorporate his preferences and judgments. This assertion does not of course imply that the decision-maker should ignore objective evidence that is relevant and available.

Stated in another way, the reason why a decision-maker might want help in analyzing a decision problem like our oil-drilling example, when Jones needed no help in deciding whether or not to try for the order from the XYZ Company, is that Jones could easily see the *implications* of his preferences and judgments whereas the wildcatter cannot. The wildcatter may feel quite sure that, for example, he would decide to drill if he knew that the structure was of Type *A* or *B* and would decide not to drill if he knew that the structure was of Type *C;* however, his immediate problem is to decide whether or not to spend $10,000 in order to learn what the structure is, and while it is obvious that this information has value, it is not at all clear whether the value is greater or less than the $10,000 the information will cost.

Any decision problem, no matter how complex, can in principle be reduced to a number of problems each of which individually has the same simple structure as the problem described by the tree of Figure 2.

If, in each of these simple problems, the decision-maker will

1. Quantify his *preference* by telling us how good the chances of obtaining C_3 *would have to be* to make him willing to gamble on C_2 or C_3 rather than to take C_1 for certain, and

2. Quantify his *judgment* by telling us how good in his opinion the chances of obtaining C_3 *actually are,*

and if, in addition, he accepts certain simple principles of "reasonable," "consistent," or "coherent" behavior, then it is possible by purely logical deduction to find that solution of the complex problem which is *logically consistent with the decision-maker's own preferences and judgments.*

Naturally we are concerned with decision problems where this kind of analysis by decomposition and evaluation produces fruitful results. There are, of course, many problems—some would say "most problems"—where although in principle such an analysis could be made it would not be profitable to do so. In many situations, the incremental advantage to be gained from formal analysis cannot be expected to repay the effort, time, and cost of the analysis; in others, the decision maker may not be able, especially without training, to quantify his preference and judgments in the way required for a formal analysis; in still others, the decision problem may be faithfully abstracted into the proper form only to prove to be too complicated for the analytical tools we have available. Even after granting all these exceptions, however, there remain many problems in which formal analysis can be of considerable help to a businessman who wishes to take advantage of it.

A Note on Decision-making under Uncertainty

MARTIN SHUBIK

Martin Shubik is Professor of Industrial Administration at Yale University. This is an excerpt from his article, "Approaches to the Study of Decision-making Relevant to the Firm," which appeared in The Journal of Business *in 1961.*

By introducing considerations of probability, an attempt can be made to extend the economic theory of choice to conditions involving uncertainty. The heroic assumption must be made that the situations to be modeled are such that it is valid and useful to utilize the theory of probability. This has given rise to discussions concerning subjective probability and a large literature on probabilistic preferences and the theory of utility. Problems concerning gambling and risk preference have been examined, and several alternatives for optimal behavior have been suggested. For example, Savage has offered a man who wishes to minimize regret. In other words, after the event, when he looks back, he wishes to have acted in such a manner that he will be least sorry concerning the outcome.

Bayesian and "maximin" principles[1] have also been suggested as manners in which the individual should cope with lack of

1. [The "maximin" principle is often called the "minimax" principle. *Editor*]

knowledge. The simple examples given here illustrate the behaviors manifested in following these different principles. In Figure 1 a simple 2×2 payoff matrix is presented. The decision-maker must choose between one of two actions, knowing that "Nature," or the environment, may also make a choice which affects him. For example, if both select their second alternative, the payoff is 7 to the decision-maker. The principle he follows will depend upon his view of the forces and motivations present in his environment.

"Nature"

The Decision-maker   1   2

	1	2
1	1	9
2	2	7

FIGURE 1

The Bayesian assumption says that all the actions of "Nature" are equiprobable, and thus the optimal behavior under this assumption will be to select the first alternative, with an expected payoff of:

$$\tfrac{1}{2}\,(1) + \tfrac{1}{2}\,(9) = 5.$$

The maximin assumption has the decision-maker believe that the environment is "out to get him." In this case he will select his second alternative, assuming that, since the worst will happen, he can at least guarantee 2 for himself.

"Nature"

The Decision-maker   1   2

	1	2
1	1	0
2	0	2

FIGURE 2

The "regret payoff" is illustrated in Figure 2 for the same situation. If he selected his second alternative and the environment did likewise, he would obtain 7 (Fig. 1) but could have obtained 9 (by selecting his first alternative); hence his regret is 2.

Shackle has constructed a "potential surprise function" which he feels dominates many major decisions which must be made in face of uncertainty which cannot be adequately portrayed by considerations of probability. All the methods noted above depend upon assumptions as to how to deal with uncertainty. Which is the "best" assumption depends upon the application and knowledge of human behavior.

In spite of the limitations of models of probability, operations research and industrial statistics have, however, flourished by applying normative models of economic man acting under probabilistically portrayed uncertainty. Theoretical models of inventory, sequential sampling, and various queueing problems have been actively applied. These have already influenced the inventory levels of the whole economy and have had an effect on the understanding of reliability and risk in areas as diverse as individual credit risks, quality control in production, and stockpiling for emergency.

One area in which the applications have been fewer but the implications deeper is that of dynamic programming. This methodology deals with situations where at each period the decision-maker chooses an action which influences a sequence of events stretching off into the possibly indefinite future. In subsequent periods he has the opportunity to modify the effects of previous decisions by current action. Although this theory still deals with statistical uncertainty and mathematical expectations, the rules of decision generated as dynamic program solutions have more of the flavor of over-all long-range strategic decisions. Dividend and investment policies can be studied as dynamic programs. However, the mathematics of functional equations used in dynamic programming is, unfortunately, difficult and still relatively underdeveloped.

Decision Theory: An Example

A. A. WALTERS

A. A. Walters is Professor of Econometrics and Social Statistics at the University of Birmingham. This piece comes from his book Introduction to Econometrics, *published by* Norton in 1970.

It is often claimed that the ultimate purpose of any investigation is to enable us to make better decisions. From a judgment of the state of the world we evaluate the consequences of each potential course of action. We then decide to pursue one of these courses of action according to our view of the attractiveness of the consequences. For example, suppose we are concerned with finding the optimum tax to impose on confectionery and that we know that the elasticity of supply is infinite; then the question turns on the elasticity of demand. With the traditional approach we would either estimate the elasticity of demand or examine certain hypotheses about the elasticity. Let us suppose, for simplicity, that the elasticity of demand is *either* unity *or* 0.5. We might then set up our experiment to discover which hypothesis has the highest likelihood—using either Bayesian methods or the traditional methods of hypothesis testing. At this stage the statistician's job *per se* is completed and the decision-maker takes over.

With decision theory, however, the statistical problem is extended to consider the costs of making various decisions if certain hypotheses hold. Again let us simplify and assume that there are only two possible courses of action—to tax at 10 percent or not to tax at all. Then we can characterize the four outcomes by the following costs:

	Elasticity	
	1	0.5
Tax	$10 million	0
No tax	0	$5 million

Now if the main purpose of the tax is to raise revenue, it is clear that taxing confectionery when the elasticity is unity involves expense and no tax revenue—so we have supposed that the cost is $10 million which has been entered in the appropriate box of the table of outcomes. If, on the other hand, we impose a tax and the elasticity is only 0.5, we have taxed 'correctly' and we reckon the cost at zero. Similarly, if we do not tax when we should not, the cost can be taken as zero. If we miss an opportunity for taxing, i.e. no tax when the elasticity is 0.5, we incur a cost of $5 million.

Now let us suppose that we have *already carried out the survey* and found that the chance of unit elasticity is 0.2 and the likelihood of 0.5 elasticity is 0.8. Then we can find the expected costs of adopting the tax as

$$[(\$10 \text{ million}) \times 0.2] + [(\$0 \text{ million}) \times 0.8] = \$2 \text{ million}.$$

This is simply the sum of the outcome multiplied by the likelihood of that outcome. Similarly, the expected costs of not adopting the tax is

$$[(\$0 \text{ million}) \times 0.2] + [(\$5 \text{ million}) \times 0.8] = \$4 \text{ million}.$$

So we have

Strategy	*Expected costs*
Tax	$2 million
No tax	$4 million

and it is clearly the best strategy to tax confectionery.

This result is, however, critically dependent on the criteria we have adopted—that is, the minimizing of expected costs. There is nothing sacrosanct about this aim; and it is natural to consider alternative approaches. One such is to find the strategy which results in as low a value as possible for the *maximum* loss. In short the strategy is concerned with minimizing the maximum loss—or even shorter "minimax."

In our table we see that, if we tax, the maximum possible loss is $10 million. If we do not tax, the maximum possible loss is $5 million. Clearly the maximum loss is minimized if we then choose not to tax confectionery—and we are ensured that the maximum loss is $5 million. This is a different solution from that developed for the "expected loss" criterion. The minimax strategy represents a "safety-first" attitude to decision-making. In this strategy the numerical value of the likelihoods, provided they exceed zero, do not play a part—whereas in the "expected loss" case they play a critical role.

There are, of course, many other criteria for decision-making. But there is no obvious rule for choosing between the criteria available. Each must be chosen according to the "utility function" of the decision-maker. An ultra-cautious individual may choose "minimax," a less cautious man the "expected loss" criterion. If it is possible to describe each situation by means of a utility function we can generalise the choice criterion to one of maximizing expected utility (or minimizing expected disutility). This will then enable us to take account of the fact that a large loss, for example, has enormous disutility, while a small loss has proportionately less disutility. For example, we may assume that the disutility function is simply the *square* of the loss so that we have the disutility table in "utils":

| | Elasticity | |
	1	0
Tax	100	0
No tax	0	25

Units: utils.

And now calculating expected disutility

for tax $(100 \times 0.2) + (0 \times 0.8) = 20$ utils;

for no tax $(0 \times 0.2) + (25 \times 0.8) = 20$ utils.

There is a tie! It does not matter whether we choose to tax confectionery or not—they have equal disutility. If the disutility function had been the *cube* of the loss, then we should have been better off *not* introducing a tax. For the rest of this discussion we shall adopt only one of the various criteria discussed above—we shall use the simple "expected loss" formulation.

Up to now we have supposed that the experiment (the survey) had already taken place and that we were concerned with making a decision on the basis of its results about the likelihoods. But frequently we find ourselves in the situation where *whether to do a survey or not is actually part of the decision-making procedure.* In other words we start our decision-making process *before* the sample; we ask whether it is worthwhile sampling or not. This is a question in addition to those about choosing an action strategy, i.e. whether to tax or not.

Obviously the question of whether to sample or not will depend on two things: first the cost of the sample itself and secondly our ideas about how the sample result is likely to affect our views about the likelihoods of the elasticities. To develop the latter point suppose that *if the elasticity is actually unity* there is a very high chance (say 0.9) that the experiment will produce the correct result (elasticity = 1.0), and only a low chance (0.1) that the experiment will produce the wrong result, i.e. falsely allege that the elasticity is 0.5.

Now let us suppose that, as before, we can, before we decide whether or not to sample, ascribe probabilities to the hypotheses elasticity = 1, and 0.5, and let us suppose that these are respectively 0.3 and 0.7. These figures measure our degree of belief in the validity of the hypothesis before the sample is carried out. (They correspond to the values of 0.8 and 0.2 which we assumed in the previous example, when we assumed that we had already sampled and incorporated the results in these two likelihoods.) We can now calculate the chances of *both* the elasticity being unity *and* the experiment producing evidence showing that it is unity (and we use the mnemonic "prob" for probability):

$$\text{prob}\left[\begin{array}{cc} \text{elasticity}=1, & \text{sample} \\ & \text{indicates unity} \end{array}\right]$$
$$=\text{prob}\left[\begin{array}{c|c} \text{sample} & \text{elasticity} \\ \text{indicates unity} & =1 \end{array}\right] \cdot \text{prob}[\text{elasticity}=1]$$

by the ordinary laws of conditional probability.[1]

---

1. Prob [event x | event y] is the probability that event x occurs *given that event y occurs*: it is a conditional probability. On the other hand, prob [event x, event y] is the probability that *both* event x and event y occur. Clearly, prob [event x, event y] = prob [event x | event y] · prob [event y] · [*Editor.*]

Numerically

$$\text{prob} \left[\text{elasticity} = 1, \begin{array}{l} \text{sample} \\ \text{indicates unity} \end{array} \right] = 0.9 \times 0.3$$
$$= 0.27.$$

Similarly

$$\text{prob} \left[\text{elasticity} = 1, \begin{array}{l} \text{sample} \\ \text{indicates } 0.5 \end{array} \right] = 0.1 \times 0.3$$
$$= 0.03$$

—this shows the likelihood that *both* the elasticity is unity *and* the sample evidence indicated that it is (wrongly) 0.5.

We have dealt with the case when the elasticity is unity; now we examine the case when the elasticity is 0.5. Suppose now that in fact the elasticity were 0.5. Then let us assume that the likelihood of the sample survey pointing to the correct result (i.e. elasticity = 0.5) is 0.6, and the likelihood of it indicating the wrong result (unity) is 0.4. One can then construct the chances of the outcomes:

$$\text{prob} \left[\text{elasticity} = 0.5, \begin{array}{l} \text{sample indicates} \\ \text{elasticity} = 0.5 \end{array} \right]$$

$$= \text{prob} \left[\begin{array}{l} \text{sample indicates} \\ \text{elasticity} = 0.5 \end{array} \Big| \text{elasticity} = 0.5 \right] \cdot \text{prob} \left[\text{elasticity} = 0.5 \right]$$

$$= 0.6 \times 0.7 = 0.42.$$

Similarly

$$\text{prob} \left[\text{elasticity} = 0.5, \begin{array}{l} \text{sample indicates} \\ \text{elasticity} = 1 \end{array} \right]$$

$$= \text{prob} \left[\begin{array}{l} \text{sample indicates} \\ \text{elasticity} = 1 \end{array} \Big| \text{elasticity} = 0.5 \right] \cdot \text{prob} \left[\text{elasticity} = 0.5 \right]$$

$$= 0.4 \times 0.7 = 0.28.$$

These chances give us a measure of how the sample is likely to influence our views of the elasticity. We can portray them in a table which gives us the chances of outcomes when it is *assumed that we have decided to sample*. Notice that the sum of the joint chances over the sample outcomes gives us the prior probabilities

TABLE 1

JOINT CHANCE OF SAMPLE OUTCOME AND ACTUAL ELASTICITY

		Actual elasticity:		*Sum* Prior probability of sample outcomes
		0.5	1.0	
Sample indicates elasticity to be	0.5	0.42	0.03	0.45
	1.0	0.28	0.27	0.55
Sum	Prior probability of actual elasticity	0.70	0.30	1.00

of the elasticities, 0.7 and 0.3. The sum horizontally gives the prior probabilities of the sample outcomes.

Now we can specify the decisions open to us and the costs associated with each eventuality. Let us assume that the survey costs \$2 million. The costs of the various outcomes can be tabulated as follows:

Costs in \$ million

Strategy	Elasticity	
	0.5	1.0
Sample and tax	2	12
Sample and no tax	7	2
No sample and tax	0	10
No sample and no tax	5	0

We have simply incorporated the cost of the sample in this Table. Thus when we sample and tax and the elasticity is actually unity we incur the total cost of \$12 million, of which \$2 million was spent on the sample.

We might set out the process of decision-making in the form of a "tree." We begin on the left with the problem whether or not to sample—and there are two branches, the upper one representing no sample and the bottom one representing the decision to sample. The bottom branch is then split into two according to the results of the sample—the upper one indicating the sample outcome favorable to the elasticity being 0.5, and the lower one favorable to the elasticity being 1.0. To each of these outcomes of the sample we can attach the prior probabilities (given that the sample has been carried out) indicated in the last column of Table 1—0.45 for the elasticity=0.5, and 0.55 for the elasticity=1.0. We then continue our tree with the *action* branch—to tax or not to tax. The two sample branches, as well as the upper "do not-sample" branch, are each split into two, so that we have six possible positions at the end of the action stage. Note that there are no probabilities attached to the action stage—we choose one course or another, just as we choose whether or not to sample. The last stage is the actual *realization* of the elasticity, i.e. whether it is 0.5 or 1.0. The costs of each of the outcomes, as described in the table above, is now attached to each of the final branch-ends. (Note that we have assumed that the outcome of the sample makes no difference to the branch-end costs.)

The problem is now tackled in reverse. We start at the branch-ends and work backwards to the root of the tree. Consider, for example, the topmost action branch—(do not sample)→(tax). Now we know that two possibilities arise—the elasticity may be 0.5 with prior probability 0.7 and the elasticity may be 1.0 with prior probability 0.3. So we can find the expected costs as

$$(\$0 \text{ million}) \times 0.7 + (\$10 \text{ million}) \times 0.3 = \$3 \text{ million}.$$

Now consider the "no tax" strategy, the second action branch, and we calculate expected costs as

$$(\$5 \text{ million}) \times 0.7 + (\$0 \text{ million}) \times 0.3 = \$3.5 \text{ million}.$$

We insert these values on the diagram at the appropriate junctions and encircle them. Clearly this calculation makes the no-tax strategy (when we have already decided *not* to sample) redundant—the expected costs of taxing are \$0.5 *less*. Thus, effectively, the expected costs of not sampling—and then following the best policy of taxing—are \$3 million, so enter that value, duly encircled at the junction at the beginning of the action branch.

More difficulties are involved with the sampling branches. Again let us start at the top branch-end—the process of: (sample) —(outcome favorable to elasticity=0.5—(tax)—(elasticity=0.5). Working backwards from the branch-ends we see that the final process is the probabilistic realization that the elasticity is either

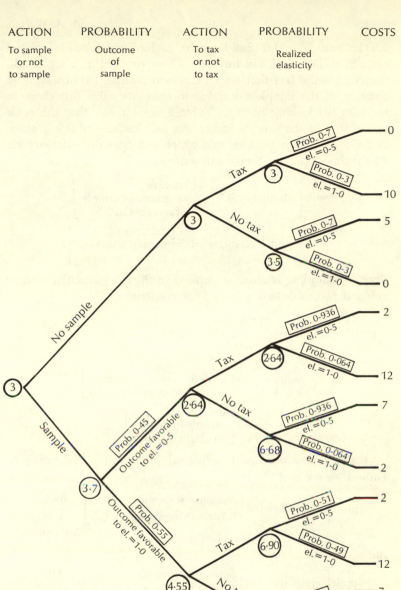

ACTION	PROBABILITY	ACTION	PROBABILITY	COSTS
To sample or not to sample	Outcome of sample	To tax or not to tax	Realized elasticity	

0.5 (1st branch) or 1.0 (2nd branch), each of which has associated
costs $2 million and $12 million. These probabilities are conditional upon the fact that we (i) chose to sample; (ii) observed an
outcome of the sample favorable to elasticity $=0.5$; (iii) chose to
tax. On (ii) looking back to Table 1 we can see that the prior
probability of the sample indicating an elasticity of 0.5 is given
as 0.45. (And if we get a sample which indicates this elasticity we
would choose to tax.) So we can write

$$\text{prob}\left[\text{elasticity}=0.5\left|\begin{array}{l}\text{(i) sample}\\\text{(ii) outcome of sample}\\\text{favorable to 0.5}\end{array}\right.\right]$$
$$=\text{prob}\left[\text{elasticity}=0.5\left|\begin{array}{l}\text{outcome of}\\\text{sample favorable}\\\text{to 0.5}\end{array}\right.\right],$$

since (i) sampling is already implied in (ii) the particular sample
outcome favorable to 0.5. So we can construct:

$$\text{prob}\left[\text{elasticity}=0.5\left|\begin{array}{l}\text{outcome of}\\\text{sample favorable}\\\text{to 0.5}\end{array}\right.\right]$$
$$=\frac{\text{prob}\left[\text{elasticity}=0.5,\ \begin{array}{l}\text{outcome of}\\\text{sample favorable}\\\text{to elasticity}=0.5\end{array}\right]}{\text{prob}\left[\begin{array}{l}\text{outcome of}\\\text{sample favorable}\\\text{to elasticity}=0.5\end{array}\right]},$$

by the ordinary rules of conditional probability. Returning to
Table 1 we see that this is

$$\text{prob}\left[\text{elasticity}=0.5\left|\begin{array}{l}\text{outcome of sample}\\\text{favorable to elasticity}=0.5\end{array}\right.\right]=\frac{0.42}{0.45}$$
$$=0.936,$$

and

$$\text{prob}\left[\text{elasticity}=1.0\left|\begin{array}{l}\text{outcome of sample}\\\text{favorable to elasticity}=0.5\end{array}\right.\right]=\frac{0.03}{0.45}$$
$$=0.064.$$

One can now calculate the expected costs of the strategy of
sampling and taxing if the outcome is favorable to 0.5. We have,
as expected, costs

($2 million) × 0.936 + ($12 million) × 0.064 = $2.64 million,

which we enter, duly encircled, at the appropriate junction. Secondly let us examine the no-tax branch of the "outcome-favorable-to-0.5" case. This, of course, should be the same as the case considered immediately above. Only the decision tax or no tax differs.

Now consider the other main branch of the sample result where the evidence favors an elasticity of 1.0. Taking the "tax" branch first, we calculate the probability of an elasticity of 0.5 emerging, given that the sample outcome favored 1.0.

$$\text{prob}\left[\text{elasticity}=0.5 \,\middle|\, \begin{array}{l}\text{outcome of sample} \\ \text{is favorable to 1.0}\end{array}\right]$$

$$= \frac{\text{prob}\left[\begin{array}{l}\text{elasticity}=0.5, \quad \text{outcome of sample is} \\ \qquad\qquad\qquad\quad \text{favorable to 1.0}\end{array}\right]}{\text{prob}\left[\begin{array}{l}\text{outcome of sample is} \\ \text{favorable to 1.0}\end{array}\right]},$$

which from Table 1 is

$$\frac{0.28}{0.55}=0.51.$$

The probability of the other branch where elasticity is unity is then $1 - 0.51 = 0.49$. These two probabilities are repeated for the last "no tax" branches. To find the expected costs at this last stage we repeat the operation—for example, for the last two branches

$$\{(7 \text{ million}) \text{ with prob}=0.51\} + \{(\$2 \text{ million}) \text{ with prob}=$$
$$0.49\} = 3.57 + 0.98 = \$4.55 \text{ million}$$

which we enter in a circle at the junction.

In the action of choosing to tax or not we clearly wish to consider only those which have the lowest cost. Thus if we find ourselves at the point of having sampled and found that the evidence favored the elasticity of 0.5 we should clearly tax, since the expected cost $2.64 million would be lower than not taxing. We enter then $2.64 million at the junction of sample outcome and tax. Similarly if the sample outcome were favorable to elasticity=1.0, then the choice is clearly "no tax" with an expected cost of $4.55 million.

Lastly we see whether it is worth while sampling. From the sample branch there are two outcomes:

> (i)   an expected cost of $2.64 million with an associated probability of 0.45;
> (ii) an expected cost of $4.55 million with an associated probability of 0.55.

We then form the expected costs of sampling as

$$(\$2.64 \text{ million}) \times 0.45 + (\$4.55 \text{ million}) \times 0.55 = \$3.7 \text{ million.}$$

Now it is clearly not efficient to sample the population since the expected costs of sampling are $3.7 million whereas, in the no-sample branch the expected costs are only $3 million. The optimum policy, therefore, is *not* to sample, and to introduce the tax. This completes the analysis of the decision-making process.

One of the results of this example is that it is not worth while to sample. We can get a more direct measure of why this is the case. The sample, we assumed, costs us $2 million, and if we sampled the minimum costs, including the sample costs, are $3.7 million, i.e.

Sample costs	$2 million
Other expected costs	$1.7 million
Total	$3.7 million

To be worth while the sample would have to cost less than $1.3 million; this would give a total cost less than $3 million—so it would be then preferable to sample before making the decision. As it stands, however, the sample information is worth less than it costs to acquire it.

We must now touch on some of the problems of the decision-theory approach. One which will certainly have occurred to the reader is that of attributing costs to each possible outcome. Often one just cannot formulate what the costs are likely to be. It is, however, a compelling argument that one always in fact behaves *as if* there were costs attributable to every outcome. Surely it is a good discipline to have to formulate them explicitly. In practice one often uses useful shortcuts; one commonly used rule is to use the square of the deviation of the estimate of the unknown parameter from its true value as the "loss function." Thus in our example the relative 'loss' would be measured by the square of the estimated elasticity from its true value, e.g.

Loss when elasticity $= 1.0$ and we judge it to be $0.5 = (0.5 - 1.0)^2$

$$= 0.25.$$

When the elasticity is estimated at its correct value, the loss is zero. This loss function is, of course, quite arbitrary, but statisticians have found in practice that this is a useful loss function to use in the absence of any detailed cost specification.

Another major difficulty lies in attaching values to the probabilities which need to be quantified in using decision functions. This involves specifying the prior probabilities of the elasticities assuming certain values, and the more complex task of stating the probabilities of the sample indicating the correct and incorrect elasticities. This is merely a way of evaluating what the sample is going to tell us—but it is not at all easy to put quantities on the probability of the sample results revealing the true facts.

Our example is extremely simple. We have not considered the enormous number of opportunities which occur in practical cases. For example, we might consider many samples of various size, complexity and cost. Formally it is easy to extend the theory to deal with multiple opportunities, but the problems of specifying the probabilities of the outcomes are not simplified! Even so, it is often useful to draw a decision tree, or at least certain of the main branches, to clear one's mind about the decision problem.

The "Game" of Business

JOHN MCDONALD

John McDonald is an editor of Fortune
Magazine. *This article is taken from his
book,* Strategy in Poker, Business, and War,
first published in 1950.

The core of business is the market. The core of the market is
the relationship of buyer and seller, whether either is an individual or a corporation. The theory of games investigates the interior
of this relationship with game models.

From the standpoint of the individual there are three possible
economic situations on earth: one man alone, two men, or three
or more men. One man is Robinson Crusoe alone on an island.
He plays there the game of solitaire, maximizing his gain uncom-
plicated by anything but the forces of nature, which are predictable, at least in such terms as probable rainfall and the probability
of a tornado.

If there are two men on earth, the individual enters into the
relation of exchange (buyer-seller), in which the problem of the
other fellow appears; he can no longer maximize his gain but
must seek a limitation of the possibilities in an optimum. But if
there are three men, the novelty occurs that two of them may
gain more by combining against the third (e.g., two sellers against
a buyer, or vice versa). These three situations are the same as
those found in games.

Any industry serves as an example of strategical game play. Take the liquor industry, which like steel, oil or automobiles has only a few sellers. The following story was told at length in *Fortune* magazine. Samuel Bronfman of Seagram had come down from Canada at the time of repeal and built his organization on blended whiskey in the tradition of Canadian and Scotch whiskeys. U.S. distillers, slow to adopt blends, preferred to sell the traditional American rye and bourbon. But blended whiskey could be nationally advertised to better advantage (rye and bourbon being largely regional); and Bronfman made the most of it. His marketing strategy consisted of blends, brand names and mild taste. Eventually there was a contest for leadership in the industry between Seagram and Schenley. Lewis Rosenstiel of Schenley, an old-school U.S. distiller, divided his attention between blends and straights. Now whiskey is made at one time to be sold four or more years later, and there is a corresponding risk in the inventory. Keep too little and you may run short. Keep too much and you may get stuck (whiskey consumption roughly follows the income curve; and as in any industry total inventories can get out of hand, resulting, in the absence of mandatory fair trade laws, in occasional price wars). "Holidays" during World War II had eliminated several crops of whiskey and inventories generally were low. Rosenstiel is known as an inventory strategist. He came out of the war period with brand sales off but with perhaps half of the remaining aged whiskey inventory in the U.S. Bronfman of Seagram had used up a large part of his whiskey inventory in gaining record brand sales. In this situation, they had a contest for the leadership, a kind of two-man game within the industry.

Facing a forthcoming shortage, Bronfman could either buy scarce bulk whiskey at a losing price and maintain Seagram's brand sales with a decline in profits, or maintain his rate of profit out of his remaining inventory with a decline in brand sales—or follow a mixed policy. In any event he could not maximize both brand sales and profits. Rosenstiel could sell the inventory to Bronfman at high bulk prices and no sales cost and thus maximize profits in the immediate circumstance; or he could put the inventory into Schenley brands with an expensive and risky sales campaign to raise brand sales at less profit. Like Bronfman, but for different reasons, he could not maximize both brand sales and profits.

Nor could the policies of the antagonists fail to conflict; for Rosenstiel, who, having the better inventory, had the dominant choice, could reconcile their difference only by taking profit and giving Bronfman the market (brand sales), i.e., take short-term gains at the cost of long-term losses. Within limits, Bronfman would have been glad to buy the market (take short-term losses with long-term gains)—if Rosenstiel would let him. But Rosenstiel wouldn't. Each sought an optimum move on a strategical basis. The game broadened out with larger numbers as Bronfman got some whiskey from another source. Rosenstiel opened a "back-label" campaign to make his aged stocks pay off. The consequences of the struggle have not been told, but whatever they are, they are the consequences of conscious strategy. Theoretically, Seagram and Schenley had another alternative, namely, to combine. There are good reasons why they would not, yet each of these corporate individuals like so many others in industry had grown large through combination.

The three-man coalition game can be played as an auction with one seller and two buyers. The seller has a reserve price of, say, $10 on the object to be sold. The first buyer is willing to go to not more than $15; the second buyer to not more than $20. Clearly the second buyer being the stronger will get the object. Ordinarily he is expected to get it for something over $15. But suppose the second buyer approaches the first and makes a deal to eliminate competitive bidding. He can then get the object for something over $10. The deal, however, requires a division of the spoils. The second, stronger buyer must pay the first, weaker buyer something for making the coalition. That payment must be enough to yield the second buyer the "best" profit, and yet enough to ensure that his partner will remain in the coalition: two maximums which must be resolved. For another, rival deal is possible —in game theory but not in classical economics—namely this: The seller may cross the market and break up the coalition by paying something to the second buyer to restore the bidding and thereby push the selling price back above $15. Thus each two-man game in this three-man game is under the influence of the other possible two-man games, in arriving at the distribution payment.

In the theory of games a number of solutions, i.e., distribution schemes, are possible, some of which are enforceable and therefore dominate others. In classical theory the weaker buyer gets nothing; in game theory he gets a bribe, and the bribe will be expressed in the price. Here the difference between classical economics and game theory can be shown with simple numbers. In classical theory the price is between $15 and $20 (all going to the seller). In game theory it is between $10 and $20, depending on the bargaining ability of the players.

The basic strategy of organizers of industry from the beginning has been to substitute combination for large-number competition. The value which J. P. Morgan put on combination was indicated in the capitalization of the United States Steel Corporation in 1901. The Corporation, which brought together about 65 percent of the steel capacity of the United States, was capitalized at about twice the tangible value given to its separate properties before combination. The specific combinative value (about three-quarters of a billion dollars minus an unknown value put on "good will") was expressed in the new common stock—attacked as "watered stock"—which eventually paid off as the technical and strategical market advantages of combination were realized. The Corporation later met rivalry from other combinations which were organized in opposition to it.

Rockefeller's genius similarly expressed itself in combinations. But some of these early combinations, as they were organized, were unwieldy. Standard Oil stockholders probably benefited from the trust's court-ordered dissolution in 1911. It became impolitic thereafter, under the Sherman Act, for one organization to hold an overwhelming share of the market. For that reason or because its ability to compete against counter-combinations was injured by organizational and management defects, the Steel Corporation retreated to its present holdings of about one-third of the industry's ingot capacity. Its present leadership of the industry is maintained by modern market techniques described in oligopoly and game theory.

Introduction to Game Theory

J. D. WILLIAMS

J. D. Williams is head of the mathematics department at the RAND Corporation. This article comes from his book, The Compleat Strategyst, *published in 1954.*

The number of persons involved is one of the important criteria for classifying and studying games, 'person' meaning a distinct set of interests. Another criterion has to do with the payoff: What happens at the end of the game? Say at the end of the hand in poker? Well, in poker there is usually just an exchange of assets. If there are two persons, say you (Blue) and we (Red), then if you should win $10, we would lose $10. In other words,

$$\text{Blue winnings} = \text{Red losses}$$

or, stated otherwise,

$$\text{Blue winnings} - \text{Red losses} = 0$$

We may also write it as

$$\text{Blue payoff} + \text{Red payoff} = \$10 - \$10 = 0$$

by adopting the convention that winnings are positive numbers and that losses are negative numbers.

It needn't have turned out just that way; i.e., that the sum of the payoffs is zero. For instance, if the person who wins the pot has to contribute 10 percent toward the drinks and other incidentals, as to the cop on the corner, then the sum of the payoffs is not zero; in fact

$$\text{Blue payoff} + \text{Red payoff} = \$9 - \$10 = -\$1$$

The above two cases illustrate a fundamental distinction among games: It is important to know whether or not the sum of the payoffs, counting winnings as positive and losses as negative, to all players is zero. If it is, the game is known as a *zero-sum game*. If it is not, the game is known (mathematicians are not very imaginative at times) as a *non-zero-sum game*. The importance of the distinction is easy to see: In the zero-sum case, we are dealing with a good, clean, closed system; the two players and the valuables are locked in the room. It will require a certain effort to specify and to analyze such a game. On the other hand, the non-zero-sum game contains all the difficulties of the zero-sum game, plus additional troubles due to the need to incorporate new factors. This can be appreciated by noting that we can restore the situation by adding a fictitious player—Nature, say, or the cop. Then we have

$$\text{Blue payoff} = \$9$$
$$\text{Red payoff} = -\$10$$
$$\text{Cop payoff} = \$1$$

so now

$$\text{Blue payoff} + \text{Red payoff} + \text{Cop payoff} = \$9 - \$10 + \$1 = 0$$

which is a *three-person zero-sum* game, of sorts, where the third player has some of the characteristics of a millstone around the neck. But recall that we don't like three-person games so well as we do two-person games, because they contain the vagaries of coalitions. So non-zero-sum games offer real difficulties not present in zero-sum games, particularly if the latter are two-person games.

Parlor games, such as poker, bridge, and chess, are usually zero-sum games, and many other conflict situations may be treated as if they were. Most of the development of game theory to date has been on this type of game. Some work on non-zero-sum games has been done, and more is in progress, but the subject is beyond our scope. A troublesome case of particular interest is the two-person game in which the nominally equal payoffs differ in utility to the players; this situation occurs often even in parlor games.

STRATEGIES

Just as the word "person" has a meaning in game theory somewhat different from everyday usage, the word 'strategy' does too. This word, as used in its everyday sense, carries the connotation of a particularly skillful or adroit plan, whereas in game theory it designates any *complete* plan. *A strategy is a plan so complete that it cannot be upset by enemy action or Nature;* for everything that the enemy or Nature may choose to do, together with a set of possible actions for yourself, is just part of the description of the strategy.

So the strategy of game theory differs in two important respects from the conventional meaning: It must be utterly complete, and it may be utterly bad; for nothing is required of it except completeness. Thus, in poker, all strategies must make provision for your being dealt a royal flush in spades, and some of them will require that you fold instantly. The latter are not very glamorous strategies, but they are still strategies—after all, a bridge player once bid 7 no-trump while holding 13 spades. In a game which is completely amenable to analysis, we are able— conceptually, if not actually—to foresee all eventualities and hence are able to catalogue all possible strategies.

We are now able to mention still another criterion according to which games may be classified for study, namely, the number of strategies available to each player. Thus, if Blue and Red are the players, Blue may have three strategies and Red may have five; this would be called a 3×5 game (read 'three-by-five game').

When the number of players was discussed, you will recall that certain numbers—namely, one, two, and more-than two—were especially significant. Similarly, there are critical values in the number of strategies; and it turns out to be important to distinguish two major categories. In the first are games in which the player having the *greatest* number of strategies still has a finite number; this means that he can count them, and finish the task within some time limit. The second major category is that in which at least one player has infinitely many strategies, or, if the word 'infinitely' disturbs you, in which at least one player has a number of strategies which is larger than any definite number you can name. (This, incidentally, is just precisely what 'infinitely large' means to a mathematician.)

While infinite games (as the latter are called) cover many interesting and useful applications, the theory of such games is difficult. 'Difficult' here means that there are at least some problems the mathematician doesn't know how to solve, and further that we don't know how to present any of it within friendly pedagogical limits; such games require mathematics at the level of the calculus and beyond—mostly beyond. Therefore we here resolve to confine our attention to finite games.

THE GAME MATRIX

We are now in a position to complete the description of games, i.e., conflict situations, in the form required for game theory analysis. We will freely invoke all the restrictions developed so far. Hence our remarks will primarily apply to finite, zero-sum, two-person games.

The players are Blue and Red. Each has several potential strategies which we assume are known; let them be numbered just for identification. Blue's strategies will then bear names, such as Blue 1, Blue 2, and so on; perhaps, in a specific case, up to Blue 9; and Red's might range from Red 1 through Red 5. We would call this a nine-by-five game and write it as '9×5 game.' Just to demonstrate that it is possible to have a 9×5 game, we shall state one (or enough of it to make the point). Consider a game played on the following page.

The rules require that Blue travel from B to R, following the system of roads, without returning to B or using the same segment twice during the trip. The rules are different for Red, who must travel from R to B, always moving toward the west. Perhaps Blue doesn't want to meet Red, and has fewer inhibitions about behavior. You may verify that there are nine routes for Blue and five for Red.[1]

1. To avoid even the possiblity of frustrating you this early in the game,

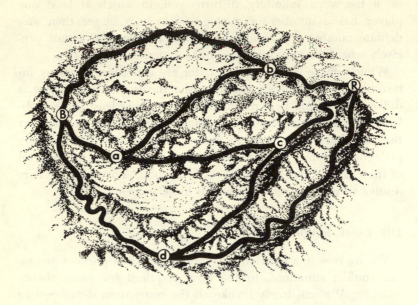

The rules must also contain information from which we can determine what happens at the end of any play of the game: What is the payoff when, say, Blue uses the strategy Blue 7 (the northern route, perhaps) and Red uses Red 3 (the southern route, perhaps)? There will be $9 \times 5 = 45$ of these pairs and hence that number of possible values for the payoff; and these must be known. Whatever the values are, it is surely possible to arrange the information on the kind of bookkeeping form shown on Chart 1, page 188.

Such an array of boxes, each containing a payoff number, is called a *game matrix*. We shall adopt the convention that a positive number in the matrix represents a gain for Blue and hence a loss for Red, and vice versa. Thus if two of the values in the game matrix are 3 and -8, as shown in Chart 2 (page 188), the

---

we itemize the routes. Blue may visit any of the following sets of road junctions (beginning with *B* and ending with *R* in each case):

         b, bac, bacd, ab, ac, acd, dcab, dc, d

Red may visit

         b, ba, ca, cd, d

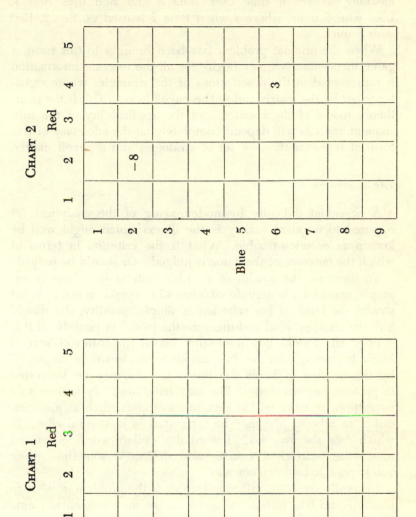

meaning is: When Blue uses Blue 6 and Red uses Red 4, Blue wins 3 units, whereas when Blue 2 is used vs. Red 2, Red wins 8 units.

When the original problem has been brought to this form, a game theory analysis may begin, for all the relevant information is represented in the descriptions of the strategies whose signatures border the matrix and in the payoff boxes. This is the game theory model of the conflict, and the applicability of the subsequent analysis will depend completely on the adequacy of this form of representation—a set of strategies and a payoff matrix.

THE CRITERION

A perennial difficulty in modelmaking of the analytical (as opposed to wooden) variety is the illness which might well be known as criterion-trouble. What is the criterion in terms of which the outcome of the game is judged? Or should be judged?

To illustrate the wealth of possible criteria in a homely example, consider a housewife who has $5 to spend on meat. What should she buy? If her criterion is simply quantity, she should buy the cheapest kind and measure the payoff in pounds. If it is variety, she should buy minimum, useful quantities of several kinds, beginning with the cheapest kinds; she measures the payoff by the number of kinds she buys. Or she may be interested in protein, fat, or calories. She may have to satisfy various side conditions, or work within certain constraints, such as allergies, tastes, or taboos. She may be interested in least total effort, in which case she may say, "I want five dollars worth of cooked meat—the nearest, of course—and deliver it sometime when you happen to be down our way."

Generally speaking, criterion-trouble is the problem of what to measure and how to base behavior on the measurements. Game Theory has nothing to say on the first topic, but it advocates a very explicit and definite behavior-pattern based on the measurements.

It takes the position that there is a definite way that rational people should behave, if they believe in the game matrix. The notion that there is some way people ought to behave does not refer to an obligation based on law or ethics. Rather it refers to a kind of mathematical morality, or at least frugality, which claims that the *sensible object of the player is to gain as much from the game as he can, safely, in the face of a skillful opponent who is pursuing an antithetical goal.* This is our model of rational behavior. As with all models, the shoe has to be tried on each time an application comes along to see whether the fit is tolerable; but it is well known in the Military Establishment, for instance, that a lot of ground can be covered in shoes that do not fit perfectly.

Let us follow up the consequences of this model in a zero-sum game, which, you will recall, is a closed system in which assets are merely passed back and forth between the players. It won't affect anything adversely (except Red), and it will simplify the discussion, if we assume for a moment that all payoffs in the game matrix are *positive;* this means that the strategy options available to the players only affect how many valuables Red must give to Blue at the end of a play of the game; this isn't a fair game for Red, but we will let him suffer for the common weal.

Now the viewpoint in game theory is that *Blue wishes to act in such a manner that the least number he can win is as great as possible, irrespective of what Red does;* this takes care of the safety requirement. *Red's comparable desire is to make the greatest number of valuables that he must relinquish as small as possible, irrespective of Blue's action.* This philosophy, if held by the players, is sufficient to specify their choices of strategy. If Blue departs from it, he does so at the risk of getting less than he might have received; and if Red departs from it, he may have to pay more than he could have settled for.

The above argument is the central one in game theory. There is a way to play every two-person game that will satisfy this criterion. However, as in the case of the housewife buying meat, it is not the only possible criterion; for example, by attributing to the enemy various degrees of ignorance or stupidity, one could devise many others. Since game theory does not attribute these attractive qualities to the enemy, it is a conservative theory.

You will note an apparent disparity in the aims of Blue and Red as stated above; Blue's aims are expressed in terms of winning and Red's in terms of losing. This difference is not a real one, as both have precisely the same philosophy. Rather, it is a consequence of our convention regarding the meaning of positive and negative numbers in the game matrix. The adoption of a uniform convention, to the effect that Blue is always the maximizing player and Red the minimizing player, will reduce technical confusion (once it becomes fixed in your mind); but let's not pay for this mnemonic by coming to believe that there is an essential lack of symmetry in the game treatment of Blue and Red.

Introduction to the Lot-size Formula

THOMSON M. WHITIN

Thomson M. Whitin is Professor of Economics at Wesleyan University. This is an excerpt from his article, "Inventory Control in Theory and Practice," which appeared in the Quarterly Journal of Economics in 1952.

The best known "scientific" inventory control system involves the calculation of economical purchase quantities and reorder point quantities. Several authors independently arrived at the same basic formula for determining economical purchase quantities in the 1920s. A number of different factors contributed to the development of such formulas.

First of all, the increasing size of business establishments has played an important role. It was possible for most firms in the past to make use of highly inefficient inventory control methods and yet still maintain profit margins. Modern large-scale enterprises often operate with small profit margins which might well be eliminated by poor inventory control methods. Furthermore, size in itself makes obvious the existence of possibilities of substantial savings through improvement in inventory control.

Secondly, during the past century, there has been an enormous increase in the amount of business training. High schools now offer some business preparatory courses, and the growth of business administration colleges has been extremely rapid. This

255

additional training has made recent generations of businessmen more aware of improvement possibilities. Also, trade publications on market research, purchasing, retailing, standardization, and many other topics have contributed much to businessmen's understanding of the various problems which confront them.

A third factor that has aided the transition to modern inventory control methods is the increased emphasis that has been placed on the importance of engineers in business. The entrance of many trained engineers into business has brought with it the "scientific" approach, including scientific methods of production control, factory layout, standardization, etc. Also, cost accounting has helped entrepreneurs to evaluate the performance of various departments of their establishments, thus indicating specific areas where better control may be needed.

A final factor that gave impetus to research on inventory control was the "inventory depression" of 1921, which taught businessmen to be extremely wary of inventory accumulation. As a result of these factors, formulas for determining economic purchase quantities have been derived. These formulas involve a simple application of elementary differential calculus to inventory control.

The economic purchase quantity may be determined in the following manner. Two different sets of cost factors must be considered, namely, those which increase as purchase quantities increase and those which decrease as purchase quantities increase. Among those costs which increase are interest, obsolescence, risk, depreciation, storage, etc., while the forces making for decreasing costs include such items as quantity discounts, freight differentials, and procurement costs. In the following example, assume that the expense of procurement is constant and that interest, risk, depreciation, obsolescence, etc., may be lumped into one percentage figure (I). Let Y designate expected yearly sales (in \$), Q be the economic purchase quantity (in \$) and S be the procurement expense (in \$). Then total annual variable costs involved in ordering and carrying purchase quantities may be expressed as follows: $TVC = \dfrac{Q}{2}I + \dfrac{Y}{Q}S$. Differentiating with respect to the purchase quantity, Q, and setting the derivative equal to zero, the solution

$$Q = \sqrt{\frac{2YS}{I}}$$

results, where Q is the purchase quantity that minimizes combined ordering costs and carrying charges. This economical purchase quantity is thus seen to vary with the square root of sales and inversely with the square root of the carrying charges. This formula has been used in business and its use has been accompanied by good results.

Queuing Analysis and Monte Carlo Methods

WILLIAM J. BAUMOL

William Baumol is Professor of Economics at Princeton University. This article is taken from his book, Economic Theory and Operations Analysis, *published in 1961.*

QUEUING ANALYSIS

Queuing theory is one of the subjects which has loomed large in the literature of operations research. Any operation in which the objects to be dealt with arrive at irregular intervals, and in which the operating facilities are of limited capacity, is a queuing problem. Automobiles waiting to be serviced in a garage, subway riders waiting to get through a turnstile, and telephone callers waiting for a clear line all constitute queues. Among the real problems to which queuing theory has been applied are the landing of aircraft, the parking of automobiles, the timing of traffic lights, the processing of films, and the servicing of travelers through customs.

One of the key characteristics of a queue is the random pattern of arrivals, which can therefore only be described in probabilistic terms. There will be times, which cannot be predicted precisely, when the number of arrivals will be unusually large, and as a result, it will then take longer to be serviced. For example, in a supermarket, customer delays at the checkout counters may be caused by the arrival of a large number of customers at the same time, or by the coincidental arrival of several customers each of whom has many groceries in her shopping basket, so that the average checkout time is materially increased.

Suppose the manager of the supermarket wishes to know what sort of delays his customers are likely to encounter. The analyst requires information about two frequency distributions, one describing customer arrivals and the other the length of time it takes a clerk to handle a customer's purchases. Once both of these have been found, mathematical analysis permits us, in many cases, to find out such things as the expected average customer waiting time, the expected length of the waiting lines at different times of the day or week, etc.

The basic idea of the calculation is relatively simple, although the details are ingenious and complicated. The probability that there will be, say, 25 customers waiting now is equal to the sum of probabilities of the several alternative series of events which can produce this result. For example, there would now be 25 customers in line if 24 customers were there one minute ago, none has since been serviced, and one more customer has just arrived. Since we know the probability of a customer's having been serviced during any one minute and of a customer's arriving during any one minute, we can find out the relationship between the probability that there were 24 customers a minute ago and the probability that there are 25 customers in line now. Similarly, we can find the probability that the lines will grow from 25 to 26 customers in this way; and we can trace, customer by customer, the expected growth of the queues in the supermarket from the time it opens in the morning with zero customers.

One of the most interesting results of the theory states, in effect, that service facilities must have excess capacity built into them if service is not to break down altogether. More specifically, suppose the service facilities, if they were always kept fully occupied, were just sufficient to meet the needs of all the store's customers. Then queues would just grow longer and longer, without limit, and ultimately the operations would collapse. The basic reason for this result is, of course, that customer arrivals are *not* spread evenly in time, and so during some periods the facility will temporarily be idle whereas at other times it will be overcrowded. But, by assumption, the facilities would be of sufficient capacity only if there were no such oscillations in customer arrival time. To permit them to cope with bunched arrivals, therefore, the capacity of service facilities must be increased.

The theory also permits us, at least in principle, to investigate how much the expected length of queue lines will be reduced when a number of new checkout counters are added in our supermarket. This immediately raises an optimality question— just how many checkout counters should the supermarket have? More counters cost money to install and operate. Too many counters will therefore be wasteful, but too small a number of counters will slow down service and lose customers. The optimality problem, then, is to determine the intermediate number of counters which best serves management's purposes. Unfortunately, these probabilistic optimality calculations are often likely to grow very complex; therefore, instead of a direct approach to the problem, the operations researcher frequently resorts to the methods described in the following section.

ARTIFICIAL EXPERIMENTATION: MONTE CARLO TECHNIQUES

Before we can hope to find out the consequences of a course of action, it is necessary to have some sort of data. For example, suppose, as before, that it is desired to test some proposed service facilities to see how often customers will be kept waiting, and how long they will have to wait, on the average. These figures, of course, depend on the fluctuations in the number of customer arrivals—how frequently their number will exceed a particular magnitude.

In solving such a problem, experimentation is not a real possibility. It can be costly in customer relations to try very much more meager service facilities just to see what will happen. It may be that some information can be obtained from the experience of other supermarkets. But this may be too limited in range and in quantity to be of much assistance.

The operations researcher has, however, invented another very effective way to gather the relevant data: that is, to make them up himself, or rather to let the mathematical statistician make them up for him! But one may well ask, how can improvised statistics help us to foresee what will happen in the real world?

The answer is that the numbers are invented in a manner which carefully employs the analytical methods of mathematical statistics in order to stretch as far as possible such few actual data as are available to begin with. At some particular moment in the week we may assume that customers will arrive randomly, in a pattern somewhat similar to outcomes in successive throws of a pair of dice. The pattern of customer arrivals may then be described in terms of a frequency distribution, which indicates how many weeks in a year customer arrivals per hour can be expected to fall between 100 and 110 units, how often the number will lie in the 110 to 120 range, etc.

Now, from the available information *and the nature of the problem*, the statistician can often decide which frequency distribution best describes the pattern of expected customer arrivals. From this frequency distribution it is then possible to construct an artificial history of customer arrivals by choosing randomly among all the possibilities, but in a way which is "loaded" to produce the right frequencies. To give a very simple illustration, suppose we consider two possibilities: A, fewer than 100 arrivals per hour and B, at least 100 arrivals. If, on some basis, the odds are computed to be 2 to 1 in favor of A, we can generate an artificial demand history as follows: Toss the (unbiased) die. If it falls, 1, 2, 3, or 4, put down an A; if it falls 5 or 6, put down a B. This might yield a pattern for weekly demands such as the following:

TABLE 1

"Week"	Face of die	Arrival "history"	
		Under 100	100 or more
First	3	A	
Second	1	A	
Third	3	A	
Fourth	5		B
Fifth	6		B
Sixth	2	A	
Seventh	2	A	

This, incidentally, indicates the reason for the term "Monte Carlo method."

In practice, it is not actually necessary to toss any dice. Instead, we can use tables called "tables of random numbers" which have been worked out in advance. Moreover, the computations can be made by high-speed electronic computers which are able, in a few minutes or hours, to run off thousands of cases and manufacture data whose collection would, otherwise, require many years. But although this method is economical and powerful, it must be used only with the greatest care and caution. As we have seen, everything depends on the choice of frequency distribution (i.e., the odds of the various outcomes), and unless there is some assurance that these have been picked well, the entire calculation can be worthless.

Once this artificial experience has been generated, it can be used to find approximate solutions to optimality problems such as that of determining the number of checkout counters which was described in the last section—problems where straightforward computational methods are too complex. To illustrate the approach, consider the (unrelated) problem of finding an approximate root of the equation

$$X^2 - 6X + 9.1 = 0.$$

Instead of using the standard formula, we can go about it indirectly by trial and error, first, say, substituting $X = 1$ to find that the expression takes the value

$$(1)^2 - 6(1) + 9.1 = 4.1.$$

Clearly, $X = 1$ is not our root. So we try again, this time using, say, $X = 0$, and we see that this value of X makes the expression equal 9.1—i.e., it has only made things worse. We therefore infer that we have been going in the wrong direction, so this time we go up and try $X = 2$, etc. The results of several such trials can be tabulated as follows:

Trial value of X	1	0	2	3	4
Value of $X^2 - 6X + 9.1$	4.1	9.1	1.1	0.1	1.1

Clearly, this suggests that there is a root located very close to $X = 3$, at which the value of the expression is very close to zero, and we can take this as the approximate value of the root we are seeking.

The finding of optimal solutions in queuing problems and many other difficult operations problems can be approached in somewhat the same spirit with the aid of Monte Carlo methods. A number of alternative possibilities (number of possible checkout counters) can be postulated, and their consequences over a long period can then be simulated and reported on by the computer with the aid of Monte Carlo predictions of customer arrivals. If our objective is to minimize some sort of over-all cost function (which includes the costs of operating additional checkout counters as well as the costs of customer delays), we would take the optimal solution to be approximated by that trial (number of checkout counters) for which the machine reported the lowest over-all expected costs.

Unfortunately, this description, although correct in essence, is somewhat misleading in its simplicity. Particularly where decisions involve the assignment of values to a number of interrelated variables and where the ranges of possible values are considerable, there are difficult problems in deciding on what combination of values to try out next. It is by no means easy to design a procedure which converges with reasonable rapidity toward an optimal solution.

It is to be emphasized that the use of Monte Carlo methods is not limited to queuing problems. They can be used in inventory analysis, replacement analysis (when to stop repairing a piece of equipment and replace it with a new one), and a wide variety of other situations in which a prominent role is played by probabilistic elements such as the timing and magnitudes of customer demands or of the need for repairs.

Part Six

The Role of the Computer in Industrial Management

THE electronic computer has had an enormous impact on management practices, and its full influence has yet to be felt. The computer allows the manager to control the firm and assess its environment with new effectiveness because it enables him to get the relevant facts quickly and to understand their changing relationships. The papers in Part Six are concerned with the role of the computer in industrial management. The article by Gilbert Burck of *Fortune* describes the Westinghouse Electric Corporation's use of computers, both to reduce the length of time required to obtain management information and to simulate various aspects of its business.

Harold Leavitt and Thomas Whisler try to predict the impact of the electronic computer on managerial organization. In their judgment, the boundary between planning and performance will move upward, and their will be a tendency toward recentralization and a radical reorganization of middle management. John Dearden, in the following article, argues that the Leavitt-Whisler conclusions are incorrect. Herbert Simon is also concerned with the changes that will take place in the job of the manager during the next generation. He concludes that "the change in occupational profile depends on a well-known economic principle, the doctrine of comparative advantage. . . . [Thus,] if computers are a hundred times faster than executives in making investment decisions, but only ten times faster in handling employee grievances (the quality of the decisions being held constant), then computers will be employed in making investment decisions, while executives will be employed in handling grievances."

"On Line" in "Real Time"

GILBERT BURCK

*This article appeared in the April 1964 issue
of* Fortune. *Its author, Gilbert Burck, is an
editor of that magazine.*

Members of Westinghouse Electric Corporation's executive
committee recently filed into a small room in the company's new
Tele-Computer Center near Pittsburgh and prepared to look
at their business as no group of executives had ever looked at
business before. In front of them was a large video screen, and
to one side of the screen was a "remote inquiry" device that
seemed a cross between a typewriter and a calculator. As the
lights dimmed, the screen lit up with current reports from many
of the company's important divisions—news of gross sales, orders,
profitability, inventory levels, manufacturing costs, and various
measures of performance based on such data. When the officers
asked the remote-inquiry device for additional information or
calculations, distant computers shot back the answers in seconds.

This was only an experimental performance, designed to show
how the corporation's decision makers could someday be provided with practically all the timely and relevant information they
need to run the company. No computer system can do that yet,
and a few academicians doubt that such a system will ever do it.
But top managers in companies like Westinghouse are enthusi-
astically supporting the efforts of their systems men to convert
common business data into useful knowledge with the computer.

The computer is making such rapid, continuous progress in converting knowledge into efficiency and dollar savings that no man can yet be sure of its potential.

Knowledge is power and control, provided it is timely, ample, and relevant. Only a businessman who knows what is happening inside his company as soon as it happens can truly adjust his means to his aims; and only one who understands what is happening in the marketplace as soon as it happens can really make sound decisions about his aims. But even a lot of timely facts is not enough. Most facts are either dead the moment they are born, or are the remnants of autopsies on history. Unless a man understands how they are related, and particularly how their relationships are changing, he knows very little.

Today's advanced electronic computer enables a man to control his business and to assess its environment with incomparable effectiveness because it enables him both to lay hands on relevant facts swiftly and to understand their changing relationships. Besides supplying him with facts in historical time, or after they have happened, it supplies him with facts "on line," i.e., as soon as they are born, and in "real time," i.e., promptly and abundantly enough to control the circumstances they describe while those circumstances are developing. The computer helps the businessman understand the changing relationships of facts chiefly by a technique known as simulation, or the imitation of experience with models. Without the computer, he must build many models and compare them laboriously, or even construct pilot plants, and both methods cost much time and money. With the computer he needs only to translate an appropriate number of models into mathematical formulas and instruct the computer to compare them and pick the likeliest. He can also simulate part or all of his operation in a computer, and test it in dozens of different situations.

The simulation technique grows in effectiveness when a corporation can repeatedly inspect its past performance and gauge its objectives accordingly—that is, after the business has become "computerized," and the records of its "transactions" over the years have been stored in the machine's memory. Given such a "continuum" of information, the businessman can keep on refining his model by taking it apart, nailing down its variables, rejiggering its weights. As time passes, his model gets better and better, and he can make millions of telling comparisons in a few minutes. He knows precisely what has happened and why, what should be happening and why, and he has an excellent notion of what is likely to happen, and what is the best way of capitalizing on it all. He can rely less and less on guesses and hunch and more and more on analysis. As somebody once remarked hyperbolically, an executive is a genius if he is right fifty-two percent of the time. Whatever the correct percentage, computer men argue, the machine can help him expand and elevate his native intuitive powers to new levels.

The vast bulk of United States businesses' fourteen thousand computer installations are still confined to routine data processing —preparing payrolls and paychecks for nearly every kind of business, recording and sorting bank checks, making out bills for telephone and electric utilities, analyzing personnel data, preparing financial results for corporate annual reports, and performing all manner of scientific calculations. But now that the practicality of real-time applications has been demonstrated, more and more corporations are starting the arduous process of putting themselves at least partly on real time lest competitors get the jump on them. By 1970, computer sages predict, nearly all new electronic data-processing systems will be on line in real time.

Westinghouse Electric Corporation is said to use computers in a wider range of applications than any other United States company; whether it does or not, it has a clear notion of what it wants to do with them. The aim of the company's business-systems department, says Lou Hague, its director, is to shrink the lead time in the management information cycle to practically nothing, and eventually to be able to prepare a final report that will include just about everything top management needs to make its decisions. Some are skeptical. John Dearden of the Harvard Business School argues that flooding high-level management with operational information is "sheer nonsense." But Hague points out that no competent computer-system man proposes to inundate managers with useless information, and anyway no good top manager would stand for it. The phrase for what he and other systems men want to present to managers is "exception information," or information that calls for attention and action.

How the computer monitors exception information is illustrated by an example the business-systems department uses for internal education. Costs in a certain plant have been normal for a while, but begin to rise steeply. Without the computer, these costs would get far out of line before being noticed, and would not be brought back for a week or more; but with real-time control they get only a little out of line before being noticed, and are brought back promptly. The cumulative effect on profits can be enormous.

Westinghouse's business-systems department is tackling one problem at a time; Hague says it doesn't yet know enough to do the job all at once, and he doubts that anyone else does. And the company keeps expansion within realistic limits by making computer operations pay off in identifiable savings. Last year Westinghouse spent $16,200,000 for machine rentals and programing and research. But it realized $20,700,000 and thus saved $4,500,000 or nearly 30 percent on its outlays, not including indirect benefits such as better customer service and improved cash flow.

Westinghouse's adventure with the computer began seven years ago, when Hague hired James Emery, now teaching production and cost control at M.I.T., to tackle the problem of adjusting inventory supply to demand in the transformer plant at Sharon, Pennsylvania. The job only sounds easy. Inventories of distribution transformers, which are mass produced, had a habit of piling up unless demand was estimated correctly.

Emery and his associates resorted to simulations of demand based on such things as historical buying cycles, abnormal regional growth, and interest-rate levels. They fed the data into an I.B.M. 705, which forecast demand by size, type, and location. Thus simulating demand on a weekly basis, they sharply reduced inventories while giving customers better service. "We replaced a lot of discussion over the conference table with the computer," says Hague. "If we had known years before what we learned in 1958, we would have saved millions."

Don Burnham, the president of Westinghouse and then manufacturing vice president, was enthusiastic about the computer experiment from the start. In 1960, owing to his support, the business-systems department was founded, and plans were made for the Tele-Computer Center. Inventory control is now only part of a large-scale simulation operation that relates factory operation to buying patterns. At the Tele-Computer Center two Sperry Rand Univac 490's link 360 offices, factories, and warehouses in real time. They handle an average of 2,000 orders a day. Not only do they prepare invoices and bookkeep all transactions, they send incoming orders to the nearest warehouse, and pick the next nearest warehouse if (as is unlikely) the nearest is out of the item they are looking for. Because they automatically adjust warehouse stocks to optimum level by sending a reorder to the factory, they have enabled the company to close six of its twenty-six warehouses and to slash inventories by roughly 35 percent as well as to provide better service.

Like many commercial real-time installations, this one uses a standby computer to take over if the on-line machine fails. The standby computer solves engineering problems, turns out payrolls and annual-report figures, pays dividends, and prepares various financial and sales data. This sort of chore, however, can also be done by the on-line computer. Given an urgent query, say one asking if there is a left-handed pink refrigerator in stock, the on-line computer interrupts its routine duties to answer the question or even to make out an order and appropriately adjust inventory. But then it goes right back to the routine job it was doing.

Simulation is a standard procedure at Westinghouse. In scheduling its work, for example, the management of the South Philadelphia turbine plant draws up dozens of alternative plans. Given the plans plus the actual orders on hand and the sequence in which they must be filled, the computer runs through the equivalent of two or three years of operation, and so helps decide on the best schedule. "It often only verifies our hunches," says Hague. "But it can be a real shocker at times." Simulation is also being used to evaluate plant sites and appraise other capital investment, but the most effective use of the technique will occur after more activities or "transactions" have been put on real time.

Westinghouse is now augmenting order and inventory control with production control. In its Elmira, New York, electronic-tube plant and in its South Philadelphia turbine plant the company is installing electronic data-gathering equipment that keeps accurate and timely records of various stages of production; Westinghouse estimates that such systems will pay off at 50 percent.

While all this is going on, the business-systems department keeps its eye on the goal: shrink the management information cycle. To this end it has developed what it claims is a unique technique for retrieving information from a computer's memory. So-called random-access devices, which are standard peripheral equipment, enable a man to retrieve specific facts. But when he wants to find *all* the relevant information on a given subject, random-access devices don't help much. Business systems' solution to the problem, oversimplified considerably, is to instruct the computer to file information under dozens of different headings, and then to use a "list processor" to retrieve the information by scanning appropriate categories serially. Suppose, for example, an official wants to find out how many Westinghouse people working in cryogenics have done graduate work at M.I.T. Working against three variables, the computer would have to labor through the whole random-access file to come up with the answer. But using the processor, it is back with the reply in twelve minutes: two out of 117,000 employees.

Management in the 1980's

HAROLD J. LEAVITT AND
THOMAS C. WHISLER

*Harold Leavitt is Professor of Industrial Ad-
ministration at the Graduate School of Business at Stanford University. Thomas Whisler
is Professor of Industrial Relations at the
University of Chicago's Graduate School of
Business. This paper appeared in the
Harvard Business Review, December 1958.*

Over the last decade a new technology has begun to take hold
in American business, one so new that its significance is still
difficult to evaluate. While many aspects of this technology are
uncertain, it seems clear that it will move into the managerial
scene rapidly, with definite and far-reaching impact on managerial organization. We would like to speculate about these
effects, especially as they apply to medium-size and large business
firms of the future.

The new technology does not yet have a single established
name. We shall call it *information technology*. It is composed
of several related parts. One includes techniques for processing
large amounts of information rapidly, and it is epitomized by
the high-speed computer. A second part centers around the
application of statistical and mathematical methods to decision-
making problems; it is represented by techniques like mathematical programing, and by methodologies like operations research. A third part is in the offing, though its applications have

not yet emerged very clearly; it consists of the simulation of higher-order thinking through computer programs.

Information technology is likely to have its greatest impact on middle and top management. In many instances it will lead to opposite conclusions from those dictated by the currently popular philosophy of "participative" management. Broadly, our prognostications are along the following lines:

1. Information technology should move the boundary between planning and performance upward. Just as planning was taken from the hourly worker and given to the industrial engineer, we now expect it to be taken from a number of middle managers and given to as yet largely nonexistent specialists: "operations researchers," perhaps, or "organizational analysts." Jobs at today's middle-management level will become highly structured. Much more of the work will be programed, i.e., covered by sets of operating rules governing the day-to-day decisions that are made.

2. Correlatively, we predict that large industrial organizations will recentralize, that top managers will take on an even larger proportion of the innovating, planning, and other "creative" functions than they have now.

3. A radical reorganization of middle-management levels should occur, with *certain classes* of middle-management jobs moving downward in status and compensation (because they will require less autonomy and skill), while other classes move upward into the top-management group.

4. We suggest, too, that the line separating the top from the middle of the organization will be drawn more clearly and impenetrably than ever, much like the line drawn in the last few decades between hourly workers and first-line supervisors.

THE NEW TECHNOLOGY

Information technology has diverse roots—with contributions from such disparate groups as sociologists and electrical engineers. Working independently, people from many disciplines have been worrying about problems that have turned out to be closely related and cross-fertilizing. Cases in point are the engineers' development of servomechanisms and the related developments of general cybernetics and information theory. These ideas from the "hard" sciences all had a direct bearing on problems of processing information—in particular, the development of techniques for conceptualizing and measuring information.

Related ideas have also emerged from other disciplines. The mathematical economist came along with game theory, a means of ordering and permitting analysis of strategies and tactics in purely competitive "think-" type games. Operations research fits in here, too; OR people made use of evolving mathematical concepts, or devised their own, for solving multivariate problems without necessarily worrying about the particular context of the variables. And from social psychology ideas about communication structures in groups began to emerge, followed by ideas about thinking and general problem-solving processes.

All of these developments, and many others from even more diverse sources, have in common a concern about the systematic manipulation of information in individuals, groups, or machines. The relationships among the ideas are not yet clear, nor has the wheat been adequately separated from the chaff. It is hard to tell who started what, what preceded what, and which is method and which theory. But, characteristically, application has not, and probably will not in the future, wait on completion of basic research.

Distinctive Features · We call information technology "new" because one did not see much use of it until World War II, and it did not become clearly visible in industry until a decade later. It is new, also, in that it can be differentiated from at least two earlier industrial technologies:

1. In the first two decades of this century, Frederick W. Taylor's *scientific management* constituted a new and influential technology—one that took a large part in shaping the design of industrial organizations.

2. Largely after World War II a second distinct technology, *participative management*, seriously overtook—and even partially displaced—scientific management. Notions about decentralization, morale, and human relations modified and sometimes reversed earlier applications of scientific management. Individual incentives, for example, were treated first

as simple applications of Taylorism, but they have more recently been revised in the light of "participative" ideas.

The scientific and participative varieties both survived. One reason is that scientific management concentrated on the hourly worker, while participative management has generally aimed one level higher, at middle managers, so they have not conflicted. But what will happen now? The new information technology has direct implications for middle management as well as top management.

Current Picture · The inroads made by this technology are already apparent, so that our predictions are more extrapolations than derivations.[1] But the significance of the new trends has been obscured by the wave of interest in participative management and decentralization. Information technology seems now to show itself mostly in the periphery of management. Its applications appear to be independent of central organizational issues like communication and creativity. We have tended until now to use little pieces of the new technology to generate information, or to lay down limits for subtasks that can then be used within the old structural framework.

Some of this sparing use of information technology may be due to the fact that those of us with a large commitment to participative management have cause to resist the central implications of the new techniques. But the implications are becoming harder to deny. Many business decisions once made judgmentally now can be made better by following some simple routines devised by a staff man whose company experience is slight, whose position on the organization chart is still unclear, and whose skill (if any) in human relations was picked up on the playground. For example:

> We have heard recently of an electric utility which is considering a move to take away from generating-station managers virtually all responsibility for deciding when to use stand-by generating capacity. A typical decision facing such managers develops on hot summer afternoons. In anticipation of heavy home air-conditioning demand

1. Two examples of current developments are discussed in "Putting Arma Back on Its Feet," *Business Week*, February 1, 1958, p. 84; and "Two-Way Overhaul Rebuilds Raytheon," *Business Week*, February 22, 1958, p. 91.

at the close of working hours, the manager may put on extra capacity in late afternoon. This results in additional costs, such as overtime premiums. In this particular geographical area, rapidly moving cold fronts are frequent. Should such a front arrive after the commitment to added capacity is made, losses are substantial. If the front fails to arrive and capacity has not been added, power must be purchased from an adjacent system at penalty rates—again resulting in losses.

Such decisions may soon be made centrally by individuals whose technical skills are in mathematics and computer programing, with absolutely no experience in generating stations.

Rapid Spread · We believe that information technology will spread rapidly. One important reason for expecting fast changes in current practices is that information technology will make centralization much easier. By permitting more information to be organized more simply and processed more rapidly it will, in effect, extend the thinking range of individuals. It will allow the top level of management intelligently to categorize, digest, and act on a wider range of problems. Moreover, by quantifying more information it will extend top management's control over the decision processes of subordinates.

If centralization becomes easier to implement, managers will probably revert to it. Decentralization has, after all, been largely negatively motivated. Top managers have backed into it because they have been unable to keep up with size and technology. They could not design and maintain the huge and complex communication systems that their large, centralized organizations needed. Information technology should make recentralization possible. It may also obviate other major reasons for decentralization. For example, speed and flexibility will be possible despite large size, and top executives will be less dependent on subordinates because there will be fewer "experience" and "judgment" areas in which the junior men have more working knowledge. In addition, more efficient information-processing techniques can be expected to shorten radically the feedback loop that tests the accuracy of original observations and decisions.

Some of the psychological reasons for decentralization may remain as compelling as ever. For instance, decentralized organizations probably provide a good training ground for the top manager. They make better use of the whole man; they encourage more active cooperation. But though interest in these advantages should be very great indeed, it will be counterbalanced by interest in the possibilities of effective top-management control over the work done by the middle echelons. Here an analogy to Taylorism seems appropriate.

> In perspective, and discounting the counter-trends instigated by participative management, the upshot of Taylorism seems to have been the separating of the hourly worker from the rest of the organization, and the acceptance by both management and the worker of the idea that the worker need not plan and create. Whether it is psychologically or socially justifiable or not, his creativity and ingenuity are left largely to be acted out off the job in his home or his community. One reason, then, that we expect top acceptance of information technology is its implicit promise to allow the top to control the middle just as Taylorism allowed the middle to control the bottom.

There are other reasons for expecting fast changes. Information technology promises to allow fewer people to do more work. The more it can reduce the number of middle managers, the more top managers will be willing to try it.

We have not yet mentioned what may well be the most compelling reason of all: the pressure on management to cope with increasingly complicated engineering, logistics, and marketing problems. The temporal distance between the discovery of new knowledge and its practical application has been shrinking rapidly, perhaps at a geometric rate. The pressure to reorganize in order to deal with the complicating, speeding world should become very great in the next decade. Improvisations and "adjustments" within present organizational frameworks are likely to prove quite inadequate; radical rethinking of organizational ideas is to be expected.

Revolutionary Effects · Speculating a little more, one can imagine some radical effects of an accelerating development of information technology—effects warranting the adjective "revolutionary."

Within the organization, for example, many middle-management jobs may change in a manner reminiscent of (but faster than) the transition from shoemaker to stitcher, from old-time craftsman to today's hourly worker. As we have drawn an

organizational class line between the hourly worker and the foreman, we may expect a new line to be drawn heavily, though
jaggedly, between "top management" and "middle management,"
with some vice presidents and many ambitious suburban junior
executives falling on the lower side.

In one respect, the picture we might paint for the 1980's bears
a strong resemblance to the organizations of certain other societies—e.g., to the family-dominated organizations of Italy and
other parts of Europe, and even to a small number of such firms
in our own country. There will be many fewer middle managers,
and most of those who remain are likely to be routine technicians
rather than thinkers. This similarity will be superficial, of course,
for the changes we forecast here will be generated from quite
different origins.

What organizational and social problems are likely to come
up as by-products of such changes? One can imagine major
psychological problems arising from the depersonalization of relationships within management and the greater distance between
people at different levels. Major resistances should be expected in
the process of converting relatively autonomous and unprogramed middle-management jobs to highly routinized programs.

These problems may be of the same order as some of those
that were influential in the development of American unions and
in focusing middle management's interest on techniques for overcoming the hourly workers' resistance to change. This time it
will be the top executive who is directly concerned, and the problems of resistance to change will occur among those middle managers who are programed out of their autonomy, perhaps out of
their current status in the company, and possibly even out of their
jobs.

On a broader social scale one can conceive of large problems
outside the firm, that affect many institutions ancillary to industry. Thus:

- What about education for management? How do we educate people for routinized middle-management jobs, especially if the path from those jobs up to top management gets
  much rockier?

- To what extent do business schools stop training specialists and start training generalists to move directly into top management?

- To what extent do schools start training new kinds of specialists?

- What happens to the traditional apprentice system of training within managerial ranks?

- What will happen to American class structure? Do we end up with a new kind of managerial elite? Will technical knowledge be the major criterion for membership?

- Will technical knowledge become obsolete so fast that managers themselves will become obsolete within the time span of their industrial careers?

MIDDLE-MANAGEMENT CHANGES

Some jobs in industrial organizations are more programed than others. The job that has been subjected to micromotion analysis, for instance, has been highly programed; rules about what is to be done, in what order, and by what processes, are all specified.

Characteristically, the jobs of today's hourly workers tend to be highly programed—an effect of Taylorism. Conversely, the jobs shown at the tops of organization charts are often largely unprogramed. They are "think" jobs—hard to define and describe operationally. Jobs that appear in the big middle area of the organization chart tend to be programed in part, with some specific rules to be followed, but with varying amounts of room for judgment and autonomy.[2] One major effect of information technology is likely to be intensive programing of many jobs now held by middle managers and the concomitant "deprograming" of others.

As organizations have proliferated in size and specialization, the problem of control and integration of supervisory and staff levels has become increasingly worrisome. The best answer until now has been participative management. But information technology promises better answers. It promises to eliminate the risk of less than adequate decisions arising from garbled com-

2. See Robert N. McMurry, "The Case for Benevolent Autocracy," HBR January–February 1958, p. 82.

munications, from misconceptions of goals, and from unsatisfactory measurement of partial contributions on the part of dozens of line and staff specialists.

Good illustrations of this programing process are not common in middle management, but they do exist, mostly on the production side of the business. For example, the programmers have had some successes in displacing the judgment and experience of production schedulers (although the scheduler is still likely to be there to act out the routines) and in displacing the weekly scheduling meetings of production, sales, and supply people. Programs are also being worked out in increasing numbers to yield decisions about product mixes, warehousing, capital budgeting, and so forth.[3]

Predicting the Impact · We have noted that not all middle-management jobs will be affected alike by the new technology. What kinds of jobs will become more routinized, and what kinds less? What factors will make the difference?

The impact of change is likely to be determined by three criteria:

1. *Ease of measurement.* It is easier, at this stage, to apply the new techniques to jobs in and around production than in, say, labor relations, one reason being that quantitative measurement is easier in the former realms.

2. *Economic pressure.* Jobs that call for big money decisions will tend to get earlier investments in exploratory programing than others.

3. *The acceptability of programing by the present jobholder.* For some classes of jobs and of people, the advent of impersonal rules may offer protection or relief from frustration. We recently heard, for example, of efforts to program a maintenance foreman's decisions by providing rules for allocating priorities in maintenance and emergency repairs. The foreman supported this fully. He was a harried and much blamed man, and programing promised relief.

Such factors should accelerate the use of programing in certain areas. So should the great interest and activity in the new tech-

3. See the journals, *Operations Research* and *Management Science.*

niques now apparent in academic and research settings. New journals are appearing, and new societies are springing up, like the Operations Research Society of America (established in 1946), and the Institute of Management Sciences (established in 1954), both of which publish journals.

The number of mathematicians and economic analysts who are being taken into industry is impressive, as is the development within industry, often on the personal staffs of top management, of individuals or groups with new labels like "operations researchers," "organization analysts," or simply "special assistants for planning." These new people are a cue to the emergence of information technology. Just as programing the operations of hourly workers created the industrial engineer, so should information technology, as planning is withdrawn from middle levels, create new planners with new names at the top level.

So much for work becoming more routinized. At least two classes of middle jobs should move *upward* toward *de*programedness:

1. The programmers themselves, the new information engineers, should move up. They should appear increasingly in staff roles close to the top.
2. We would also expect jobs in research and development to go in that direction, for innovation and creativity will become increasingly important to top management as the rate of obsolescence of things and of information increases. Application of new techniques to scanning and analyzing the business environment is bound to increase the range and number of possibilities for profitable production. Competition between firms should center more and more around their capacities to innovate.

Thus, in effect, we think that the horizontal slice of the current organization chart that we call middle management will break in two, with the larger portion shrinking and sinking into a more highly programed state and the smaller portion proliferating and rising to a level where more creative thinking is needed. There seem to be signs that such a split is already occurring. The growth of literature on the organization of research activities in industry is one indication.⁴ Many social scientists and industrial research managers, as well as some general managers, are worrying more and more about problems of creativity and authority in industrial research organizations. Even some highly conservative company presidents have been forced to break time-honored policies (such as the one relating salary and status to organizational rank) in dealing with their researchers.

Individual Problems · As the programing idea grows, some old human relations problems may be redefined. Redefinition will not necessarily solve the problems, but it may obviate some and give new priorities to others.

Thus, the issue of morale versus productivity that now worries us may pale as programing moves in. The morale of programed personnel may be of less central concern because less (or at least a different sort of) productivity will be demanded of them. The execution of controllable routine acts does not require great enthusiasm by the actors.

Another current issue may also take a new form: the debate about the social advantages or disadvantages of "conformity." The stereotype of the conforming junior executive, more interested in being well liked than in working, should become far less significant in a highly depersonalized, highly programed, and more machine-like middle-management world. Of course, the pressures to conform will in one sense become more intense, for the individual will be required to stay within the limits of the routines that are set for him. But the constant behavioral pressure to be a "good guy," to get along, will have less reason for existence.

As for individualism, our suspicion is that the average middle manager will have to satisfy his personal needs and aspirations off the job, largely as we have forced the hourly worker to do.

---

4. Much of the work in this area is still unpublished. However, for some examples, see Herbert A. Shepard, "Superiors and Subordinates in Research," *Journal of Business of the University of Chicago*, October 1956, p. 261; and also Donald C. Pelz, "Some Social Factors Related to Performance in a Research Organization," *Administrative Science Quarterly*, December 1956, p. 310.

In this case, the Park Forest of the future may be an even more interesting phenomenon than it is now.

CHANGES AT THE TOP

If the new technology tends to split middle management—thin it, simplify it, program it, and separate a large part of it more rigorously from the top—what compensatory changes might one expect within the top group?

This is a much harder question to answer. We can guess that the top will focus even more intensively on "horizon" problems, on problems of innovation and change. We can forecast, too, that in dealing with such problems the top will continue for a while to fly by the seat of its pants, that it will remain largely unprogramed.

But even this is quite uncertain. Current research on the machine simulation of higher mental processes suggests that we will be able to program much of the top job before too many decades have passed. There is good authority for the prediction that within ten years a digital computer will be the world's chess champion, and that another will discover and prove an important new mathematical theorem; and that in the somewhat more distant future "the way is open to deal scientifically with ill-structured problems—to make the computer coextensive with the human mind." [5]

Meanwhile, we expect top management to become more abstract, more search-and-research-oriented and correspondingly less directly involved in the making of routine decisions. Allen Newell recently suggested to one of the authors that the wave of top-management game playing may be one manifestation of such change. Top management of the 1980's may indeed spend a good deal of money and time playing games, trying to simulate its own behavior in hypothetical future environments.

Room for Innovators · As the work of the middle manager is programed, the top manager should be freed more than ever from internal detail. But the top will not only be released to

5. See Herbert A. Simon and Allen Newell, "Heuristic Problem Solving: The Next Advance in Operations Research," *Operations Research*, January–February 1958, p. 9.

think; it will be *forced* to think. We doubt that many large companies in the 1980's will be able to survive for even a decade without major changes in products, methods, or internal organization. The rate of obsolescence and the atmosphere of continuous change which now characterize industries like chemicals and pharmaceuticals should spread rapidly to other industries, pressuring them toward rapid technical and organizational change.

These ideas lead one to expect that researchers, or people like researchers, will sit closer to the top floor of American companies in larger numbers; and that highly creative people will be more sought after and more highly valued than at present. But since researchers may be as interested in technical problems and professional affiliations as in progress up the organizational ladder, we might expect more impersonal, problem-oriented behavior at the top, with less emphasis on loyalty to the firm and more on relatively rational concern with solving difficult problems.

Again, top staff people may follow their problems from firm to firm much more closely than they do now, so that ideas about executive turnover and compensation may change along with ideas about tying people down with pension plans. Higher turnover at this level may prove advantageous to companies, for innovators can burn out fast. We may see more brain picking of the kind which is now supposedly characteristic of Madison Avenue. At this creating and innovating level, all the current work on organization and communication in research groups may find its payoff.

Besides innovators and creators, new top-management bodies will need programmers who will focus on the internal organization itself. These will be the operations researchers, mathematical programmers, computer experts, and the like. It is not clear where these kinds of people are being located on organization charts today, but our guess is that the programmer will find a place close to the top. He will probably remain relatively free to innovate and to carry out his own applied research on what and how to program (although he may eventually settle into using some stable repertory of techniques as has the industrial engineer).

Innovators and programmers will need to be supplemented by "committors." Committors are people who take on the role of approving or vetoing decisions. They will commit the organization's resources to a particular course of action—the course chosen from some alternatives provided by innovators and programmers. The current notion that managers ought to be "coordinators" should flower in the 1980's, but at the top rather than the middle; and the people to be coordinated will be top staff groups.

Tight Little Oligarchy · We surmise that the "groupthink" which is frightening some people today will be a commonplace in top management of the future. For while the innovators and the programmers may maintain or even increase their autonomy, and while the committor may be more independent than ever of lower-line levels, the interdependence of the top-staff oligarchy should increase with the increasing complexity of their tasks. The committor may be forced increasingly to have the top men operate as a committee, which would mean that the precise individual locus of decision may become even more obscure than it is today. The small-group psychologists, the researchers on creativity, the clinicians—all should find a surfeit of work at that level.

Our references to a small oligarchy at the top may be misleading. There is no reason to believe that the absolute numbers of creative research people or programmers will shrink; if anything, the reverse will be true. It is the *head men* in these areas who will probably operate as a little oligarchy, with subgroups and sub-subgroups of researchers and programmers reporting to them. But the optimal structural shape of these unprogramed groups will not necessarily be pyramidal. It is more likely to be shifting and somewhat amorphous, while the operating, programed portions of the structure ought to be more clearly pyramidal than ever.

The organization chart of the future may look something like a football balanced upon the point of a church bell. Within the football (the top staff organization), problems of coordination, individual autonomy, group decision making, and so on should arise more intensely than ever. We expect they will be dealt with quite independently of the bell portion of the company, with distinctly different methods of remuneration, control, and communication.

CHANGES IN PRACTICES

With the emergence of information technology, radical changes in certain administrative practices may also be expected. Without attempting to present the logic for the statements, we list a few changes that we foresee:

- With the organization of management into corps (supervisors, programmers, creators, committors), multiple entry points into the organization will become increasingly common.

- Multiple sources of potential managers will develop, with training institutions outside the firm specializing along the lines of the new organizational structure.

- Apprenticeship as a basis for training managers will be used less and less since movement up through the line will become increasingly unlikely.

- Top-management training will be taken over increasingly by universities, with on-the-job training done through jobs like that of assistant to a senior executive.

- Appraisal of higher management performance will be handled through some devices little used at present, such as evaluation by peers.

- Appraisal of the new middle managers will become much more precise than present rating techniques make possible, with the development of new methods attaching specific values to input-output parameters.

- Individual compensation for top staff groups will be more strongly influenced by market forces than ever before, given the increased mobility of all kinds of managers.

- With the new organizational structure new kinds of compensation practices—such as team bonuses—will appear.

Immediate Measures · If the probability seems high that some of our predictions are correct, what can businessmen do to prepare for them? A number of steps are inexpensive and relatively easy. Managers can, for example, explore these areas:

1. They can locate and work up closer liaison with appropriate

research organizations, academic and otherwise, just as many companies have profited from similar relationships in connection with the physical sciences.

2. They can re-examine their own organizations for lost information technologists. Many companies undoubtedly have such people, but not all of the top executives seem to know it.

3. They can make an early study and reassessment of some of the organizationally fuzzy groups in their own companies. Operations research departments, departments of organization, statistical analysis sections, perhaps even personnel departments, and other "odd-ball" staff groups often contain people whose knowledge and ideas in this realm have not been recognized. Such people provide a potential nucleus for serious major efforts to plan for the inroads of information technology.

Perhaps the biggest step managers need to take is an internal, psychological one. In view of the fact that information technology will challenge many long-established practices and doctrines, we will need to rethink some of the attitudes and values which we have taken for granted. In particular, we may have to reappraise our traditional notions about the worth of the individual as opposed to the organization and about the mobility rights of young men on the make. This kind of inquiry may be painfully difficult, but will be increasingly necessary.

Computers and Profit Centers

JOHN DEARDEN

John Dearden is Professor of Business Administration at the Harvard Business School. This article was published in The Impact of Computers on Management, *which appeared in 1967.*

The purpose of this paper is to consider the potential impact of computers and related information technology on the profit-center type of business organization.

In 1958, Leavitt and Whisler published an article describing what they believed to be the impact of computers and information technology on business organization in the 1980's.[1] This article predicted that significant changes would occur in business management. One of these changes would be a movement toward recentralization made possible by the new information technology. Specifically, they stated:

> We believe that information technology will spread rapidly. One important reason for expecting fast changes in current practices is that information technology will make centralization much easier. By permitting more information to be organized more simply and processed more rapidly it will, in effect, extend the thinking range of individuals. It will allow the top level of management intelligently to categorize, digest, and act on a wider range of problems. More-

1. Harold J. Leavitt and Thomas L. Whisler, "Management in the 1980's," *Harvard Business Review*, 1958, 36, No. 6. Reprinted in this book, pp. 273–288.

over, by quantifying more information it will extend top management's control over the decision processes of subordinates.

If centralization becomes easier to implement, managers will probably revert to it. Decentralization has, after all, been largely negatively motivated. Top managers have backed into it because they
have been unable to keep up with size and technology. They could
not design and maintain the huge and complex communication systems that their large, centralized organizations needed. Information
technology should make recentralization possible. It may also
obviate other major reasons for decentralization. For example, speed
and flexibility will be possible despite large size, and top executives
will be less dependent on subordinates because there will be fewer
"experience" and "judgment" areas in which the junior men have
more working knowledge. In addition, more efficient information-
processing techniques can be expected to shorten radically the feedback loop that tests the accuracy of original observations and
decisions.[2]

Another, more recent, article was published in *Fortune*.[3] One
of the principal themes in this article is that the computer will
cause increased centralization of decision-making. Specifically,
Burck states:

The machine's power to help U.S. managers control their operations has generated what appears to be nothing less than a pervasive
recentralization or reintegration movement. For twenty-five years or
so decentralization has been the word for corporations all over the
world and the reason seemed obvious enough. As companies grew
larger and more complex or more diversified, one man or a small
group was no longer able to run them directly. So top managers
broke down their organization functionally, and delegated authority
to divisional managers who were often assigned divisional profit
goals, and often spurred by profit sharing.[4]

On the following page, Burck states:

. . . the computer is now radically altering the balance of advantage between centralization and decentralization. It organizes and
processes information so swiftly that computerized information systems enable top management to know every thing important that
happens as soon as it happens in the largest and most dispersed
organizations.[5]

2. *Ibid.*
3. Gilbert Burck, "Management Will Never Be the Same Again," *Fortune*,
August 1964, 124–126ff.
4. *Ibid.*, p. 125.
5. *Ibid.*, p. 126.

In this paper, I will first examine the validity of the prediction that computers and the new information technology will cause a recentralization of authority. I will do this by testing this prediction as it applies to the profit-center form of organization, because this form of organization generally represents the greatest degree of decentralization. Secondly, I will examine the potential of the computer to improve the ability of top management to control profit-center activity. Thirdly, I will speculate on the changes that are likely to occur *within* the individual profit centers as a result of developments in computers and related technology.

WILL PROFIT CENTERS BE ELIMINATED?

In order to decide the potential impact of computers on the profit-center form of organization, we must first look at why a profit-center system was established in the first place. Then, we can see whether the computer has made changes that would affect that original reason. If it does, a change in organization may logically result; if it does not, the computer should have no impact on the organization structure. There are two different types of profit-center organization. In this part of the article, I would like to look at each of these types and analyze the changes, if any, that the developments in computer technology might create.

Profit Center: A Natural Organization Unit · One main reason for organizing an activity into profit centers has nothing to do with size or complexity; it is simply that the activity logically divides into a number of more-or-less independent profit-generating responsibilities, and the centralized control of these activities is artificial and inefficient. Take, for example, an automobile dealership. It can logically be divided into new-car business, used-car business, and service business. Many automotive dealers are organized successfully by making each of these a separate profit center. Since all three profit centers are usually located in the same place, there is no problem with information transmittal. Certainly, a typical automobile dealership is not so complex that one man could not control the entire profit responsibility. They are organized into profit centers because it is convenient and effective; thus, this type of organization will not be affected by computer developments.

There are, of course, other types of businesses where the same conclusion also holds. Gasoline service stations are one; venture-capital companies are another. I believe, therefore, that we can conclude that where a business is naturally divided into separate independent, profit-determining units, the computer will cause no change from the profit-center type of organization.

Large, Complex Business · What about the large, complex businesses referred to earlier in the article? Many of these deliberately established profit centers in what was originally a centralized business. General Motors did this in the thirties and General Electric in the forties, to name two out of a great many. It is clear that as a business grows in complexity and size, top management must delegate more responsibility for decisions simply because they do not have the time or the knowledge to make these decisions. Ultimately, management must delegate all but the most vital operating decisions.

Of course, in any business, there is a gradual delegation of authority. Periodically, however, a growing company examines the state of its organization and decides whether it should be changed. Basically, the delegation of authority could take a functional form (manufacturing, marketing, research, finance, and so forth) or a profit-center form. The functional form frequently just evolves, whereas a change to a profit-center system takes a specific decision in those companies not naturally divided into profit centers.

In order for a business organized on a functional basis to change to a profit-center system, it must be possible to separate it into profit-determining units. That is, in order to hold a manager responsible for profit performance, he must have control over the principal determinants of that profit. (Complete autonomy is usually not practicable. It becomes, therefore, a decision in many companies as to whether there is a sufficient degree of autonomy to make it reasonable to hold the manager responsible for profits.) In other words, if a business can be more logically broken down by type of business than by type of activity (manufacturing, marketing, etc.), a profit-center system is appropriate. Under these conditions, a profit-center system will have the following main advantages:

1. Each profit-center manager can become a specialist in a particular type of business.
2. Each manager will be motivated to maximize the return on his investment and thus contribute to the profit goals of the company. In other words, his goals will be consistent with those of the company. (The problem of establishing goal congruence will be discussed later in this paper.)
3. A profit center is a good training ground for future top managers.

To summarize, then, two conditions are necessary before a centralized company will change to a profit-center form of organization: (1) the company must be sufficiently large and complex to require a considerable amount of delegation on the part of top management; and (2) the business must be such that it can logically be divided into profit-responsible units. If computers are going to affect the profit-center system of organization, it must affect one or both of these conditions. Let us look at each.

Delegation of Authority. Will the computer allow management to decrease significantly the degree of delegation? In the quotations given earlier in the article, Leavitt and Whisler as well as Burck obviously believe this to be so. My own investigation of this problem, however, has led me to a different conclusion. It is not lack of *information* that has required delegation; it is two other factors. The first is that management lacks the *time* to make all but the important decisions. As the president of a multi-billion-dollar corporation told me, "My scarcest resource is my time. I have to allocate my time to those activities where my contribution is greatest. In fact, as a rule of thumb, I try to make no decisions that involve less than a million dollars." Secondly, managers have had to delegate authority because they are unable to maintain expertise in all of the different businesses in which their company is engaged. They cannot, therefore, make as good decisions as the expert *even with the same information.* It is not, therefore, lack of information or timeliness of information that has made it necessary to delegate authority; it is the lack of the knowledge necessary to use the information most effectively. As a result, I do not see how the increased use of computers and more sophisticated information technology will have any significant effect on the degree of the delegation of authority in our large, complex, decentralized concerns. It will, of course, have some minor impact. For example, inventory levels will tend to be more closely controlled centrally. In some instances, however, the computer could result in an *increase* in decentralization. If information is available to check more closely on what is happening, it might be practical for top management to delegate certain operating decisions formerly made centrally.

The method usually proposed to overcome the problems of executive time is called the "exception" principle. That is, management will be provided with information only when it exceeds some predetermined norm. The real problem, however, is to determine this norm and to prescribe the conditions where the norm has not been met. If this could be done, a limited delegation of authority would have been possible in the first place. The reason for delegation is that the establishment of satisfactory standards for most aspects of a business *are not now practical*. Further, as will be indicated later in the paper, the computer does not appear to have increased significantly the ability of management to set such standards or determine meaningful deviations from them. Consequently, in most situations, management by exception is *not* an answer to the problem of executive time.

Profit-Center Structure. If the computer will not affect significantly the necessity to delegate authority, will it affect the profit-center system by making a functional breakdown more desirable? As will be explained later, the computer will affect two principal areas of organization: (1) the data-processing activity will tend to become centralized; and (2) there will be much more centralization of the logistics systems (the flow of goods through the company). The impact of these two changes on organization will be considered below. For the present, let us see if they will affect the typical profit-center organization. Will these changes make it less logical to delegate profit responsibility?

Data-Processing. I do not see how the centralization of data-processing can have any effect on the decentralization of profit responsibility. If the same information is available at the same time, the place where it is processed makes no difference. Further, it is not necessary for a profit-center manager to control directly the processing of the information that is reported to him, as long as he can determine what that information will be.

Logistics. The centralization of the logistics systems may, of course, reduce the authority of the profit-center manager. The question is: Will it change it enough to make the delegation of profit responsibility unreasonable? I believe that it will not. It seems to me that it is entirely reasonable for a profit-center manager to participate in a centralized control of material flow and still retain most of his authority over profit determination. As evidence that this can be done, I would like to cite the General Motors Corporation as an example. They have had centralized control over most of their automotive scheduling while enjoying an extremely successful profit-center organization. Note, also, that many companies may only centralize logistics *within* profit centers rather than between profit centers. This is true where each profit center produces and markets more-or-less independent products.

To summarize, I do not see how the centralization of logistics will have any serious impact on profit-center responsibilities. Even when the centralization of logistics is extreme (as in the case of the automotive industry), profit centers can and do operate effectively. About the only exception to this generalization that I can think of would be the case where the logistics function was the *major* responsibility of the profit-center manager. This situation would be most unusual, however, because, if a manager's main responsibility is logistics, it is generally illogical to make him responsible for profit performance.

Conclusion · My conclusion is that we can expect no significant change in the degree of delegation of authority by top management or in the profit-center system of organization as a result of developments in computers and information technology. Profit-center decentralization has been somewhat of a fad in the past few years, and many companies have established profit-center organizations when they should have maintained centralized profit responsibility. Furthermore, many companies have gone to extremes in giving autonomy to profit-center managers. Consequently, we can expect some changes in the new few years away from profit centers and to less autonomy by the profit-center manager. These changes, however, will not be caused by computers, although they may be attributed to them by many.

WILL COMPUTERS HELP PROFIT-CENTER CONTROL?

If, as I believe, computers and information technology will have no significant impact on the profit-center form of organization, to what extent will the computer improve top management's control over the profit-center manager? I shall examine this question by reviewing the critical problems of controlling a group of profit centers and determining if the computer can be of significant help in solving these problems.

Critical Problems of Profit-Center Systems · Top management typically controls profit-center activity by setting a goal (usually an annual profit budget) for each profit center and periodically (usually monthly) by evaluating actual performance against this goal. Presumably, if the division is meeting its budget, top management need take no action. If the budget is missed, top management must decide what, if any, steps it should take to correct the situation. The profit budget is, first, an instrument for coordinating all divisional plans with over-all company plans. After approval, it is a means of evaluating the divisional manager and motivating him to maximize company profits.

Although simple in concept, the proper execution of profit-center control is very difficult, requiring a high degree of managerial judgment. In this part of the paper, I shall examine each of the problems that I have found to cause these difficulties and try to see to what extent computers will be helpful in solving these problems.

Establishing Goals. The evaluation of a profit-budget proposal is frequently a very difficult matter. Does the proposed profit represent an adequate goal? Is it comparable in difficulty to other profit centers? Should more research costs have been budgeted? And so forth. The profit budget is the key to the control system, yet frequently, top management has no real notion as to how much profit potential a division has. Consequently, management settles for a budgeted profit that is somewhat higher than last year's actual profit.

There has been some experimental work done in developing models of profit centers to help to predict their profitability. Also, companies have developed computer models of the budget and, then, have manipulated this model to show the effect of various alternatives proposed by management. (This is called the "what if" game.) This is of help to management in that it allows them to examine more alternatives. It is a little hard to say how much the computer can help management in setting goals. There are frequently intangible factors that are impossible to quantify. Furthermore, even where quantification is possible, the necessary information is not available. My conclusion is that the computer will help management to set better profit goals in some cases and that it will make it practicable for management to look at more alternatives. I believe, however, that the computer is a long way from providing a universal answer to the question, "How much should this division earn this year?" Furthermore, as you go into the details that make up the profitability, the computer tends to become progressively less useful.

Evaluating Performance. Perhaps the most difficult problem in profit-center management is the evaluation of divisional performance. The reason for this is that it is frequently nearly impossible to decide the extent to which unfavorable variances from budget are caused by the inadequacies of the profit-center manager and the extent to which they are beyond his control. Where performance is favorable, the same problem exists in deciding how much of the favorable variance is due to good performance and how much is due to fortuitous circumstance. This condition occurs because many variances are semicontrollable or controllable only under certain conditions. Frequently, one of top management's more difficult tasks is to decide what action is warranted from a report of actual profits compared to budget.

Clearly, much work needs to be done to improve management's ability to evaluate profit performance. To what extent the computer will be necessary to these improvements is a little difficult to say. As in the case of goal setting, I think the computer will be helpful in implementing new methods for analyzing variances. I believe, however, the computer will provide help only in limited situations. The evaluation of performance will still be one of management's principal problems in most instances.

Personnel. Somewhat related to profit-performance evaluation is the entire problem of personnel selection. Whom to hire, promote, discharge, or demote, as well as when these actions should be made, are critical to the successful operation of a decentralized company. Except for some convenience in the retrieval of personnel information, I see no impact on the solution of personnel problems by the computer.

Goal Congruence. In setting up a profit-center control system, one of the principal requirements is that the goals of the profit-center manager should be congruent with the goals of the company. That is, what improves profit-center performance should also improve the company performance by the same amount. The problems of developing a system that does this are quite technical. Even if a system is as technically perfect as we know how to make it, there will be, however, instances where the goals of the manager will not be consistent with the goals of the company. In this part of the paper I shall examine three major goal-congruence problems to see if the computer will help to solve them.

1. *Short-Run Profits.* A profit-center manager tends to be motivated to maximize short-term profits. This results from his belief (often justified) that he will not be around for the long run if his division is not profitable in the short run. This problem is overcome by such things as education, insistence on a certain level of research, and so forth. Consequently, I do not see how the computer and related technology will have any impact on solving this problem.

2. *Cooperation Among Divisions.* A second goal-congruence problem is that it is to a division's advantage *not* to cooperate with those divisions of the company with which it is in competition, even though such cooperation would be to the benefit of the company. (Even where divisions are not in direct competition, there are instances where the best interests of the company will require a profit sacrifice on the part of a division in favor of another.) As in the case of a short-term profitability, I see no

way in which the computer can be used to help solve this problem.

3. *Early Warning of Trouble.* When a divisional manager begins to run into serious problems, it is to the company's interests that this condition be communicated to top management as soon as possible. Frequently, however, the divisional manager is not only reluctant to call for help but may even try to hide the condition. Usually he hopes that he can correct it or that the condition will change for the better before he has to report he is having difficulties.

Top management needs a system to indicate when a division is in trouble as soon as it is in trouble. This problem comes up when conditions degenerate *between* reporting periods to such an extent that management should know about it. (Most serious divisional problems are of a long-run nature and cover several reporting periods.) The problem is usually solved by requiring the profit-center manager to report immediately when certain conditions exist or, more importantly, are expected to exist.

The computer has only limited ability to monitor the happenings within a division. In the first place, it can only monitor historical data, when often the important information is known only to the manager (e.g., a threatened strike). Secondly, it can only monitor on a daily basis certain kinds of data (e.g., profits on a daily basis are not practical). Consequently, I do not see how the computer will improve significantly present methods of early warning.

Conclusions · Computers will reduce the cost of data-processing; they will make it possible to have performance information earlier; they will make it possible to have somewhat more accurate and complex variance analysis; they will be of help in determining profit goals. It is my conclusion, however, that computers and related technology will not have a great impact in the typical company on ability of top management to control divisional operations.

HOW WILL COMPUTERS AFFECT MANAGEMENT?

As indicated above, I believe that the top management of a decentralized company will be relatively unaffected by the computer. The purpose of this part of the article will be to consider what changes might take place at the divisional level.

Logistics and Data-Processing · There are two pronounced trends taking place in industry today that are related to computer developments. The first is the centralization of logistics systems and the second is the centralization of the data-processing activity. I will now describe each of these trends and speculate on their impact on divisional management.

Logistics. Recent developments in time-sharing, cheap random access equipment, and cheap and fast data transmission have made the automation and centralization of logistics systems economically feasible. (Logistics are the flow of material through a company, from the purchase of the raw material and components to the delivery of the finished goods to the customer.) For example, a household-appliance company will have raw-material and work-in-process inventories at the factory and finished-goods inventories at warehouses, at distributors, and at dealers. There is an almost continuous flow from the purchase of the material to the delivery of the appliance to the ultimate consumer. In some instances, it is now economically practicable to keep track of the flow of all of the inventory in a central computer. In the future, I believe that we will find the centralization of logistics systems commonplace. This will, of course, result in marked improvements in inventory control, customer service, and distribution costs, because the computer can help solve the critical logistics problems—knowing quickly the amount and flow of products through the company.

Logistics will tend to be centralized by product. Where a company is divisionalized by product line, logistics will tend to be centralized by division. Where several divisions are involved in the same product line (as in the automobile business), the logistics systems will tend to be centralized at the group or corporate level.

Data-Processing. Data-processing will tend to be centralized, at least at the divisional level, and frequently at the corporate level. This will be true of such activities as accounting, scheduling, and personnel information. The reason for this is purely economic. It is cheaper to maintain a large central computer than to maintain several small computers. Also, where two or more locations use the same data, a common data base may be maintained more efficiently.

Management Changes · Within the division, the main changes that will occur from the automation and centralization of logistics and data-processing will be at the plant or warehouse level. As I see it, the following four changes can be expected:

1. The divisional manager will tend to spend less time co-ordinating and solving logistics problems because these will be handled automatically at a lower level.
2. Anyone at a plant, warehouse, or geographically decentralized office who is principally concerned with the supervision of data-processing personnel may have his job either changed or eliminated. For example, the plant controller who is now concerned mostly with maintaining accounting records will have to become more of an interpreter of data and a financial adviser to the divisional manager.
3. Anyone at the plant or warehouse who is largely engaged in making logistics decisions (i.e., ordering parts or scheduling production) may have his job down-graded or eliminated. For example, the manager of a parts warehouse may well become merely a supervisor of stock handlers, receiving and shipping parts in accordance with a schedule received from the divisional office.
4. Anyone who is partially concerned with making logistics decisions may have that part of his job eliminated. (Because most jobs are becoming more complex, I do not think that generally the elimination of logistics decisions will affect the job status.)

Notice that these changes will have a limited impact on most managers at any level. They will be confined to relatively two types—managers engaged primarily in supervising decentralized data-processing or logistics activities. Further, not all of these managers will be affected. With respect to logistics, they must be engaged in the type of activity that can be logically centralized. In some situations, local conditions are so important that a centralization of these decisions is not practical. With respect to data-processing, the type and extent of this activity must be such that centralization is economic.

CONCLUSIONS

My conclusions are that the computer will have no impact on the organization of top and divisional management, relatively little impact on the ability of the top manager to control profit centers, and limited impact on management levels below the divisional manager. Consequently, I believe that the opinions quoted at the beginning of this paper are incorrect. There will be some centralization of data-processing and logistic systems. I do not see how this limited centralization, however, can have anywhere near the impact envisioned by many writers on the subject.

The Corporation: Will It Be Managed by Machines?

HERBERT A. SIMON

Herbert A. Simon is Associate Dean of the Graduate School of Industrial Administration at Carnegie Institute of Technology. This article is taken from his paper in Management and Corporations, 1985, *published in 1960.*

I don't know whether the title assigned to me was meant seriously or humorously. I shall take it seriously. During the past five years, I have been too close to machines—the kinds of machines known as computers, that is—to treat the question lightly. Perhaps I have lost my sense of humor and perspective about them.

My work on this paper has been somewhat impeded, in recent days, by a fascinating spectacle just outside my office window. Men and machines have been constructing the foundations of a small building. After some preliminary skirmishing by men equipped with surveying instruments and sledges for driving pegs, most of the work has been done by various species of mechanical elephant and their mahouts. Two kinds of elephants dug out the earth (one with its forelegs, the other with its trunk) and loaded it in trucks (pack elephants, I suppose). Then, after an interlude during which another group of men carefully fitted some boards into place as forms, a new kind of

303

elephant appeared, its belly full of concrete which it disgorged
into the forms. It was assisted by two men with wheelbarrows
—plain old-fashioned man-handled wheelbarrows—and two or
three other men who fussily tamped the poured concrete with
metal rods. Twice during this whole period a shovel appeared
—on one occasion it was used by a man to remove dirt that had
been dropped on a sidewalk; on another occasion it was used to
clean a trough down which the concrete slid.

Here, before me, was a sample of automated, or semiauto-
mated production. What did it show about the nature of present and future relations of man with machine in the production
of goods and services? And what lessons that could be learned
from the automation of manufacturing and construction could
be transferred to the problems of managerial automation? I
concluded that there were two good reasons for beginning my
analysis with a careful look at factory and office automation.
First, the business organization in 1985 will be a highly automated man-machine system, and the nature of management will
surely be conditioned by the character of the system being managed. Second, perhaps there are greater similarities than appear
at first blush among the several areas of potential automation—
blue-collar, clerical, and managerial. Perhaps the automated
executive of the future has a great deal in common with the automated worker or clerk whom we can already observe in many
situations today.

First, however, we must establish a framework and a point of
view. Our task is to forecast the changes that will take place
over the next generation in the job of the manager. It is fair to
ask: Which manager? Not everyone nor every job will be affected
in the same way; indeed, most persons who will be affected are
not even managers at the present time. Moreover, we must
distinguish the gross effects of a technological change, occurring
at the point of impact of that change, from the net effects, the
whole series of secondary ripples spreading from that point of
initial impact.

Many of the initial effects are transitory—important enough
to those directly involved at the time and place of change, but
of no lasting significance to the society. Other effects are neither
apparent nor anticipated when the initial change takes place but

flow from it over a period of years through the succession of reactions it produces. Examples of both transient and indirect effects of change come to mind readily enough—e.g., the unemployment of blacksmiths and the appearance of suburbia, respectively, as effects of the automobile.

Since our task is to look ahead twenty-five years, I shall say little about the transient effects of the change in the job of the manager. I do not mean to discount the importance of these effects to the people they touch. In our time we are highly conscious of the transient effects, particularly the harmful ones, the displacement of skill and status. We say less of the benefit to those who acquire the new skills or of the exhilaration that many derive from erecting new structures.

Of course, the social management of change does not consist simply in balancing beneficial transient effects against harmful ones. The simplest moral reasoning leads to a general rule for the introduction of change: The general society which stands to benefit from the change should pay the major costs of introducing it and should compensate generously those who would otherwise be harmed by it. A discussion of the transient effects of change would have to center on ways of applying that rule. But that is not the problem we have to deal with here.

Our task is to forecast the long-run effects of change. First of all, we must predict what is likely to happen to the job of the individual manager, and to the activity of management in the individual organization. Changes in these patterns will have secondary effects on the occupational profile in the economy as a whole. Our task is to picture the society after it has made all these secondary adjustments and settled down to its new equilibrium. * * *

PREDICTING LONG-RUN EQUILIBRIUM

To predict long-run equilibrium, one must identify two major aspects of the total situation: (1) the variables that will change autonomously and inexorably—the "first causes"—and (2) the constant, unchanging "givens" in the situation, to which the other variables must adjust themselves. These are the hammer and the anvil that beat out the shape of the future. The accuracy of our predictions will depend less upon forecasting exactly the course of change than upon assessing correctly which factors are the unmoved movers and which the equally unmoved invariants. My entire forecast rests on my identification of this hammer and this anvil.

The Causes of Change · The growth in human knowledge is the primary factor that will give the system its direction—in particular, that will fix the boundaries of the technologically feasible. The growth in real capital is the major secondary factor in change—within the realm of what is technologically feasible, it will determine what is economical.

The crucial area of expansion of knowledge is not hard to predict, for the basic innovations—or at least a large part of them—have already occurred and we are now rapidly exploiting them. The new knowledge consists in a fundamental understanding of the processes of thinking and learning or, to use a more neutral term, of complex information processing. We can now write programs for electronic computers that enable these devices to think and learn. This knowledge is having, and will have, practical impacts in two directions: (1) because we can now simulate in considerable detail an important and increasing part of the processes of the human mind, we have available a technique of tremendous power for psychological research; (2) because we can now write complex information-processing programs for computers, we are acquiring the technical capacity to replace humans with computers in a rapidly widening range of "thinking" and "deciding" tasks.

Closely allied to the development of complex information-processing techniques for general-purpose computers is the rapid advance in the technique of automating all sorts of production and clerical tasks. Putting these two lines of development together, I am led to the following general predictions: Within the very near future—much less than twenty-five years—we shall have the *technical* capability of substituting machines for any and all human functions in organizations. Within the same period, we shall have acquired an extensive and empirically tested theory of human cognitive processes and their interaction with human emotions, attitudes, and values.

To predict that we will have these technical capabilities says nothing of how we shall use them. Before we can forecast that, we must discuss the important invariants in the social system.

The Invariants · The changes that our new technical capability will bring about will be governed, particularly in the production sphere, by two major fixed factors in the society. Both of these have to do with the use of human resources for production.

1. Apart from transient effects of automation, the human resources of the society will be substantially fully employed. *Full employment* does not necessarily mean a forty-hour week, for the allocation of productive capacity between additional goods and services and additional leisure may continue to change as it has in the past. *Full employment* means that the opportunity to work will be available to virtually all adults in the society and that, through wages or other allocative devices, the product of the economy will be distributed widely among families.

2. The distribution of intelligence and ability in the society will be much as it is now, although a substantially larger percentage of adults (perhaps half or more) will have completed college educations.

These assumptions—of capability of automation, accompanied by full employment and constancy in the quality of the human resources—provide us with a basis for characterizing the change. We cannot talk about the technological unemployment it may create, for we have assumed that such unemployment is a transient phenomenon—that there will be none in the long run. But the pattern of occupations, the profile showing the relative distribution of employed persons among occupations, may be greatly changed. It is the change in this profile that will measure the organizational impact of the technological change.

The change in the occupational profile depends on a well-known economic principle, the doctrine of comparative advantage. It may seem paradoxical to think that we can increase the productivity of mechanized techniques in all processes without displacing men somewhere. Won't a point be reached where men are less productive than machines in *all* processes, hence economically unemployable?[1]

1. The difficulty that laymen find with this point underlies the consistent failure of economists to win wide general support for the free trade argu-

The paradox is dissolved by supplying a missing term. Whether man or machines will be employed in a particular process depends not simply on their relative productivity in physical terms but on their cost as well. And cost depends on price. Hence—so goes the traditional argument of economics—as technology changes and machines become more productive, the prices of labor and capital will so adjust themselves as to clear the market of both. As much of each will be employed as offers itself at the market price, and the market price will be proportional to the marginal productivity of that factor. By the operation of the market place, manpower will flow to those processes in which its productivity is comparatively high relative to the productivity of machines; it will leave those processes in which its productivity is comparatively low. The comparison is not with the productivities of the past, but among the productivities in different processes with the currently available technology.

I apologize for dwelling at length on a point that is clearly enough stated in the *Wealth of Nations*. My excuse is that contemporary discussion of technological change and automation still very often falls into error through not applying the doctrine of comparative advantage correctly and consistently.

We conclude that human employment will become smaller relative to the total labor force in those kinds of occupations and activities in which automatic devices have the greatest comparative advantage over humans; human employment will become relatively greater in those occupations and activities in which automatic devices have the least comparative advantage.[2]

---

ment. The central idea—that comparative advantage, not absolute advantage, counts—is exactly the same in the two cases.

2. I am oversimplifying, for there is another term in this equation. With a general rise in productivity and with shifts in relative prices due to uneven technological progress in different spheres, the demands for some kinds of goods and services will rise more rapidly than the demands for others. Hence, other things being equal, the total demand will rise in those occupations (of men and machines) that are largely concerned with producing the former, more rapidly than in occupations concerned largely with producing the latter. I have shown elsewhere how all these mechanisms can be handled formally in analyzing technological change. See "Productivity and the Urban-Rural Population Balance," in *Models of Man* (New York, John Wiley & Sons, Inc., 1957) chapter 12; and "Effects of Technological Change in a Linear Model," in T. Koopmans (ed.), *Activity Analysis of Production and Allocation*, (New York, John Wiley & Sons, Inc., 1951) chapter 15.

Thus, if computers are a thousand times faster than book-keepers in doing arithmetic, but only one hundred times faster than stenographers in taking dictation, we shall expect the number of bookkeepers per thousand employees to decrease but the number of stenographers to increase. Similarly, if computers are a hundred times faster than executives in making investment decisions, but only ten times faster in handling employee grievances (the quality of the decisions being held constant), then computers will be employed in making investment decisions, while executives will be employed in handling grievances.

Part Seven

Operations Research in the Public Sector

MODERN economic analysis and operations research are coming to play an important role in the public sector of the economy as well as in private business. For example, such techniques have been introduced on a large scale in the Department of Defense. The papers in Part Seven attempt to show how these techniques can be, and are being, applied to problems of public policy and high-level government planning.

In the first article, Charles Hitch and Roland N. McKean describe the elements of a military problem of economic choice and show that two frequently-used approaches to these problems suffer from important defects, and that an application of elementary economic principles yields more satisfactory results. In the following article, the editor describes how a standard part of economic theory—the theory of exchange—was used to help solve an important problem facing military planners in the early fifties: How should fissionable material be allocated between strategic and tactical missions?

The following three articles are concerned with program budgeting and cost-benefit analysis. Charles Schultze describes in detail the planning, programming, and budgeting system (PPB), viewed both as a set of goals and objectives and as a system for achieving these goals. Roland McKean discusses the nature and limitations of cost-benefit analyses, such analyses being "attempts to estimate certain costs and gains that would result from alternative courses of action." A. R. Prest and Ralph Turvey provide an extensive discussion of applications of cost-benefit analysis to public policy issues concerning water projects, transport projects, land usage, and health. Finally Hirshleifer, DeHaven, and Milliman discuss the economic aspects of the utilization of existing water supplies.

Economic Choice in Military Planning

Charles J. Hitch and
Ronald N. McKean

Charles Hitch was Assistant Secretary of Defense until 1965, when he became Vice President of the University of California. Roland McKean is Professor of Economics at the University of California at Los Angeles. This paper comes from their book, The Economics of Defense in the Nuclear Age, *published in 1960.*

THE ELEMENTS OF AN ECONOMIC ANALYSIS

The essence of economic choice in military planning is not quantitative analysis: calculation may or may not be necessary or useful, depending upon the problem and what is known about it. The essential thing is the comparison of all the relevant alternatives from the point of view of the objectives each can accomplish and the costs which it involves; and the selection of the best (or a "good") alternative through the use of appropriate economic criteria.

The elements of a military problem of economic choice, whether its solution requires advanced mathematics, high speed computing equipment, or just straight hard thinking, are therefore the following:

1. An objective or objectives. What military (or other national) aim or aims are we trying to accomplish with the forces, equipments, projects, or tactics that the analysis is designed to compare? Choice of objectives is fundamental: if it is wrongly made, the whole analysis is addressed to the wrong question.

2. Alternatives. By what alternative forces, equipments, projects, tactics, and so on, may the objective be accomplished? The alternatives are frequently referred to as *systems*[1] because each combines all the elements—men, machines, and the tactics of their employment—needed to accomplish the objective. System A may differ from System B in only one respect (for example, in number of bombs per bomber), or in several (number of bombs per bomber, number of strikes, and so on), but both are complete systems, however many elements they have in common. The great problem in choosing alternatives to compare is to be sure that all the good alternatives have been included. Frequently we lack the imagination to do this at the beginning of an analysis; we think of better alternatives (that is, invent new systems) as the analysis proceeds and we learn more about the problem. The invention of new and better systems in this fashion is indeed one of the principal payoffs from this kind of analysis.

3. Costs or resources used. Each alternative method of accomplishing the objective, or in other words each system, involves the incurring of certain costs or the using up of certain resources (these are different phrases to describe the same phenomena). Costs are the negative values in the analysis (as the objectives are positive values). The resources required may be general (as is commonly the case in problems of long-range planning), or highly specific (as in most tactical problems), or mixed.

4. A model or models. Models are abstract representations of reality which help us to perceive significant relations in the real world, to manipulate them, and thereby predict others. They may take any of numerous forms. Some are small-scale physical representations of reality, like model aircraft in a wind tunnel. Many are simply representations on paper—like mathematical models. Or, finally, they may be simple sets of relationships that are sketched out in the mind and not formally put down on paper.

---

1. Hence "systems analysis," a term frequently applied to complex quantitative analyses.

In no case are models photographic reproductions of reality; if they were, they would be so complicated that they would be of no use to us. They have to abstract from a great deal of the real world—focusing upon what is relevant for the problem at hand, ignoring what is irrelevant. Whether or not one model is better than another depends not on its complexity, or its appearance of reality, but solely on whether it gives better predictions (and thereby helps us to make better decisions).[2] In systems analyses models of one type or another are required to trace the relations between inputs and outputs, resources and objectives, for each of the systems to be compared, so that we can predict the relevant consequences of choosing any system.

5. A criterion. By "criterion" we mean the test by which we choose one alternative or system rather than another. The choice of an appropriate economic criterion is frequently the central problem in designing a systems analysis. In principle, the criterion we want is clear enough: the optimal system is the one which yields the greatest excess of positive values (objectives) over negative values (resources used up, or costs). But as we have already seen, this clear-cut ideal solution is seldom a practical possibility in military problems.[3] Objectives and costs usually have no common measure: there is no generally acceptable way to subtract dollars spent or aircraft lost from enemy targets destroyed. Moreover, there may be multiple objectives or multiple costs that are incommensurable. So in most military analyses we have to be satisfied with some approximation to the ideal criterion that will enable us to say, not that some system A is optimal, but that it is better than some other proposed systems B, C, and so on. In many cases we will have to be content with calculating efficient rather than optimal systems, relying on the intuitive judgment of well-informed people (of whom the analyst may be one) to

2. Bombardiers once bombed visually, using simple models in their heads to estimate the bomb's trajectory in relation to the target. Modern bomb-sights use mathematical models, requiring high speed computers for solution, to make the same estimate. The model used by the modern bombsight is better only if its predictions are more accurate—a question of fact which has to be tested by experiment.

3. In private industry this "ideal" criterion is the familiar one of profit maximization.

select one of the efficient systems in the neighborhood of the optimum.

It cannot be stated too frequently or emphasized enough that economic choice is *a way of looking at problems* and does not necessarily depend upon the use of any analytic aids or computational devices. Some analytic aids (mathematical models) and computing machinery are quite likely to be useful in analyzing complex military problems, but there are many military problems in which they have not proved particularly useful where, nevertheless, it is rewarding to array the alternatives and think through their implications in terms of objectives and costs. Where mathematical models and computations are useful, they are in no sense alternatives to or rivals of good intuitive judgment; they supplement and complement it. Judgment is always of critical importance in designing the analysis, choosing the alternatives to be compared, and selecting the criterion. Except where there is a completely satisfactory one-dimensional measurable objective (a rare circumstance), judgment must supplement the quantitative analysis before a choice can be recommended.

THE REQUIREMENTS APPROACH

In the absence of systematic analysis in terms of objectives and costs, a procedure that might be called the "requirements approach" is commonly used in the military departments and throughout much of the government. Staff officers inspect a problem, say, the defense of the continental United States or the design of the next generation of heavy bomber, draft a plan which seems to solve the problem, and determine requirements from the plan. Then feasibility is checked: Can the "required" performance characteristics, such as some designated speed and range, be achieved? Can the necessary budget be obtained? Does the nation have the necessary resources in total? If the program passes the feasibility tests, it is adopted; if it fails, some adjustments have to be made. But the question: What are the payoffs *and the costs* of alternative programs? may not be explicitly asked during the process of setting the requirement or deciding upon the budget. In fact, officials have on occasion boasted that their stated "requirements" have been based on need alone.

This, of course, is an illusion. Some notion of cost (money, resources, time), however imprecise, is implicit in the recognition of any limitation. Military departments frequently determine "requirements" which are from 10 to 25 percent higher than the available budget, but never ten times as high, and seldom twice as high. But this notion of cost merely rules out grossly infeasible programs. It does not help in making optimal or efficient choices.

For that purpose it is essential that alternative ways of achieving military objectives be costed, and that choices be made on the basis of payoff and cost. How *are* choices made by military planners prior to any costing of alternatives? We have never heard any satisfying explanation. The derivation of requirements by any process that fails to cost alternatives can result in good solutions only by accident. Probably military planners sometimes weigh relative costs in some crude manner, at least subconsciously, even when they deny they do; or they make choices on the basis of considerations which ought to be secondary or tertiary, such as the preservation of an existing command structure, or the matching of a reported foreign accomplishment.

The defects of the requirements approach can be seen clearly if we think of applying it to our problems as a consumer. Suppose the consumer mulls over his transportation problem and decides, "on the basis of need alone," that he requires a new Cadillac. It is "the best" car he knows, and besides Jones drives one. So he buys a Cadillac, ignoring cost and ignoring therefore the sacrifices he is making in other directions by buying "the best." There are numerous alternative ways of solving the consumer's transportation problem (as there are always numerous ways of solving a military problem), and a little costing of alternatives prior to purchase might have revealed that the purchase of "the best" instrument is not *necessarily* an optimal choice. Perhaps if the consumer had purchased a Pontiac or a secondhand Cadillac he would have saved enough to maintain and operate it and take an occasional trip.[4] Or if he had purchased a Chevrolet he could have afforded to keep his old car and become head of a two-car family. One of these alternatives, properly costed and compared,

4. Costing in our sense is never simply the cost of a unit of equipment; it is always the cost of a complete system including everything that must be purchased with the equipment and the cost of maintaining and operating it.

might have promised a far greater amount of utility for the consumer than the purchase of a new Cadillac "on the basis of need alone." Or the exercise might have reassured the consumer that the new Cadillac was indeed optimal. While expensive unit equipment is not necessarily optimal, in some cases it can be proved to be.

THE PRIORITIES APPROACH

Another procedure that seems to have a great deal of appeal, in both military planning and other government activities, is the "priorities approach." To facilitate a decision about how to spend a specified budget, the desirable items are ranked according to the urgency with which they are needed. The result is a list of things that might be bought, the ones that are more important being near the top and the ones that are less important being near the bottom. Lists that rank several hundred weapons and items have sometimes been generated in the military services.

At first blush, this appears to be a commendable and systematic way to tackle the problem. When one reflects a bit, however, the usefulness and significance of such a list begins to evaporate. Consider the following items ranked according to their (hypothetical) priorities: (1) Missile X, (2) Radar device Y, (3) Cargo aircraft Z. How do you use such a ranking? Does it mean that the entire budget should be spent on the first item? Probably not, for it is usually foolish to allocate all of a budget to a single weapon or object. Besides, if a budget is to be so allocated, the ranking of the items below the first one has no significance.

Does the ranking mean that the money should go to the first item until no additional amount is needed, then to the second item until no further amount is needed, and so on? Hardly, because there could be some need for more of Missile X almost without limit. Even if only a limited amount of Missile X was available, to keep buying right out to this limit would usually be a foolish rule. After quite a few Missile X's were purchased, the next dollar could better be spent on some other item. Even using lifeboats for women and children first is foolish if a sailor or doctor on each lifeboat can save many lives.

Perhaps a priority list means that we should spend more money on the higher-priority items than on those having a lower priority.

But this makes little sense, since some of the items high on the list, for example, the radar device, may cost little per unit and call at most for a relatively small amount of money; while some lower-ranking purchases, such as the cargo aircraft, may call for comparatively large sums if they are to be purchased at all. In any event, the priorities reveal nothing about how much more should be spent on particular items.

Just how anyone can use such a list is not clear. Suppose a consumer lists possible items for his monthly budget in the order of their priority and he feels that in some sense they rank as follows: (1) groceries, (2) gas and oil, (3) cigarettes, (4) repairs to house, (5) liquor, and (6) steam baths. This does not mean that he will spend all of his funds on groceries, nor does it mean that he will spend nothing on liquor or steam baths. His problem is really to allocate his budget among these different objects. He would like to choose the allocation such that an extra dollar on cigarettes is just as important to him as an extra dollar on groceries. At the margin, therefore, the objects of expenditure would be equally important (except for those that are not purchased at all).

The notion of priority stems from the very sensible proposition that one should do "first things first." It makes sense, or at least the top priority does, when one considers the use of a small increment of resources or time. If one thinks about the use of an extra dollar or of the next half-hour of his time, it is sensible to ask, "What is the most urgent—the first-priority—item?" If one is deciding what to do with a budget or with the next eight hours, however, he ordinarily faces a problem of *allocation,* not of setting priorities. A list of priorities does not face the problem or help solve it.

Thus in formulating defense policy and choosing weapon systems, we have to decide how much effort or how many resources should go to each item. The "priorities approach" does not solve the allocation problem and can even trap us into adopting foolish policies.[5]

5. For a revealing discussion of priority lists, see *Military Construction Appropriations for 1958,* Hearings before the Subcommittee of the Committee on Appropriations, House of Representatives, 85th Congress, 1st Session, U.S. Government Printing Office, Washington, D.C., 1957, pp. 420-427.

The Allocation of Fissionable Materials and the Theory of Exchange

Edwin Mansfield

Edwin Mansfield is Professor of Economics at the University of Pennsylvania. This article is from his book Microeconomics: Theory and Applications, *published by Norton in 1970.*

1. INTRODUCTION

Economic analysis has proved useful in many aspects of decision-making concerning military problems. The purpose of this paper is to describe how a standard part of economic theory —the theory of exchange—was used to solve an important problem facing military planners in the early fifties. In the following section, we present the relevant aspects of the theory of exchange. In the next section, we describe the nature of the problem that faced the military planners. In the final section, we indicate how the theory of exchange was used to help solve the problem.

2. EXCHANGE BETWEEN CONSUMERS

Let's begin by analyzing the exchange that can fruitfully take place between consumers. The essential elements of our theory can be presented if we assume that there are only two consumers, Bill and Joe, and only two commodities, good X and good Y.

We assume that Bill has a certain amount of each of the goods and that Joe has a certain amount of each of the goods. Moreover, we assume that they meet and discuss the possibility of trading. The question is: what sort of trading or exchange will occur?

To answer this question, we construct a special diagram, called an *Edgeworth box diagram*. This diagram is shown in Figure 1.

FIGURE 1

THE EDGEWORTH BOX DIAGRAM

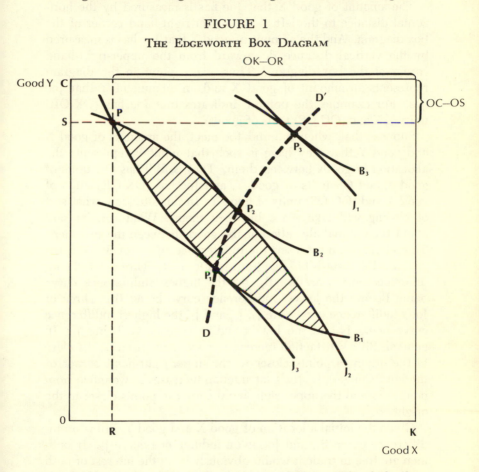

It is constructed in the following way: The width of the box, which is equal to OK, is the total amount of good X that Bill and Joe together have. The height of the box, which is equal to OC, is the total amount of good Y that Bill and Joe together have. The amount of good X that Bill has is measured horizontally from the origin at O. The amount of good Y that Bill has is measured vertically from the origin at O. Thus any point in the box diagram indicated a certain amount of good X and a certain amount of good Y that Bill has. For example, the point, P, indicates that Bill has OR units of good X and OS units of good Y.

The amount of good X that Joe has is measured by the horizontal distance to the left of the upper-right-hand corner of the box diagram. And the amount of good Y that Joe has is measured by the vertical distance downward from the upper-right-hand corner of the box diagram. Thus, every point in the diagram represents an amount of good X and an amount of Y that Joe has. For example, the point P indicates that Joe has (OK-OR) units of X and (OC-OS) units of good Y.

Suppose that, when Bill and Joe meet, the amounts of good X and good Y that they have is such that point P represents the allocation of goods between them. That is, Bill has OR units of good X and OS units of good Y, and Joe has (OK-OR) units of good X and (OC-OS) units of good Y. In this situation, what sort of trading will take place between them? What can be said about the optimal allocation of the goods between the two men? To find out, we must insert the indifference curves of Bill and Joe into the Edgeworth box diagram in Figure 1. Three of Bill's indifference curves are B_1, B_2, B_3, the highest indifference curve being B_3 and the lowest indifference curve being B_1. Three of Joe's indifference curves are J_1, J_2, and J_3, the highest indifference curve being J_3 and the lowest indifference curve being J_1. In general, Bill's satisfaction increases as we move from points close to the origin to points closer to the upper-right-hand corner of the box. Conversely, Joe's satisfaction increases as we move from points close to the upper-right-hand corner to points closer to the origin.

Given the initial allocation of good X and good Y, Bill is on indifference curve B_1, and Joe is on indifference curve J_2. If both men are free to trade it would obviously be in the interest of both parties for Bill to trade some good Y in exchange for some good X. Unless there is coercion, the point at which they will finally end up is somewhere in the shaded area in Figure 1; this area includes all points at which both men are no worse off than at P. The exact point to which they will move cannot be predicted, however. If Joe is the more astute bargainer, he may get Bill to accept the allocation at Point P_1, where Bill is no better off than before (since he is still on indifference curve B_1) but Joe is much better off (since he moves to indifference curve J_3). If Bill is the more astute bargainer, he may get Joe to accept the allocation at P_2, where Joe is no better off than before (since he is still on indifference curve J_2) but Bill is much better off (since he moves to indifference curve B_2). The ultimate outcome is likely to be a point between P_1 and P_2.

If after some exchange occurs a point is reached at which Bill's indifference curve is tangent to Joe's indifference curve, then there is no opportunity for further mutually advantageous exchange. One man can be made better off only by making the other man worse off—and surely such a situation would not result in further exchange. The locus of points where such a tangency occurs is called the *contract curve*. Some points on the contract curve are points P_1, P_2, and P_3 in Figure 1. Because of obstinacy or ineptness, exchange may cease at a point off the contract curve, but this would not be optimal in the following sense: If the consumers are at a point off the contract curve, it is always preferable for them to move to a point on the contract curve, since one or both can gain from the move while neither incurs a loss. Clearly, such a move results in a net gain. In this sense, the contract curve is an optimal set of points.

3. FISSIONABLE MATERIALS: AN APPLICATION OF THE THEORY OF EXCHANGE

Back around 1950, one of the key problems in the defense establishment was the allocation of fissionable material—U258 and Pu 239. In particular, how much of our supply of fissionable material should be used for strategic purposes, and how much should be used for tactical purposes? The strategic forces, principally long-range bombers at that time, were the foundation of our capability to strike back at an enemy's cities and bases. The tactical forces were concerned with more limited engagements with enemy forces. At that time, the strategic mission had exclusive claim on the national stockpile of fissionable materials, and an urgent question was whether some tactical air squadrons should be equipped with small-yield atomic weapons. As you can imagine, this was a very, very important question— one which occupied and concerned the minds of some of the nation's highest officials.

Both for the strategic and tactical mission, the two most important determinants of the effectiveness of the mission were (1) the amount of fissionable material used, and (2) the number of aircraft used. Within limits, it was possible to substitute airplanes for fissionable material and vice versa. For example, if the object of an Air Force operation was the expected destruction of a certain number of targets, fewer aircraft would be required to destroy these targets if atomic weapons, rather than conventional weapons, were used. Also, one way of increasing the probability that a bomb would get to the target was to have several empty decoy bombers accompanying each aircraft with an atomic bomb—which clearly was a way of substituting aircraft for fissionable materials.

In the very short run, it was sensible to view the total number of aircraft available for either strategic or tactical missions as fixed. It was also sensible to view the total amount of fissionable material available for either strategic or tactical missions as fixed. However, this was appropriate only in analyzing the problem in the short run; in the long run, it was possible to add to our supplies of aircraft and fissionable materials. Also, it is important to note that there was no way to establish the relative importance of strategic and tactical targets. For example, no one was willing to say that the destruction of a strategic target was worth the destruction of two tactical targets. Instead, strategic and tactical targets were regarded as incommensurable.

4. SOLUTION TO THE PROBLEM

The reader can be forgiven if he asks in a somewhat bewildered tone: "What in the world has this problem got to do with the theory of exchange we discussed in section 1?" The answer is that, strange as it may seem, economists used the theory of exchange described in section 1 to help solve this question. The way in which they solved the problem is instructive in many respects, one being that it illustrates how simple models can be adapted to throw light on very complicated problems.

In effect, the economists said: "Let's view the strategic mission as one consumer and the tactical mission as another consumer. Let's regard airplanes and fissionable material as two goods to be allocated between these two consumers, the total amount of these two goods being fixed in the very short run. Let's use as indifference curves for the strategic mission the combinations of aircraft and fissionable material that will result in the expected destruction of a particular number of strategic targets. Let's use as indifference curves for the tactical mission the combinations of aircraft and fissionable material that will result in the expected destruction of a particular number of tactical targets. Then let's use the Edgeworth box diagram to indicate which allocations of aircraft and fissionable materials between strategic and tactical missions are on the contract curve. This will tell us whether the existing allocation is on the contract curve. If it isn't, the allocation can be improved."

To actually attack the problem in this way, the first step was, of course, to construct the appropriate Edgeworth box diagram. Figure 2 shows what the resulting box diagram looked like. As in Figure 1, any point in the diagram represented a possible allocation of the two goods, airplanes and fissionable material, between the two "consumers," the strategic mission and the tactical mission. For example, point P in Figure 2 represents a case where the strategic mission gets OU units of aircraft and OV units of fissionable material, and the tactical mission gets (OA-OU) units of aircraft and (OM-OV) units of fissionable material.

The two "consumers" are not ordinary consumers. They are military missions. What do indifference curves mean in such a situation? Consider the tactical mission's indifference curve, T_1. Each point on T_1 represents a combination of aircraft and fissionable material that results in the same number of *tactical* targets expected to be destroyed. The fictitious consumer, "the tactical mission," is viewed as being interested in maximizing the expected number of tactical targets that can be destroyed. In other words, the expected number of tactical targets that can be destroyed is a measure of this consumer's "utility." Thus, he is indifferent among all of the points on T_1. And he clearly prefers indifference curve T_2 to indifference curve T_1. Similarly, consider the strategic mission's indifference curve, S_1. Each point on S_1

FIGURE 2

ALLOCATION OF FISSIONABLE MATERIALS AND
AIRPLANES BETWEEN STRATEGIC AND TACTICAL MISSIONS

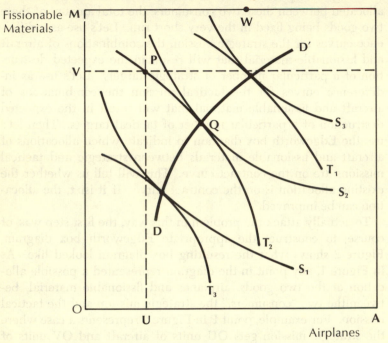

represents a combination of aircraft and fissionable material that
results in the same number of *strategic* targets expected to be
destroyed. The fictitious consumer, "the strategic mission," is
viewed as being interested in maximizing the expected number of
strategic targets that can be destroyed. In other words, the expected number of strategic targets that can be destroyed is a
measure of the consumer's utility. Thus, he is indifferent among
all of the points of S_1, and he prefers S_2 to S_1.

From the discussion in section 1, we know that any allocation
of aircraft and fissionable materials that is represented by a point
that is not a point of tangency between an indifference curve of
the tactical mission and an indifference curve of the strategic
mission is not an optimal allocation. For example, P in Figure 2
is not an optimal allocation since it is not a point of tangency

between an indifference curve of the tactical mission and an indifference curve of the strategic mission. Why isn't P an optimal allocation? Because if we hold constant the expected number of tactical targets that can be destroyed (the "utility" of the tactical mission), we can increase the expected number of strategic targets that can be destroyed (the "utility" of the strategic mission) by moving to point Q. The locus of optimal points—the contract curve—is shown by DD′ in Figure 2.

Having constructed the contract curve, what did the economists conclude? Recall that the existing allocation assigned all of the nation's stockpile of fissionable material to the strategic mission and none to the tactical mission. Thus, the existing allocation was at point W in Figure 2. However, according to the economist's calculations, this point was not on the contract curve, DD′. Consequently, the existing allocation was shown to be sub-optimal, a movement to the contract curve being called for. Specifically, the stockpile of fissionable material needed to be reallocated, some atomic weapons being reserved for the tactical mission. However, this analysis could not indicate which particular point on the contract curve should be chosen, since this decision hinged on whether we wanted to increase our strategic capability at the expense of our tactical capability, or vice versa. On the basis of the information given here, no judgment on this score could be made.

This was an important example of the application of the theory described in previous sections. For that reason, it is interesting. In addition, it is interesting because it illustrates the fact that most aspects of microeconomics are concerned with means to achieve specified ends, not with the choice of ends. Thus, economists in the case discussed here were able to increase the destructive power of given supplies of aircraft and fissionable material. But they took as given the hypothesis that it was a good thing to increase their destructive power. In other words, they took as given the fact that the "utility" of the "consumers" should be increased. In certain circumstances, this hypothesis could be quite wrong. For example, there might be circumstances where an increase in destructive power might increase the chances of war. Of course, this does not mean that it is not valuable to have techniques like those discussed here: they obviously are of great value. What it does mean is that one cannot expect them to do more than they are designed to do.[1]

1. For further discussion, see S. Enke, "Using Costs to Select Weapons," *American Economic Review*, May 1965; and "Some Economic Aspects of Fissionable Materials," *Quarterly Journal of Economics*, May 1954.

The Planning, Programming, and Budgeting System in the Federal Government

CHARLES SCHULTZE

Charles Schultze is a senior fellow at the Brookings Institution and a former director of the Bureau of the Budget. This piece is from his book The Politics and Economics of Public Spending.

THE GOALS OF PPB

The planning, programming, and budgeting system (PPB) can be viewed as both a set of goals and objectives and a system for achieving those goals. It seeks to accomplish the following ends.

First, PPB calls for careful identification and examination of goals and objectives in each major area of governmental activity. It attempts to force government agencies to step back and reflect on the fundamental aims of their current programs. For example, what are the goals of federal manpower programs? To reduce structural unemployment and inflationary pressure by retraining programs that increase the number of workers with skills in short supply? To raise the income of hard-core disadvantaged by upgrading their skills and improving their work habits? To create more job opportunities for the unskilled? While they are not wholly incompatible, they are different and the design and composition of public manpower programs will

329

depend upon the particular combination of objectives sought.

Intercity highway programs provide another example. The objective of the intercity highway program ought not to be simply building highways. Highways are useful only to transport people and goods efficiently and safely. Once this objective is recognized, it becomes possible to analyze alternative transportation investments as means to these ends. So long as the ultimate goal of the highway program is considered the laying of x miles of concrete, comparison of the effectiveness of various investments is impossible.

At the same time, we cannot expect the perspectives of any given level in the decision hierarchy to be as broad as those of the next higher level. The federal highway administrator will not, and should not, have the same range of objectives as the secretary of transportation nor will the secretary deal with as broad a range of alternatives as the President. Each level in the decision-making process has its own role to play. In seeking to specify program objectives, PPB aims at a realistic broadening of perspective, not at making the objectives of every participant coextensive with the President's. An attempt to force too wide a span of objectives on a participant in the process may well render the whole effort fruitless. In short, PPB seeks to encourage an analysis of program objectives in order to widen but not homogenize the perspective with which agency heads view their programs, thereby broadening the range of alternatives considered for policy and program design.

The second task of PPB is to analyze the *output* of a given program in terms of its objectives. For example, the effectiveness of various manpower training programs can only be determined in relation to a particular set of objectives. "Creaming off" the manpower pool by concentrating training resources on unemployed white high school graduates may prove highly effective when measured by the proportion of trainees subsequently employed at steady jobs and higher wages. But if the objective is to improve the lot of the hard-core unemployed or underemployed in the ghetto, comparing alternative programs on the basis of such measures of effectiveness would be inappropriate and misleading. Similarly in evaluating the highway program, it is not sufficient to ask how many miles of concrete are laid, but what the program produces in terms of safer, less-congested travel—how many hours of travel time are eliminated and how many accidents are prevented.

The third objective of PPB is the measurement of total program costs, not for just one year but for at least several years ahead. Two kinds of costs are involved. The first relates to the future budgetary consequences of current decisions. The 1968 budget, for example, requested $10 million to design a 200 billion electron volt research accelerator for the Atomic Energy Commission at an estimated construction cost of $240 million. But over a longer time period—say ten years—the total system's cost of this decision may exceed $1 billion, since operating costs, once the machine is built, will run between $60 and $100 million per year. In terms of overall budget policy it is necessary to know the extent to which future budgetary commitments are being made by current decisions. Moreover, in comparing alternative programs designed to accomplish a given objective, the comparison should be made on the basis of all the relevant costs, not just the immediate costs.

In addition to budgetary costs, there are often other costs associated with a proposed program which should be taken into account in making a decision. The costs of urban freeways, for example, are not merely the construction costs of the freeway itself but include the cost of relocating displaced residents. Even where these costs are not reflected in the budget, they are still costs to society and should be identified in the statement of program costs.

PPB, then, seeks to provide the decision maker with all the relevant costs that his decision would entail. This sounds so sensible that to belabor the point seems unnecessary. Yet too often large federal investment decisions have been made in the annual budget on the basis of only the next year's cost—or made without taking into account any of the indirectly associated costs.

A fourth and closely related goal of PPB is the formulation of objectives and programs extending beyond the single year of the annual budget submission. Most federal programs cannot achieve their intended objectives in one year. Many, like the collection of taxes, are a continuing activity some of whose components, such as the computerization of returns, have discrete time-phased objectives spread over a number of years. Others seek goals that only make sense in terms of a multiyear effort, for example, the gradual expansion of medical schools in order to bring the size of the annual graduating class to a particular level. One of the major problems of budgeting has been and remains the limited period of time covered by annual budgetary decisions. PPB seeks to relate annual budget allocations to longer-term plans.

The long-term nature of most public programs calls for long-range planning. In practice, an equally importance *tactical* aspect of multiyear planning has become evident. In the short run, and in particular in the annual budget process, federal agencies are captives of the past. Prior commitments, inertia, promises to an appropriations subcommittee chairman, the need to "educate" interest-group constituents about program changes, and the like, often cause rigid constraints on yearly budget decisions. In any one year, therefore, the impact that an agency head can have on his operating bureaus is limited. By concentrating solely on what can be done in each annual budget, he can achieve very little. Major changes in objectives, operating practices, and budget allocations must be accomplished in the light of longer-range goals. By requiring subordinate bureaus to prepare the annual budget within the framework of broad, long-range budget allocations, however, the agency head can exert more influence on the general course of programs in his department than he could by fighting annual budget battles under severe constraints. Long-range budget allocations will, and should, be modified from year to year. Their value is not in their immutability, but in their use as a tool of secretarial influence over his own department. However, the role and meaning of long-range planning have been among the most troublesome aspects of PPB in civilian agencies.

The fifth and crucial aim of the PPB system is the analysis of alternatives to find the most effective means of reaching basic program objectives, and to achieve these objectives for the least cost. The goal is to force federal agencies to consider particular programs not as ends in themselves—to be perpetuated without challenge or question—but as means to objectives, subject to the competition of alternative and perhaps more effective or efficient programs. Looked at another way, PPB seeks to replace, at least in part, the pernicious practice of incremental budgeting, under which the budget allocation process does not involve a review of the basic structure of programs but primarily consists in making decisions about how much each existing program is to be increased or, much less frequently, decreased. Each program cannot, of course, he reviewed from the ground up each year. But the analytic steps of PPB call for a periodic review of fundamental program objectives, accomplishments, and costs while considering the effectiveness and efficiency of alternatives.

The sixth and final goal of PPB is to establish these analytic procedures as a systematic part of budget review. PPB seeks to subject policies and programs to analysis and to integrate the decisions into the budgetary process. Two considerations encourage this integration.

First, the allocation of limited budgetary resources among competing claims can be more intelligently made if fuller information and analysis of program objectives, effectiveness, and costs are available. When relatively narrow choices are involved —such as the allocation of funds among various alternative manpower training programs—analysis can contribute directly to program decisions. But even when broader questions are being considered—such as the allocation between education and housing—analyses that present the payoffs or consequences of each program can assist the decision maker in weighing the alternatives.

Second, if it is to be more than an academic exercise, program analysis must be built into the decision-making process at each level of the decision hierarchy. By its very nature, the budget, more than any other process in the federal system, forces action. The need to formulate budget requests each year compels program decisions to be made, by the President, agency heads, bureau chiefs, and their subordinates.

These then are the aims of PPB: the specification of objectives, the evaluation of program output as it relates to objectives, the measurement of total systems costs, multiyear program planning, the evaluation of alternative program designs, and the integration of policy and program decisions with the budgetary process.

PPB AS A SYSTEM

The formal structure of the PPB system as it has been established in civilian agencies consists of four elements.

Program Budgeting · The activities and budgetary costs of federal programs are grouped into program categories. The literature on the desirability of these output-oriented classifications as an aid to analysis is abundant.[1] The nature of the output produced by federal agencies is the key discriminant in defining program categories and assigning individual federal activities to them. Programs whose outputs are closely related, and therefore either close substitutes or necessary complements to each other, are grouped together. Broad categories such as "health," are subdivided into subcategories, such as "development of health resources" and "prevention and control of health problems." Each of the subcategories is, in turn, further subdivided into program elements. The subcategory "prevention and control of health problems," for example, contains such program elements as "mental retardation," "radiological health," and "air pollution control."

There is nothing sacred about these program classifications. They can and should be changed as analytical need dictates. Several different kinds of classifications may be needed for different analytical purposes. Their main function is to emphasize that government programs have an output, and that they should be analyzed and evaluated on the basis of how effectively and efficiently that output meets program objectives.

The effectiveness of PPB does not depend on reorganizing operating units to conform to program categories, as is often claimed. In fact, this would be harmful in some cases and im-

1. See, for example, Charles J. Hitch, "On the Choice of Objectives in Systems Studies," P–1955 (processed; Santa Monica, Calif.: RAND Corporation, 1960), and Arthur Smithies, "Conceptual Framework for the Program Budget," in David Novick (ed.), *Program Budgeting: Program Analysis and the Federal Budget* (Harvard University Press, 1965), pp. 24–60.

possible in others. Organizations are characterized, chiefly, by the type of operations they carry out. For efficient management this is an appropriate organizational criterion. But each organization usually contributes to several different kinds of output. To split the Agricultural Research Service into five or six components and to recombine one of those components with parts of the Soil Conservation Service just because they both contribute to raising farm productivity makes little managerial sense.

The set of categories appropriate to strategic planning and analysis is often quite different from the categories appropriate to the control or management efficiency functions of budgeting. A good example is found in the various classifications of the Coast Guard budget.

Appropriation categories (objects of expenditure): operating expenses; acquisition, construction, and improvements; retired pay; reserve training.

Activity schedule (types of operational processes): vessel operations; aviation operations; shore stations and aids operations; repair and supply facilities; training and recruiting facilities; administration and operational control; other military personnel expense; supporting programs.

Program budget (program outputs and objectives): search and rescue; aids to navigation; law enforcement; military readiness; merchant marine safety; oceanography and other operations; supporting services.

Since appropriations are made to the Coast Guard by type of expenditure, the budget system must provide controls to insure that obligations and expenditures stay within appropriation limits. The activity schedule is a good example of performance budgeting. It groups budgetary data by the type of operational activity and is primarily a tool of operating managers who must carry out these activities. The program budget, on the other hand, is designed to focus attention on the outputs and objectives of the Coast Guard—those objectives it seeks, and the kinds and levels of output it produces.

Program and Financial Plan · Each agency is required to submit as part of the annual budget process a multiyear (usually five

years) program and financial plan according to program categories, subdivided into subcategories and program elements.
Both financial costs and, wherever possible, measures of proposed
program outputs are provided. In most cases the simple output
measures contained in the plan are only indicators of more
complicated outputs. Since the President must recommend his
budget to Congress in terms of the congressionally established
appropriation structure, the plan also provides a "crosswalk" that
translates program costs classified by ouput category into individual appropriation requests.

In effect, the program and financial plan is a tabular record of
an agency's proposed activities, measured in both physical and
financial terms and grouped by output-oriented categories.
Originally the program and financial plan was conceived as a
five-year planning document, incorporating proposals for program decisions over that five-year period. In early 1967 the
program and financial plan was modified for most agencies so
that future financial and output data reflected only the consequences of decisions proposed for the subsequent budget.

As a hypothetical case, let us assume that the Federal Aviation
Administration proposes in the 1969 budget to initiate procurement of long lead-time equipment for traffic control systems at
air terminals (radars, computers, display equipment, and the
like). The five-year, time-phased costs of procuring, installing,
and operating the system would be included in the agency's program and financial plan. These would be the future costs of current decisions. But if the agency also believed that in 1970 a series
of improvements in air navigation facilities would be desirable,
the costs and outputs of this project would not be included in the
current program and financial plan since a decision need not be
made on the matter until the next year's budget. Thus, the
program and financial plan is not a planning document in the
true sense of the word since the plan does not fully reflect
the agency's proposed course of action over the period covered
by the plan. There are, in effect, two types of forward plans:
The first covers the future budgetary consequences of current
decisions—it provides an information system whereby built-in
budgetary increases can be estimated, in the aggregate and by
individual programs; the second projects the composition of

agency programs over an extended period, including the consequences of decisions which will not be taken for several years. Such plans are, by nature, highly tentative and change periodically. But they can be an important, internal management tool through which an agency head may influence the long-range course of his department.

The program and financial plan, as I mentioned earlier, includes a bridge between the program budget and the appropriation structure. From a technical standpoint this is necessary because program decisions have to be translated into specific appropriation requests. But more importantly, it turns out that it is impossible for the department head, the budget director, or the President to make decisions solely on the basis of program categories. In most civilian agencies the individual appropriations have lives of their own. The problems that arise in integrating the PPB system into the political process can be seen from the following example. In the Department of Agriculture there is a program subcategory called "agricultural production capacity," which covers those programs aimed at increasing farm efficiency and productivity.[2] Some of the activities in this subcategory are research efforts, such as control of crop-destroying pests and research into better seed strains. Most of this research is carried on by the Agricultural Research Service, which also conducts equally important research affecting other programs—nutrition and agricultural marketing and distribution, to mention a few.

Appropriations are made directly to the Agricultural Research Service—the administering agency. There is one appropriation for operating expenses and another for facilities construction. The Appropriations Committees are vitally interested in what happens to the Agricultural Research Service as an organizational entity. The committees are particularly concerned with the dispensing of operating funds to the hundreds of small agricultural research stations judiciously scattered throughout the country—stations which are often too small to be efficient.

2. As a sidelight on the problems involved, a companion subcategory in the same program is labeled "farm income." This subcategory includes most of the price support programs—whose major objective is to *limit* farm production as a means of raising prices and income.

They are also interested in the facilities appropriation, both the overall size and the particular location of proposed facilities. Other research in the production capacity program category is carried out through formula grants to university agricultural experiment stations. These grants are administered by the Co-operative State Research Service, a separate organization with a separate appropriation. This service also makes grants for research in program categories other than production capacity. Here, again, a whole new set of interests—well-organized interests—affects the appropriation to the Cooperative State Research Service. It determines the fate of a particular set of institutions across the country.

The agricultural Extension Service provides another example. The service administers the federal grants-in-aid to the state agricultural extension programs. Agricultural extension activities are quite diverse, and in the program or output-oriented budget these activities are assigned to various categories, depending on the particular objective. The appropriations for all of these programs, however, are made to a single organization—the Extension Service. The size and language of that appropriation is again a matter of vital concern to the Appropriations Committees and to the well-organized agricultural extension interests, whose influence was felt by the administration several years ago when it tried to substitute direct project grants—determined on "merit"—for a small fraction of the formula grants. The goal of the administration was precisely to direct the extension grants toward specific program objectives, and in particular toward the alleviation of rural poverty. This attempt was defeated on grounds that the administration was seeking to seize control of program content.

Because organizations have a political importance in their own right, it has been impossible to make budget decisions solely on the basis of program categories. The allocation of budget resources cannot be decided solely on the basis of how those resources contribute to program objectives. The implicit effect of budgetary decisions on organizations remains an essential element in the decision process.

These same problems occur in almost every civilian agency. I am not simply making the point that consideration of political values must enter into major decisions on program strategy—that fact is too obvious to need comment. What is significant here is that even at the lowest level of detail, decisions about the effectiveness and efficiency of programs impinge upon the political values—and indeed the very future—of particular groups in society. This aspect of PPB is much more pervasive in most civilian agencies than in the Department of Defense. This is exemplified by the broad general structure of the Department of Defense appropriations compared to the detailed structure of appropriations for the Department of Health, Education, and Welfare.

As a consequence of this fact, PPB has not been characterized by the making of program decisions that are mechanically translated into appropriation requests. Rather, the installation of PPB has led to a parallel and interacting process under which decisions have been based on a joint consideration of program structure and appropriation structure. This should not be considered a downgrading of PPB. It simply reflects that PPB and all it entails can be an important part, but not the whole, of the decision process, no matter what level of detail is being examined.

The Program Memorandum · While the program and financial plan is a tabular record of cost and output consequences of proposed budgetary decisions, the program memorandum provides the strategic and analytical justification for these decisions. Each major program is covered by a program memorandum. Ideally, it summarizes the analytic basis for important policy and budget choices. Since every program area encompasses a multitude of individual program elements, each of which requires some budgetary decisions, the program memorandum is designed to cover only the major issues. Indeed, the number of major issues requiring analysis far exceeds the capacity of existing staffs. In areas where no analytical work has been done, the program memorandum simply identifies major decision proposals and provides a statement of why particular choices are recommended. Thus, the PPB system tries from the start to force an *explicit* statement of broad program strategy as the basis for detailed budget decisions, even where limitations on staff resources make detailed analysis impossible. This is part of the constant attempt to integrate broad policy and program decisions into the budgetary process rather than having the two proceed on separate tracks, with a forced reconciliation at the end.

Special Issues · The program memorandum, to be a useful tool of decision making, cannot incorporate the in-depth analytical studies of program issues, but can only summarize the basic program strategy, and, where relevant, the analysis on which it is based. Each year the Bureau of the Budget and the individual federal agencies jointly agree on a number of program issues for which detailed analytic studies are to be carried out. The results of these studies are themselves the subject of discussion and debate, and form the basis for program memoranda. Often these studies relate to issues that cut across many program categories—federal policy in distributing research grants among various kinds of institutions, the role of federal hospitals in improving hospital design and management, criteria for setting user charges in federal recreation areas, and so forth.

MISCONCEPTIONS ABOUT PPB

Several misconceptions surround PPB and its objectives. To many people, the use of program or output-oriented categories in the budgetary process is the chief element and distinguishing characteristic of PPB. The program grouping of budgetary data is indeed, a most important aid in the analytic decision-making process, since program budgets, when properly conceived, almost force the decision maker to think in output terms. But other elements of PPB are equally, if not more, important.

Another misconception is that there is a single "ideal" program structure. Program structures are not immutable and should be changed as circumstances change. Moreover, for the analysis of certain problems several crosscutting sets of program categories are needed. A program structure that provides across-the-board information on federal support for basic research, or on all federal funds flowing to universities, is quite useful for some purposes. But the components of these programs are also included in the mission-oriented programs of different agencies.

For some purposes veterans' housing programs are viewed as veterans' benefits; for others this program must be combined with other housing programs. Program structures, therefore, need be neither unidimensional nor immutable. While the program structure is an important part of PPB, it is by no means the be-all and end-all of the system.

One of the most important aspects of the whole PPB system— and the one that still causes a good deal of trouble—is its relationship to the annual budget cycle within the executive. Budgetary decisions are crowded into the months of October through December. There is literally no time for extended analysis of program proposals. More important, the detailed preparation of budget requests in the thousands of bureaus, offices, and field establishments of the federal government must begin much earlier than the October-December period. Analytic studies, initial drafts of program memoranda, and basic outlines of proposed financial plans should be available by midsummer if they are to have a meaningful impact on subsequent budget formulation. Ideally, a series of major decisions would be ready in midsummer, on the basis of which detailed budgetary requests could be written. Realistically, this is impossible. No President, budget director, or agency head is likely to make decisions about the size of the poverty budget, the new housing program, or the pace of the postlunar landing effort until the overall size of the budget and the expected shape of future economic conditions are known. This information is not available in midsummer. But the availability of the results of special studies and of draft program memoranda earlier in the budget cycle are critical to the success of the system. These documents, even in draft form, can be a vehicle for isolating differences in major issues, for discovering what additional information is required, and, most important, for putting the agency head's perspective on the detailed budget requests that his subordinates send to him. For numerous reasons, however, a proper time cycle has not yet been established. In too many cases, program memoranda and special studies are available only *after* the subordinate units of the agency have submitted their budget requests to the secretary. As a consequence, they often come too late to have any impact on those requests and lose some of their effectiveness as a vehicle for critical discussion of alternative courses of action and for decisions on overall program strategy.

This, then, is the basic nature of the planning, programming, and budgeting system as it is being developed and applied in the civilian agencies of the federal government. In one sense, it is a systematic organization of the third step in the budgetary reform which began more than fifty years ago: financial control, managerial efficiency, and, now, strategic planning. But its basic aims are substantially different from those of the preceding steps. It brings both the budgetary process and the analytic problem-solving approach into the specification of objectives and the selection of alternatives among programs, and these are the very essence of the political process. Although PPB does not seek to replace the political decision-making process, it will—if successful—modify that process. And, equally, it must adapt itself to the essentially political nature of program decision making.

Cost-Benefit Analysis

ROLAND N. MCKEAN

*This selection by Roland N. McKean of the
University of California (Los Angeles) appears in his book* Public Spending, *published
in 1968.*

"Cost-benefit analyses" are attempts to estimate certain costs
and gains that would result from alternative courses of action.
For different applications, other names are often used: "cost-
effectiveness analysis" when courses of action in defense planning
are compared; "systems analysis" when the alternatives are relatively complex collections of interrelated parts; "operations research" when the alternatives are modes of operation with more
or less given equipment and resources; or "economic analysis"
when the alternatives are rival price-support or other economic
policies. The term "cost-benefit analysis" was originally associated with natural-resource projects but has gradually come to be
used for numerous other applications. The basic idea is not new:
individuals have presumably been weighing the pros and cons
of alternative actions ever since man appeared on earth; and in
the early part of the nineteenth century, Albert Gallatin and
others put together remarkably sophisticated studies of proposed
U.S. government canals and turnpikes. But techniques have improved, and interest has been growing. All these studies might
well be called economic analyses. This does not mean that the
economist's skills are the only ones needed in making such
analyses or, indeed, that economists are very good at making

them. It merely means that this analytical tool is aimed at helping decision makers—consumers, businessmen, or government
officials—economize.

In recent years, the Bureau of the Budget, the National Bureau
of Standards, many other U.S. agencies, and governments and
agencies in other nations have been exploring possible uses of
cost-benefit analysis. Sometimes the analyses are essentially
simple arithmetic. Sometimes high-speed computers are used—
as they were, for instance, in the search by a Harvard group for
the best way to use water in the Indus River basin in Pakistan.
One of the major applications of cost-benefit analysis will continue to be the comparison of alternative natural-resources policies—proposals to reduce air and water pollution, to divert water
from the Yukon to regions further south, to do something about
the rapidly declining water level in the Great Lakes, and so on.
But other applications are appearing with growing frequency—
comparisons of such things as alternative health measures, personnel policies, airport facilities, education practices, transportation systems, choices about the management of governmental
properties, and antipoverty proposals.

All such analyses involve working with certain common elements: (1) objectives, or the beneficial things to be achieved;
(2) alternatives, or the possible systems or arrangements for
achieving the objectives; (3) costs, or the benefits that have to
be foregone if one of the alternatives is adopted; (4) models, or
the sets of relationships that help one trace out the impacts of
each alternative on achievements (in other words, on benefits)
and costs; and (5) a criterion, involving both costs and benefits,
to identify the preferred alternative. In connection with each
of these elements there are major difficulties. Consider a personal problem of choice that an individual might try to analyze—
selecting the best arrangements for his family's transportation.
Spelling out the relevant objectives, that is, the kind of achievements that would yield significant benefits, is no simple task. The
objectives may include commuting to work, getting the children
to school, travel in connection with shopping, cross-country trips,
and so on. Part of this travel may be across deserts, along
mountain roads, in rainy or icy or foggy conditions. The family
may attach a high value to the prestige of traveling in style (or

of being austere, or of simply being different from most other people). Another objective that is neglected all too often is a hard-to-specify degree of flexibility to deal with uncertainties. Adaptability and flexibility are particularly important objectives if one is examining alternative educational programs, exploratory research projects, or R&D policies. Overlooking any of the relevant objectives could lead to poor choices.

The second element, the alternative ways of achieving the benefits, also deserves careful thought, for selecting the best of an unnecessarily bad lot is a poor procedure. In choosing a family's transportation system, the alternatives might include various combinations of a compact automobile, a luxury automobile, a pickup truck, a jeep, a motor scooter, an airplane, a bicycle, the use of a bus system, and the use of taxicabs.

In many problems of choice, the alternatives are called "systems," and the analyses are called "systems analyses." This terminology is quite appropriate, because the word "system" means a set of interrelated parts, and the alternative ways of achieving objectives usually are sets of interrelated parts. At the same time, the word "system" is so general that this usage is often confusing. In defense planning, for example, the term "system" can be used to refer to such sets of interrelated parts as the following:

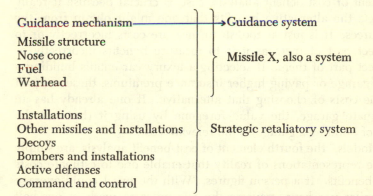

All three of these systems are collections of interrelated parts. How large should systems be for their comparison to be called a "systems analysis" or for their comparison to be a useful aid?

There are no correct answers; one must exercise judgment in deciding how large the systems should be to provide worthwhile assistance in tracing out the costs and benefits. (In effect, one must weigh the costs against the benefits of preparing alternative cost-benefit analyses.) Where interrelationships are relatively important, one is usually driven to consider large systems. Thus to choose between two engines for a supersonic airliner, one can hardly compare thrusts alone and make an intelligent selection, for weight, reliability, cost, noise, etc., may have diverse effects on overall desirability. The power plants must be fitted (at least on paper) into rival aircraft designs, and thence into airline and airport systems to see their net impact on the real objectives and the full costs. Moreover, other components of the projected systems may have to be modified so as not to use either engine stupidly. Suppose one engine would make possible the use of relatively short runways. To use an aircraft with this power plant in an intelligent way, one might have to modify many parts of the proposed airports, traffic patterns, ground installations for instrument-landing systems, and even proposed airline schedules. Hence one would end up comparing rather broad systems having many common components but also having several components that differed.

So much for the alternative systems to be compared. The third element of cost-benefit analysis, cost, is crucial because it really reflects the alternative benefits that one might obtain from the resources. It is just as foolish to measure costs incorrectly or to neglect part of them as it is to measure benefits incorrectly or neglect part of them. If selecting a luxury car entails building a new garage or paying higher insurance premiums, these are part of the costs of choosing that alternative. If one already has an adequate garage, the value foregone by using it (but *not* the cost of building a garage) is the relevant cost.

"Models," the fourth element of cost-benefit analysis, are simply crude representations of reality that enable one to estimate costs and benefits. If a person figures, "With the bus I could average ten miles per hour, traverse the five miles to work in one-half hour, spend five hours per week commuting to work, and would stand up 50 percent of the distance on 50 percent of the trips," he is using a model. If he says, "With Automobile X, I would get a motor tune-up every 5,000 miles and would therefore spend $50 per year on that item," he visualizes these events and uses a set of relationships, that is, a model, to estimate this cost. When one tries to perceive how something would work, it has become convenient and fashionable to say, "Let's build a model," though one could simply say, "Let's devise a way to predict what would happen (or a new way to estimate costs and benefits)."

The fifth element of cost-benefit analysis is the criterion or test of preferredness by means of which one points to the best choice. People tend to make a variety of criterion errors. One error, the use of the ratio of benefits to costs, is such a perennial favorite that it merits a brief discussion. Suppose at first that both benefits and costs can be measured *fully and correctly* in monetary terms and that one must choose among the following three discrete (and not mutually exclusive) alternatives:

	A	B	C
Cost	$100	$100	$200
Benefit one year later	$150	$105	$220
Ratio of benefits to costs	1.5	1.05	1.10

Suppose further that the constraint is that funds can be borrowed at 6 percent. Which projects should be undertaken, and what is the criterion? A and C, both of which yield more than 6 percent, should be undertaken, and the proper criterion is to maximize the present value of net worth or, its surrogate, to undertake projects wherever the marginal benefit exceeds the marginal cost. Note that the criterion is *not* to maximize the ratio of benefits to costs, which would restrict one to Project A. If the constraint is a fixed budget of $200, Projects A and B should be selected. Again, maximizing the ratio of benefits to costs would limit one to Project A.

Or consider two discrete and mutually exclusive alternatives (for example, two sizes of a dam):

	A	B
Cost	$100	$200
Benefit one year later	$150	$260
Ratio of benefits to costs	1.50	1.30

If funds can be borrowed at 6 percent, Project B should be undertaken. One should not choose A simply because the benefit-cost ratio is larger. Ratios are not irrelevant—every marginal productivity is a ratio—for one often seeks to *equalize* certain ratios as a condition for achieving a desired maximum. But the ratio itself is not the thing to be maximized.

The issue takes on a good deal of importance when the benefits can only be suggested by physical products or capabilities. In these circumstances, presumably in desperation, people frequently adopt as a criterion the maximization of some such ratio as satellite payload per dollar, hours of student instruction per dollar, or target-destruction capability per dollar. But the benefit-cost ratios of rival proposals simply cover up the relevant information. Take another example from the choices that confront the individual. If one is selecting a hose with which to sprinkle his lawn, one may have the following options:

	⅝-IN DIAMETER	1-IN. DIAMETER
Cost	$3	$5
Benefit (water put on lawn per hour)	108 gallons	150 gallons
Ratio of benefits to costs	36/1	30/1

The ratios are irrelevant. The pertinent question is whether or not the extra capability is worth the extra $2. Less misleading than showing the ratio would be showing the physical capabilities and the costs à la consumers' research. Or, where it makes sense to do so, one can adjust the scale of the alternatives so that each costs the same or achieves the same objectives. Then one can see which system achieves a specified objective at minimum cost, or achieves the greatest benefit for a specified budget. This is not a perfect criterion, for someone has to decide if the specified budget (or objective) is appropriate. But at least this sort of test is less misleading than a benefit-cost ratio.

With regard to this fifth element of cost-benefit analysis, discussing the correct way to design criteria may seem like discussing the correct way to find the Holy Grail. In a world of uncertainty and individual utility functions, judgments must help shape choices, and no operational test of preferredness can be above suspicion. Moreover, analyses vary in their quality, which is hard to appraise, and in their applicability to different decisions. For these reasons, responsible decision makers must treat cost-benefit analyses as "consumers' research" and introduce heroic judgments in reaching final decisions. In a sense, then, it may be both presumptuous and erroneous to discuss having a test of preferredness in these quantitative analyses.

Criteria should be considered, nonetheless, in connection with such analysis. First, cost-benefit analysts do apply criteria, especially in designing and redesigning the alternatives to be compared. They delete features that appear to be inefficient, add features that appear to be improvements, and probe for alternative combinations that are worth considering. This screening of possibilities and redesign of alternative systems entails the use of criteria, and these should be explicitly considered and exhibited. Second, whether or not they ought to, analysts often present the final comparisons in terms of a criterion. Thus while it may be wrong to talk as if a definitive criterion is an element of every analysis, these warnings about criterion selection should be emphasized.

Needless to say, in reaching decisions, one should attempt to take into account *all* gains and *all* costs. Some people feel that there are two types of gain or cost, economic and noneconomic, and that economic analysis has nothing to do with the latter. This distinction is neither very sound nor very useful. People pay for—that is, they value—music as well as food, beauty or quiet as well as aluminum pans, a lower probability of death as well as garbage disposal. The significant categories are not economic and noneconomic items but (1) gains and costs that can be measured in monetary units (for example, the use of items like typewriters that have market prices reflecting the marginal evaluations of all users); (2) other commensurable effects (impacts of higher teacher salaries, on the one hand, and of teaching machines, on the other hand, on students' test scores); (3) incommensurable effects that can be quantified but not in terms of a common denominator (capability of improving science test scores and capability of reducing the incidence of ulcers among students); and (4) nonquantifiable effects. Examples of the last category are impacts of alternative policies on the morale and happiness of students, on the probability of racial conflicts, and on the probability of protecting individual rights. In taking a position on an issue, each of us implicitly quantifies such considerations. But there is no way to make quantifications that would necessarily be valid for other persons. This sort of distinction between types of effects does serve a useful purpose, especially in warning us of the limitations of cost-benefit analysis.

One should recognize, too, that cost-benefit analysis necessarily involves groping and the making of subjective judgments, not just briskly proceeding with dispassionate scientific measurements. Consider the preparation of such analyses to aid educational choices. No one says, "This is the educational objective, and here are the three alternative systems to be compared. Now trace out the impacts of each on cost and on achievement of the objective, and indicate the preferred system." What happens is that those making the analysis spend much time groping for an *operational* statement of the objective, such as a designated improvement in specific test scores without an increase in the number of dropouts or nervous breakdowns. A first attempt is made at designing the alternative ways of realizing this objective. Preliminary costs are estimated. Members of the research team perceive that the systems have differential impacts on other objectives, such as flexibility, or student performance on tests two years later, or student interest in literature. Or the rival arrangements may elicit different reactions from teachers, parents, and school boards, affecting the achievement of other objectives. The analysts redesign the alternatives in the light of these impacts, perhaps so that each alternative performs at least "acceptably" with respect to each objective. Next it appears that certain additional features such as extra English-composition courses might add greatly to capability but not much to cost. Or the research team's cost group reports that certain facilities are extremely expensive and that eliminating them might reduce costs greatly with little impairment of effectiveness. In both cases the systems have to be modified again. This cut-and-try procedure is essential. Indeed, this process of redesigning the alternatives is probably a more important contribution than the final cost-effectiveness exhibits. In any event, the preparation of such an analysis is a process of probing—and not at all a methodical scientific comparison following prescribed procedures.

An appreciation of cost-benefit analysis also requires an awareness that incommensurables and uncertainties are pervasive. Consider the impacts of alternative educational policies that were mentioned above. These effects can perhaps be described, but not expressed in terms of a common denominator. Judgments about the extent of these effects and their worth have to be made. Some costs, such as the monetary measures of foregone benefits, perhaps additional sacrifices in terms of personality adjustment and ultimate effectiveness, or undesirable political repercussions that yield costs, cannot validly be put in terms of a common denominator. Furthermore, because of uncertainties, whatever estimates can be prepared should in principle be probability distributions rather than unique figures for costs and gains. The system that performs best in one contingency may perform worst in another contingency. Finally, costs and gains occur over a period of time, not at a single point in time, and there is no fully acceptable means of handling these streams of costs and gains in analyzing many options.

These difficulties are present because life is complex, and there is no unique correct choice. The difficulties are not created by cost-benefit analysis. Moreover, they do not render quantitative economic analysis useless. They simply mean that one has to be discriminating about when and how to use various tools. In general, the broader choices made by higher-level officials pose relatively great difficulties regarding what value judgments to make and what the physical and social consequences of alternative actions would be. Consider, for example, the allocation of the U.S. budget among various departments or the allocation of funds among such functions as the improvement of health, education, or postal service. Cost-benefit analysis gives relatively little guidance in making these choices, for in the end the decision maker's task is dominated by difficult personal judgments. Cost-benefit analysis may help somewhat, for it is the appropriate framework in terms of which to *think* about these broad choices, and it can usually provide *some* improved information. When personal judgments must play such a huge role, however, the improved information may not be worth much.

Consider another example of such broad choices: the government's allocation of its R&D effort between basic research and applied development. To choose between these two alternatives, officials must rely heavily on personal judgments about the consequences and judgments concerning the value of those consequences. Values cannot be taken as agreed upon, and physical-sociological effects cannot be predicted with confidence. Quantitative analysis can probably contribute only a little toward the sharpening of intuition here. Or consider the allocation of effort between improving medical care for the aged and improving it for the young. Suppose one could make extremely good predictions of the effects, which would of course aid decision makers. The final choice would be dominated in this instance by value judgments about the worth of prolonging the lives of elderly persons, the worth of lengthening the lives of persons in great pain, the worth of saving the lives of weakened or physically handicapped children, the relief of different kinds of distress, and so on.

Another broad or high-level choice that brings out these difficulties is the allocation of funds to, or for that matter within, the State Department. In the tasks of diplomacy it is hard to visualize taking a set of value tags as being clearly stated, let alone agreed upon. And disagreement is quite understandable in predicting the effects of alternative courses of action on the probabilities of stable alliances, provocations, little wars, nuclear wars, and so on. Positive science has provided few tested hypotheses about these relationships.

As one proceeds to narrower or lower-level problems of choice, these difficulties frequently, though not always, become less severe. (Actual decisions, of course, vary continuously in the extent to which they present these difficulties, but it is often economical to think in terms of such categories as broad and narrow or high-level and low-level choices). Within such tasks as education and health improvement, there are lower-level choices for which quantitative analysis may be very helpful, but there are also many middle-level choices that are fraught with difficulties. Should more effort be placed on the improvement of mental health even if it means less emphasis on the treatment of conventional ailments? Should effort be reallocated from higher education toward the improvement of elementary-school training, or vice versa? Or, as an alternative policy, should government leave such allocative decisions more than at present to the unin-fluenced choices of individuals families? Cost-benefit analysis cannot do much to resolve the uncertainties about the conse-quences of such decisions, about their relative worths to indi-vidual citizens, or about whose value judgments should be given what weights.

Within applied research and development, a choice between specific projects might appear to be a low-level choice that eco-nomic analysis could greatly assist. In such instances, it is true that values can sometimes be taken as agreed upon. In selecting research and development projects for new fuels, for instance, the values to be attached to various outcomes are not obvious, yet they are probably not major sources of divergent views. Perhaps the principal difficulty is the inability to predict the physical consequences, including "side effects," of alternative proposals. Here too, cost-benefit analysis may be destined to play a comparatively small role.

One can list many problems of choice that seem to fall some-where in this middle ground—that is, where cost-benefit analysis can be helpful but not enormously so. It would appear, for instance, that the selection of antipoverty and welfare programs depends heavily on consequences that one cannot predict with confidence and on value judgments about which there is much disagreement. Similar statements apply also to the selection of foreign-aid programs, urban-development proposals, or law-enforcement programs—the comparison of different methods of curbing the use of narcotics, say, or of different penal institutions and procedures. In education, many decisions that may appear to be low-level or relatively simple—for example, the selection among alternative curricula or teaching methods or disciplinary rules—are inevitably dominated by judgments about the conse-quences of these policies and about the value tags to be attached to those consequences.

It is in connection with comparatively narrow problems of choice that cost-benefit analysis can sometimes play a more significant role. In these instances, as might be expected, the alternatives are usually rather close substitutes. Science can often predict the consequences of govenmental natural-resource investments or choices affecting the utilization of water or land, and people can often agree on the values at stake—at least to a sufficient extent to render analyses highly useful. Competing irrigation plans, flood-control projects, swamp drainage and land reclamation ventures, and water-pollution control measures are examples of narrow problems of choice in which cost-benefit analysis can help.

Cost-benefit analysis also promises to be helpful in comparing certain transportation arrangements. The interdependencies of transportation networks with other aspects of life are formidable, yet with ingenuity extremely useful studies of some transportation alternatives can be produced. Numerous transportation alternatives have been the subject of such studies: highways, urban systems, inland waterways, modified railway networks, the utilization of a given amount of sea transport, air transport fleets, and of course many lower-level choices, such as alternative road materials, construction practices, airport facilities, and loading arrangements. In some instances, of course, the interdependencies may be too complex for analyses to be very valuable; transportation alternatives that affect a large region and its development yield chains of consequences that are extremely difficult to trace out.

At best, the difficulties of providing *valuable* information are awesome. There can always be legitimate disagreement about any of these policy decisions, and analyses must be regarded as inputs to decisions, not as oracular touchstones. Nonetheless, to think systematically about the costs and gains from alternative policies is surely more sensible than to rely on haphazard thought or intuition. Such analyses can bring out the areas of disagreement so that people can see where their differences lie. Even with considerable divergence in judgments, they can screen out the absurdly inferior alternatives, focusing the debate on subsets of relatively good alternatives. For some choices, cost-benefit analysis provides information that can help officials agree upon a course of action that is preferred or accepted by most citizens. And for all choices, it is the right framework to use in organizing the evidence and one's thoughts and intuitions regarding alternatives. Even in deciding which research project to undertake, or how much time to spend on it, a researcher consults rough cost-benefit T-accounts. In deciding anything, a person should weigh costs and gains. Preliminary weighing may suggest that the use of a tentative rule of thumb or "requirement" is preferable to further or repeated analyses, but he should not initially pull some mythical requirement out of the air.

Applications of Cost-Benefit Analysis

ALAN R. PREST AND RALPH TURVEY

Alan R. Prest and Ralph Turvey are well-known British economists. This piece is from their article in the Economic Journal, *1965.*

We [present here] illustrations of the ways in which the principles previously set out have been employed in cost-benefit studies. We shall first look at some water projects and then turn to transport—these being the two areas where cost-benefit studies have been common. Subsequently, we shall survey the application and applicability of these techniques in land-usage schemes (urban renewal, recreation, and land reclamation), health, education, research and development, and defense. Throughout, we shall be illustrative rather than comprehensive—both in the sense that we are concerned only with the main features of, say, irrigation schemes rather than detailed case studies, and in that we shall emphasize the differences in treatment rather than the similarities. This means that we examine general techniques for enumerating and evaluating costs and benefits rather than "standard" items, such as the choice of appropriate discount rates, the exclusion of superogatory secondary benefits, etc. We are not reproducing any examples in full detail, but good ones can be found in Krutilla and Eckstein on water-resource projects, Foster and Beesley on transport, and Borus on labor retraining.

1. WATER PROJECTS

Water projects take many different forms. They may differ enormously in respect of their engineering characteristics, *e.g.*, an estuarine barrage or a dam in the hills. Similarly, the purposes of water investment are many—provision of more water for an industrial area, provision of irrigation water, prevention of flood damage, and so on. In some cases there may be only one such purpose in a particular scheme; in others it may be a case of multi-purpose development. The details of cost-benefit analysis inevitably differ from project to project, and we can only cover a sample. We shall look at irrigation, flood control, and hydroelectric schemes in turn, and in this way hope to catch the smell even if not the flavor of the ingredients. Finally, we shall have a few words to add on the particular characteristics of multi-purpose schemes.

(a) *Irrigation* · Since it is seldom possible to ascertain directly the price at which water could be sold upon the completion of a proposed irrigation project, and since this price would in any case give no indication of consumers' surplus, the *direct* benefits of a project have to be estimated by:

  (i) forecasting the change in the output of each agricultural project, leaving out those outputs which, like the cattle feed, are also inputs;
  (ii) valuing and summing these changes;
  (iii) deducting the opportunity cost of the change in all farming inputs other than the irrigation water;

in order to get, as a result, the value of the net change in agricultural output consequent upon the irrigation of the area.

We now discuss each step in turn.

(i) Forecasts of additional output, whether sold in the market or consumed on the farm, can be made in countries with well-developed agricultural advisory services. But this is only the beginning of the story. Even if there were no delay in the response of farmers to new conditions, it will often be the case that the full effects of irrigation will take some years to be felt. Since, in addition, farmers will take time to adapt, it is clear that what is required here is not just a simple list of outputs but a schedule showing the development of production over time. Yet this is too complicated in practice, and usually the best that can be done is to make estimates for one or two benchmark dates and extrapolate or, alternatively, postulate a discrete lag in the response of farmers.

The forecast is difficult as well as complicated (in principle), because it is the behavior of a group of people that is involved, behavior which may depend upon peasant conservatism, superstition, political tensions, and so on, just as much or more than it depends upon any nice agronomic calculus. Thus, an Indian study (Sovani and Rath) reports that the peasants in an area irrigated by the Hirakud dam erroneously believed that planting a second crop on the valley-bottom land would lead to to waterlogging and salinization. The authors explicitly assumed that in the first ten years after irrigation began the area would settle down to irrigated agriculture with the least possible change in techniques and capital investment.

The probability that farmers will not follow an income-maximizing course of action is one reason why a farm-management or programming approach may be of little use—except in setting an outside limit to outputs. Another is that the requisite information may be lacking. Thus, it is frequently necessary either to substitute or supplement the projections based upon the assumption of maximizing behavior with projections based upon the assumption that behavior of other farmers elsewhere constitutes a useful precedent. The effect of irrigation in A is then forecast by comparing an irrigated area B either with B before irrigation or with an unirrigated area, C. There is obviously scope for judgment (and bias) here.

(ii) The amount the farmer gets for his crops may differ markedly from their value to the community where agriculture is protected or subsidized, as in the United States or the United Kingdom (Eckstein, Renshaw). In fact, some United States calculations have allowed for this by making an arbitrary 20-percent deduction in the prices of major commodities in surplus or receiving federal support. This is one example of the point that when the conditions for optimal resource allocation are not fulfilled in the rest of the economy market prices may prove a poor guide to project costs and benefits. Another general problem on which we have already touched arises when the increment in the output of any crop is large enough to affect its price, so that there is no unique price for valuation purposes. There is the further point that output should be valued at a given price-level, consistent with the valuations of other benefits and of costs, but that future changes in price relativities need to be taken into account. Thus, price projections are required, and once again there is scope for judgment, as anything from simple extrapolation to highly sophisticated supply and demand studies may be utilized. Finally, there is the old problem, much aired in social accounting literature (*e.g.*, Prest and Stewart) about the appropriate valuation of subsistence output.

(ii) The principles for valuing farm inputs are the same as those for valuing outputs, while the forecast of input quantities is clearly related to the forecast of output quantities. In an elaborate income-maximizing analysis inputs and outputs would be simultaneously determined, while in a simpler approach inputs per acre of irrigated land or per unit of output will be taken as being the same as on comparable irrigated land elsewhere. In either case, costs include the opportunity earnings, if any, of any additional farmers who come to work in the irrigated area.

The *secondary* benefits which have sometimes been regarded as appropriately included in irrigation benefit calculations reflect the impact of the project on the rest of the economy, both via its increased sales to farmers and via its increased purchases from them. We have already discussed the appropriateness of including these benefits. More important is the technological interdependence which is likely to be found in many irrigation schemes, such as when the effects on the height of the water-table in one area spill over to another district.

Any irrigation project will have a number of *minor* effects not obviously covered in the categories so far discussed. As these will vary from case to case, and no general list is possible, some examples may be of use. They are taken from an *ex-post* study of the Sarda Canal in India:

> Canal water is also used for washing, bathing, watering cattle. Silt is deposited at the outlet heads, which necessitates constant and laborious cleaning of the channels.

Some plots of land have been made untillable by unwanted water.

The canal divides the area (and sometimes individual fields) into two parts, but has few bridges, so that much time is wasted in circumnavigating it.

Many such effects will be unquantifiable, but must nevertheless be remembered in any analysis.

(b) *Flood Control* · Ever since the River and Harbor Act of 1927 the United States Army Corps of Engineers has had the responsibility of preparing plans for improving major rivers for flood control purposes—as well as irrigation, hydro-electric power and navigation. On the flood control side, the major benefits which have been categorized in this—and other—work have been the losses averted. Losses of this sort can refer to different types of assets—property, furnishings, crops, etc.; or to different types of owners—individuals, business firms, government, and so on. In all these cases the general principle is to estimate the mathematical expectation of annual damage (on the basis of the likely frequency of flood levels of different heights) and then regard such sums as the maximum annual amounts people would be willing to pay for flood control measures.

Other benefits which must be taken into account are as follows:

(i) Avoidance of deaths by drowning. We shall deal with the general principles relevant in such cases in connection with health improvements.

(ii) Avoidance of temporary costs, *e.g.*, evacuation of flood victims, emergency sand-bag work, etc., risks of sanitation breakdowns, epidemics, etc.

(iii) Possibilities of putting flood land to higher uses if the risk of inundation is eliminated.

The costs involved in flood control calculations are relatively straightforward. Obviously, the initial costs of the flood-control works and their repair and maintenance charges must be included. The most difficult point in any such compilation is likely to be the cost of land acquisition for reservoirs, etc. In the absence of anything remotely approaching a free land market in a country such as the United Kingdom there is bound to be an arbitrary element in such items.

There are some obvious reasons why private investment principles are insufficient in the case of flood-control measures. Protection for one inhabitant in a district implies protection for another, and so one immediately runs into the collective goods problem; protection for one district may worsen flood threats to another, and so this inevitably brings up technological externalities; finally, flood works often have to be on a large scale and of a complex nature, and so this brings up non-marginal and imperfect competition problems. So one simply has to try to estimate willingness to pay for flood protection by the roundabout devices described above. There is no simple-cut appeal to market principles.

(c) *Hydro-electric Power Schemes* · The standard way of measuring the value of the extra electricity generated by a public hydro-electric scheme is to estimate the savings realized by not having to buy from an alternative source. This sounds simple, but in fact raises all sorts of complicated issues: we shall look at these by, first, considering the simple alternative of a single hydro-electric source versus a single private steam plant, and secondly, by considering the implications of adding another source to a whole supply system.

In the first case the general point is to say that benefits can be measured by the costs of the most economical private alternative. As Eckstein shows at some length, this raises a number of issues, *e.g.*, a private sector station will not be working under competitive conditions, and so its charges may not coincide with opportunity costs; private sector charges will not be directly relevant to public sector circumstances in that they will reflect taxes, private sector interest rates, etc.; as we need the pattern of future, as well as current, benefits, we have to allow for the effects of future technological changes in reducing alternative costs, and hence benefits, through time. A further point arises when a new hydro-electric station provides a proportionately large net addition to the supply in a region. In this case the alternative-cost principle would produce an over-estimate of benefits, and we are forced back to a measure of what the extra output would sell for plus the increased consumers' surplus of its purchasers. Presumably a survey of the potential market for the power will provide some of the needed information, but the difficulties of making reliable estimates are clearly enormous.

We now turn to the case where a new hydro-electric station has to be fitted into a whole system.

The amount of power produced by a new hydro-electric station and the times of year at which it will be produced depend not only upon the physical characteristics of the river providing the power but also upon the cost characteristics of the whole electricity supply system and upon the behavior of the electricity consumers. The supply system constitutes a unity which is operated so as to minimize the operating costs of meeting consumption whatever its time pattern happens to be. Hence the way in which the hydro-electric station is operated may be affected by alterations in the peakiness of consumption, the bringing into service of new thermal stations, and so on.

If we now try to apply the principle of measuring benefits by the cost savings of not building an alternative station it follows from the system interdependence just described that the only meaningful way of measuring this cost saving is to ascertain the difference in the present value of total system operating costs in the two cases and deduct the capital cost of the alternatives. A simple comparison of the two capital costs and the two running costs, that is to say, will only give the right answer if the level and time pattern of the output of each would be exactly the same. In general, therefore, a very complicated exercise involving the simulation of the operation of the whole system is required (Turvey), as, for that matter, may be the case for other water-resource analysis (Maass).

Finally, there is another point, emphasized by Krutilla and Eckstein. Even if two or more hydro-electric stations are not linked in the same distribution and consumption network, there may be production interdependence. The clearest example is that when upstream stations in a river basin have reservoirs for water storage, this is highly likely to affect water flows downstream, and hence the generating pattern of stations in that area. If technological interdependence of this type is not internalized by having both types of station under the same authority it will be necessary to have some system of compensatory arrangement if we want to cut down resource misallocation.

(d) *Multi-purpose Schemes* · In practice, many river developments have a number of purposes in mind—not only those we have dealt with above but also transport improvements, etc., as well. Obviously, the range of choice now becomes much wider. Not only does one have to look at the cost-benefit data for, say, different sized hydro-electric stations, but one also has to take different combinations of, say, irrigation and navigation improvements. The calculations will also be more complicated, in that the possibilities of interdependence are clearly multiplied, and so the warnings we have already uttered about the feasibility of some calculations will be even more applicable. We shall have no more to say at this stage on multi-stage projects, but simply make the final point that these reflections are highly apposite in the case of projects such as the Morecambe Bay and Solway Firth barrage schemes (providing for industrial and domestic water supplies, transport improvements, land reclamation, improved recreation facilities, etc.), which are receiving a good deal of attention at the time of writing (in 1965).

2. TRANSPORT PROJECTS

(a) *Roads* · A great deal of work has now accumulated on the principles and methods of application of cost-benefit techniques in this field, ever since the first experiments in the State of Oregon in 1938. We shall illustrate the arguments by references to the work done on the M1 in the United Kingdom (Coburn, Beesley and Reynolds, Reynolds, Foster), this being a typical example of what one finds in this field.

The calculation of net annual savings was classified under four heads: (i) those relating to diverted traffic; (ii) those to generated traffic; (iii) savings in non-business time; and (iv) the effects of the growth of G.N.P. Under (i) (diverted traffic) estimates were made of the likely net savings of the traffic diverted from other routes to the M1, *i.e.*, positive items, such as working time savings of drivers, vehicle-usage economies, gasoline savings, accident reduction, etc., together with negative items in respect of additional mileages traveled on faster roads and maintenance costs of the motorway.

In respect of generated traffic the argument is that the opening of the motorway would in effect reduce the "price" (in terms of congestion and inconvenience of motoring) and enable demand which had hitherto been frustrated to express itself in motorway usage. As it must be assumed that benefits per vehicle-mile to frustrated consumers are of less consequence than those to actual consumers (if not, they would not remain frustrated), they were rated as half as great as the latter in the M1 calculations.

Savings in non-business time were the third main ingredient. This calculation involves many complications, to which we shall return in a moment. The fourth component was the introduction of a trend factor, to allow for the long-term growth of G.N.P. and the effects on the demand for road travel—an obvious ingredient of any calculation, whether relating to private or public investment. The upshot of the combined calculations was that the rate of return was of the order of 10 to 15 percent.

A number of comments can be made on these calculations. First, there are the obvious statistical shortcomings which are recognized by everyone, including the authors. Second, there are a number of minor omissions, such as allowances for police and administrative costs, the benefits accruing to pedestrians and cyclists, etc., the advantages of more reliable goods deliveries (Foster). Thirdly, there are some inconsistencies in these particular calculations, in that on some occasions a long-period view seems to be taken (*e.g.*, when calculating the savings resulting from reductions in road vehicle fleets) and on others a short-period one (*e.g.*, in assessing the benefits of diversion of traffic from the railways). Much more important than these points are the savings due to accident reduction and to economies in travel time, where important logical and practical issues arise. On the first of these, the economic benefits of a fall in the amount of damage to vehicles and to real property, the work done by insurance companies, the work of the police and the courts are simple enough. It is the loss of production due to death or, temporarily, to accident or illness which raises complications. However, these complications are exactly the same as those raised in cost-benefit studies of health programs, and so it will be convenient to leave discussion of this general topic until we reach that heading.

This leaves us with the problem of valuing time savings; as these savings often form a very high proportion of total estimated benefits of road improvements, they are extremely important. Unfortunately, these calculations have not so far been very satisfactory.

Whatever the valuation procedure followed, it is necessary to assume that one time saving of sixty minutes is worth the same as sixty savings each lasting one minute, since estimates of the value of time savings of different lengths are unobtainable. On the one hand, it is clear that some short-time savings are valueless, since nothing can be done in the time saved. On the other hand, however, there are cases where the extra time makes possible some activity which would otherwise be precluded, as, for instance, when arriving a little earlier at a theater means that one does not have to wait until the interval to gain one's seat. Similarly, the value of an hour gained may depend partly upon when it is gained. *Faute de mieux,* such variations have to be ignored and an average treated as meaningful.

It is customary to distinguish between working time saved and leisure time saved, valuing the former at the relevant wage-rate, *e.g.,* drivers' wages in the case of buses and lorries. The argument is simply that this is what the worker's time is worth to his employer. As Winch has pointed out, this raises certain difficulties: if the driver does the same work as before, the gain is a matter of his having more leisure, while if he works the same hours as before and does more work, the value of his marginal net product may fall. The first point matters only if leisure time is valued differently from working time, as Winch points out, but the second is awkward, if only in principle.

The various methods that have been proposed for valuing leisure time all rest upon the observation of choices which involve the substitution of leisure for some other good which, in contrast to leisure, does have a market price. Leisure can be substituted:

(i) for wages, net of tax, by workers;
(ii) for transport expenditure, by those who travel in their own time and are able to choose between alternative speeds of travel either directly (as drivers) or indirectly (*e.g.,* train versus bus);
(iii) for housing and transport expenditure, by people who

can choose the location of their dwelling in relation to that of their place of work, and hence determine the length of the journey to work.

Each of these approaches has its difficulties. One difficulty which is common to all of them is that the substitution rarely involves just leisure and money; for example:

(i)   A man may refuse to work an extra hour for an extra $1, yet value leisure at less than $1 because extra work involves missing a bus.

(ii) The driver who pays a toll alters the running cost he incurs in order to get to his destination faster by using a toll road is buying not only a time-saving but also the pleasure of driving along a restricted access highway. (A separate and trickier problem is that he may not know the true effect of the change in route and speed upon his car's running costs).

(iii) A house nearer work may be in a less or more attractive environment.

These problems are surveyed in Winch; Mohring presents the theory underlying the approach via land values and shows how difficult it is to apply in practice; and Moses and Williamson discuss the related problem of passengers' choice between alternative modes of transport and list American applications of the approach via toll-road utilization. A recent piece of research in the United Kingdom (Beesley) produces valuations of time savings on journeys by public transport on the basis of comparing different combinations of cash and time outlays for given journeys; by substituting this result into the comparison of public and private transport opportunities, an estimate of the valuation of time savings by private transport is obtained. It might be noted that those investigations yield markedly lower estimates than those quoted on previous occasions in the United Kingdom (*e.g.*, Foster and Beesley, *Report of Panel on Road Pricing*). So, at the very least, one can say that there are major unknowns which may or may not prove tractable to further analysis.

So far we have made no mention of the many American studies

of the impact of road improvements on bypassed shopping centers, on the value of adjacent property, and on the pattern of land use. This is because, as Mohring and Harwitz explain, these "studies suffer from either or both of two shortcomings: (1) they have concentrated on measuring benefits to specific population groups, and have done so in such a way that *net* benefits to society as a whole cannot be estimated from their results; and/or (2) they have concentrated on measuring highway-related changes in the nature and locus of economic activity and have not isolated those aspects of change that reflect net benefits."

We have concentrated on the application of cost-benefit analysis to a major motorway construction. The same general principles apply in other types of road investment, ranging from the "simple" kind of case such as the Channel Tunnel or the Forth Bridge to the far more complex network problems such as the whole transport system of a metropolitan area. If one wishes to include the *Buchanan Report* notion of "environment" in the calculus for urban road improvements the estimation process is likely to become very complex and laborious, if indeed it is feasible at all. The Report's own attempt to give an empirical filling to the idea is perfunctory in the extreme, but Beesley and Kain have proposed the principle of "environmental compensation" as an operational way of taking some account of environmental benefits and disbenefits in allocating budgeted expenditure on urban roads.

Finally, one might take note of the work of Bos and Koyck. They construct a complete general equilibrium model of a simple economy with three geographical areas and four goods. This involves a series of demand equations, technical equations, supply equations, and definitional equations. They show that a reduction in transport costs between two of these areas will raise national income by much more than the customary estimate of benefits, *i.e.,* the saving of transport costs of existing traffic between these areas plus half the cost of saving for the generated traffic. The essential point is that there is a much fuller allowance for ramifications, *e.g.,* they not only allow for the effects on goods transported but also on goods not transported. This system, of course, requires knowledge of all the demand and supply equations in the economy, so is scarcely capable of application by road engineers. It does, however, serve to remind us of the limitations of partial analysis.

(b) *Railways* · Railways have received a great deal less attention than roads from cost-benefit analysis, perhaps because they have, relatively if not absolutely, been a contracting sector of the transport industry in many countries. However, there have been two railway projects which have attracted attention in the United Kingdom in the last few years, and brief reference to them may be sufficient to illustrate the general principles.

In their well-known study of the new Victoria underground line in London, Foster and Beesley followed much the same principles as those employed in cost-benefit studies on the roads. The main benefits were time savings, cost savings (*e.g.*, private vehicle operating costs), extra comfort and convenience, and a variety of gains to Central London resulting from an effective widening of the catchment area. These benefits were distributed among the traffic diverted to the Victoria line, the traffic not so diverted and generated traffic. But by and large, gains by generated traffic were unimportant compared with the other two categories; and of the various categories of savings, time savings amounted to almost half the total. When compared with the totality of costs involved in constructing and maintaining the line over a fifty year period it was found that there was a "social surplus rate of return" of something of the order of 11 percent, the precise figure depending on the rate of interest chosen. The reasons why this rate of return is much greater than any financial or accounting return were said to be two-fold: first, that London Transport's policy of averaging fares over different modes of traveling from one place to another meant that potential money receipts would underestimate benefits, and second, that potential revenue was reduced by the fact that road users are not charged the full social cost of the resources they absorb.

Although the proposals in the Beeching Report for closing down sections of the United Kingdom main-line railway system were not couched in cost-benefit terms, various commentators (*e.g.*, Ray and Crum) have looked at these aspects. The financial savings of the measures in view can be classified under four heads:

improved methods of working, increased charges to some particular users (*e.g.*, National Coal Board), the savings from closing commuter lines, and the savings from rural closures. The first of these clearly represents a social as well as a financial saving, and need not detain us further. The second is more debatable; raising charges does not as such save any real resources, but it is possible that it would stimulate some savings of cost, and so to that extent would involve a social gain. In so far as the closure of commuter lines leads to further road congestion in large cities, the social saving is likely to be very small indeed, if anything at all. Finally, the closure of rural lines involves questions such as redundancies of specialist labor in out-of-the-way areas, extra road maintenance, more road accidents, lengthier journeys, etc. We are not concerned with the details of such calculations, but it might be noted that the overall result of Beeching would seem to be a substantial saving in real terms, even if not quite as large as the financial one. This does, however, leave out many intangibles, such as the more indirect and longer-term effects on particular regions, *e.g.*, the North of Scotland; and no one, to our knowledge, has suggested any unique and convincing way of quantifying and incorporating such repercussions in the analysis.

To summarize, the principles developed in the analysis of road improvements can fairly readily be applied to railway investment and in the assessment of the overall consequences of railway closures. As before, time savings are an important item in many cases, and to the extent that we are still very ignorant of how to crack this hardest of nuts, we are still in a position of intellectual discomfort.

(c) *Inland Waterways* · A good deal of work has been done in the United States on the estimation of benefits from new canals or from rendering an existing river channel navigable. It has been discussed especially by Eckstein and Renshaw. This is of interest both for its own sake and for the light it throws on other transport fields.

Let us start with some points first made by Dupuit and raised diagrammatically by Renshaw. Let DD in Figure 1 be the demand curve for transport of a given commodity along a specified route and OF_r be the present rail freight rate. Then F_rR will be the existing volume of traffic. If a canal were built

FIGURE 1

INLAND WATERWAYS

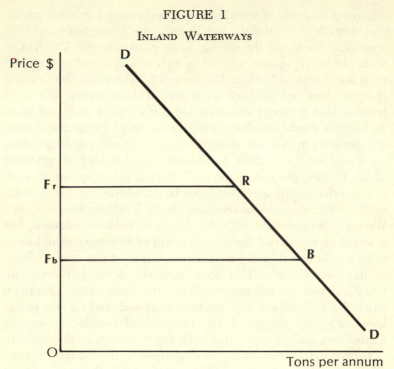

and the barge freight rate were OF_b traffic would expand to F_bB and the gain to shippers would be F_rRBF_b. This can be approximated by multiplying the existing volume of traffic F_rR by the unit freight saving F_rF_b, and this is the procedure followed in practice, *e.g.*, by the United States Corps of Engineers.

We now bring in complications.

1. The gain to shippers will not measure social gain unless freight rates adequately reflect marginal social costs. The main reason why this may not be so is that railways are frequently subject to regulation. Thus, if the freight receipts of the railway from the traffic in question exceed its avoidable costs, part of the gain to shippers is merely a transfer from the railway's owners, and must be deducted to obtain a measure of the social benefit from the canal.

2. The single demand curve of the diagram is a legitimate

construction only when neither canal nor railway are part of a network and only when they both link exactly the same points. If neither of these conditions is fulfilled a more complicated construction is required, since total system rail traffic and total system barge traffic are both functions of both rail and barge freight rates (including shippers' terminal costs). The net gain to shippers who direct traffic from rail to a canal joining points A and B will differ from the simple product of the freight rate differential between A and B and the number of tons of freight diverted to the canal because:

(i) There may be a saving or gain in transport costs beyond A and B. Consider, for example, traffic from A to C; this may previously have gone by rail all the way without going through B.

(ii) There may be a saving or gain in costs other than freight. Thus, if canal is slower than rail more working capital will be required.

(iii) The railway may cut its freight rate in response to competition from the canal, so reducing the amount of traffic diverted. This is discussed by Eckstein with examples.

Taking these three complications into account we find that the social benefit from the canal (gross of its costs) equals:

The saving in railway system costs
Less barge costs
Less increase in shippers' other costs
Plus the value to shippers of generated traffic on the canal.

This amount will be less than the product of the diverted traffic volume and the rail-canal freight rate differential unless the consumers' surplus on generated canal traffic outweighs any excess of railway rates over avoidable costs, any deficit between canal freight rates and barge costs and any increase in shippers' other costs. Thus, except where traffic generation is expected to be large, multiplying the rate differential by traffic diversion may exaggerate benefits.

An example of the application of these techniques in a particular case relates to a cross-Florida barge canal. The following figures were produced:

$000 per annum

Item	Corps of Engineers	Consultants' evaluation
Amortisation, interest, maintenance.......	5,960	8,235
Transportation savings	6,980	1,102
Commercial fishing boats' benefits........	70	0
Contractor's floating equipment benefits....	30	0
New vessel delivery benefits..............	110	0
Recreational boating benefits.............	110	0
Flood control benefits...................	240	0
Enhancement of waterfront land values....	590	0
Benefit-cost ratio	1.20	0.13

To what extent the divergence is due to the facts that the Corps likes to build canals and that the consultants were retained by the railroads, and to what extent it is due to the intrinsic impossibility of making accurate estimates is left entirely to the reader to decide!

3. LAND USAGE

(a) *Urban Renewal* · The application of cost-benefit analysis to proposals for redevelopment projects in towns has been discussed by Rothenberg and by Lichfield, both of whom have provided partial examples. The problem is complicated by the large number of types of people or institutions involved in urban development. Thus, the public acquisition of all private property in a slum area which is then redeveloped may involve more than one public agency, the dispossessed property owners, dispossessed tenants, owners, and tenants of property adjacent to the redevelopment area, owners and tenants in other areas affected by the search for alternative accommodation on the part of the dispossessed tenants, potential developers and tenants of the cleared area, and finally, the population of the town at large, both as taxpayers who meet some of the cost and (more indirectly) in so far as they suffer any adverse consequence from the slum.

Lichfield is primarily concerned to show how all the costs and benefits to all affected parties can be systematically recorded in a set of accounts. The arguments in favor of proceeding this way instead of by simply listing and evaluating the net amount of each type of cost or benefit are threefold. First, starting on an all-inclusive gross basis and then cancelling out to obtain net social benefits and costs insures against omissions. Second, the financial consequences of any project are sometimes important, and it may need to be redesigned in the light of the distribution of benefits and costs so as to compensate parties who would otherwise stand to lose from it, securing their support for it. The notion of compensation is familiar enough in welfare economics; here is a case where it can be important in practice. Third, whether or not financial transfers are used to affect the final distribution of net gains, that distribution will often be relevant to choice. In practice, that is to say, for good or bad reasons, the attitude of a county council or similar body towards a scheme will depend upon who gains as well as upon how much they gain. As the client of the cost-benefit analyst, it will therefore want to know more than just the total net figures.

Rothenberg discusses those types of benefits from urban development projects which involve slum clearance (mentioning other, aesthetic, considerations in a footnote). The first is the "internalization of market externalities," which we discuss in a moment, the second is the effect on real income distribution, and the third consists of the reduction in fire risks, crime, and other social consequences of slum living.

By internalizing market externalities, Rothenberg is thinking of the improvement of efficiency in resource allocation which can be achieved when a neighborhood is regarded as a unit where previously each of the separate owners in it had paid no regard to the adverse effects upon other owners' property of the inadequate maintenance of his own. Leaving aside a property tax complication which arises in the United States, Rothenberg's basic suggestion is that the social gain is measured by the increase in the total site value of the redevelopment area ("the value of the increased productivity of the land on the redevelopment site") corrected for any change in locational advantages brought about by redevelopment plus any increase in the value of properties adjacent to the redevelopment area resulting from its physical improvement (*i.e.*, technological externalities). The nature of the locational advantages is not very clear, and the convenient assumption that the sum of locational effects in the town as a whole is zero requires a good deal of justification.

Another difficulty relates to the increment of site values. The relevance of site values after slum clearance is obvious enough, since these values are the capitalized values of the rents to be had from the new buildings which are most appropriate, less the present value of the costs of erecting and maintaining those buildings. But the relevance of site values in the absence of a redevelopment scheme is not so clear.

A second difficulty with Rothenberg's expositions is that the illustrative example of his technique is an *ex-post* one. This introduces problems which are irrelevant to the *ex-ante* calculations that are required if the technique is ever to be of use. How different an actual past change in land value would have been if things had been different, that is to say, is no concern of the man making forward-looking estimates. His problem is to estimate how much the site would sell for if not only it but also all the surrounding sites were to be redeveloped. The way to answer this question is surely to start with an estimate of the rental or selling value of new accommodation in the improved area and then deduct for building costs. But does this not require the art of the valuer as much as the science of the economist or econometrician?

(b) *Recreation* · The problem of estimating and valuing recreational gains or losses due to projects has received a good deal of attention in the United States, where much of the discussion has been usefully surveyed by Clawson. An example of the problem is provided by the conflict between the provision of hydroelectric power and the preservation of the salmon runs in the Pacific Northwest (though this involves commercial fishing as well as sports fishing), while the gain to pleasure-boating from harbor improvements constitutes another case.

The principle is clear enough: what is needed in any particular case, on the benefit side, is measurement of the demand curve for access to the recreational facility in question. In practice, however, the choice has often lain between getting a figure by the wrong method and not getting one by the right method. Thus,

Crutchfield lists four invalid techniques that have been used in the case of sports fishing.

(a) The argument that recreational facilities should not, in principle, be measured in money terms and that some level of provision should thus be arbitrarily set regardless of competing demands.

(b) Expenditure on providing and using the fishery. This merely measures the size of the sport fishing industry, but provides no indication of the loss that would be sustained if it disappeared.

(c) Imputing to sport fishing the market value of the fish caught, which implies that the angler is simply out to get some food.

(d) Valuing anglers' fishing time at the earnings the anglers could have acquired by working. This implies, among other things, that every hour spent in any kind of recreation is equally valuable.

The method proposed by Clawson and Trice and Wood, though statistically dubious, in practice does at least attempt to get at an imputed demand curve. The basic idea is to deduce the amount of usage at different "prices" from data of differential travel (and other) costs actually incurred in utilizing recreational facilities. If visitors to a recreation area come from a series of concentric zones one can reasonably postulate that anyone coming from the nearest zone enjoys a consumer's surplus which can be measured by the difference between his travel costs and those incurred by a man coming from the farthest zone. (There is an implicit assumption that the inner-zone resident derives as much satisfaction from a visit as the outer-zone man, but in a situation where approximations have to be made this does not seem too wild a one.) It is understood that this notion is due basically to Hotelling, and that use has been made of it in an Upper Feather River basin study. Unfortunately, it ignores the point that part of the consumers' surplus derived from proximity may be swallowed up in residential rent.

(c) *Land Reclamation* · A Dutch paper describes the use of cost-benefit analysis for evaluating land-reclamation schemes.

The particular points singled out are the insistence that one must not overlook related investment expenditure (*e.g.*, for the manufacture of raw materials for use on reclaimed land or for processing) and the corresponding returns, the use of foreign exchange shadow prices for such calculations as the expected saving in imports, allowances for harm done to fisheries and for benefits to road traffic and a general recognition of the widespread nature and importance of intangibles ("indeterminables" in Dutch-English). This is in no sense a complete listing of the relevant variables, but may be sufficient to savor the flavor of the dish.

4. HEALTH

The major purpose of health programs is to save lives and reduce illness, and on this score there is some overlap with flood-prevention and road-improvement measures. There are no special problems which relate to the estimate of the costs of such programs, and the special problem of quantifying their effects is a matter for engineers and doctors rather than for economists. The interest of the latter is thus concentrated on the problem of valuing the benefits per life saved or per illness avoided, and this is all we shall consider here. And even within this limited area, we shall devote most of our time to the former. Our task is aided by the work of Weisbrod, and the useful surveys of Mushkin and Klarman. It might be further noted that this subject is a well-established one, having attracted the attention of Irving Fisher many years ago.

Before exploring the conceptual problems, it should be noted that some of the differences between authors in the way they estimate benefits stem from differences in the availability of statistics rather than from differences in what the authors would like to measure if they could. Thus, some of the simplifications in Reynolds' classic paper on the cost of road accidents were surely dictated by statistical exigencies rather than by considerations of high principle. This paper at least has the merit that after calculating the average costs in 1952 of various consequences of accidents (death, injury, property damage, insurance, administrative costs) the author went on, in an appendix, to show how his results could be used to estimate the purely economic benefits that would have accrued from new pedestrian crossing regulations and from adequate rear lighting on all vehicles and cycles.

A death avoided means that a loss of production may be avoided. Thus the present value of this is an economic benefit to be credited to the measure responsible for saving life. The first step in estimating it is to ascertain what the average person whose life is made safer will earn over the rest of his life. This depends upon age at death, the probability of survival to each higher age, the proportion of people at each age who will both be in the labor force and employed, and their contribution to production at each age.

(*a*) Age at death of those whose lives would be saved can be assumed to equal the average age of all those who die from whatever it is, unless the proposed life-saving expenditure obviously discriminates between age groups.

(*b*) The probability of survival to each age can be calculated from a life table for the group at risk, which should be amended to take account of any projected changes in its age-specific death-rates.

(*c*) Participation rates have to be forecast. It is generally agreed that the appropriate unemployment percentage to assume is that corresponding to "full employment."

(*d*) The earnings of a person are usually taken as a measure of the value of his marginal product, average product being obviously too high. Since it is future earnings which are relevant, the trend of growth in earnings should be allowed for if the analysis starts with figures of current earnings.

In practice, Weisbrod was able to construct estimates only for all men and all women and not for any particular group at risk, on account of data limitations. He and Reynolds both took earnings in a recent year without making any addition for future productivity increases.

The question whether housewives' services should be included as lost production has produced some discussion. Since there can be no question but that the loss of these services does impose a cost upon the survivors, it would sometimes bias choice to disregard the services of housewives in calculating production loss.

As Klarman points out, the distribution of diseases between the sexes is not uniform, so that the relative economic benefits of different health programs will be affected by the weight given to housewives' services. What is really at issue, therefore, is how to measure their value, not whether to measure it. One possibility is to estimate their opportunity cost, *i.e.*, what housewives could earn in paid jobs (net of taxes and extra expenses), since this provides a minimum estimate of what the services are worth to the family. Alternatively, replacement cost, *i.e.*, the cost of a housekeeper, could be used. Weisbrod develops a very ingenious measure along these lines, where the value of a housewife's services is an increasing function of the number of other persons in her family. Neither measure can be accurately estimated in practice.

An even larger question is that of consumption. If society loses the production of the decedent, does it not also gain by not having to supply his own consumption? The answer is a matter of definition. If society is defined to exclude the decedent, the loss is confined to the wealth he would have accumulated and the taxes he would have paid less the transfers he would have received, and would be borne partly by his heirs and partly by the Government on behalf of all other taxpayers. It thus constitutes the amount which society so defined would find it worthwhile to pay to save his life (leaving aside all non-materialistic considerations for later discussion). Now the society whose representatives decide whether or not to undertake a measure which would save lives includes those people who may lose their lives if the proposed measure is not undertaken. Hence, so the argument might run, society is relevantly defined as including the prospective decedent, and his consumption is part of the social loss contingent upon his death.

Those, like Weisbrod, who take the line that consumption should be deducted have to face the problem of estimating it, and Weisbrod does so with commendable ingenuity. He argues that marginal rather than average consumption is relevant, and measures this as the change in family consumption with a change in family size, given income. Using family budget data, he calculates for each age bracket a weighted mean of the marginal consumption of persons in mean-income families of all sizes. It is only fair to add that he is far from dogmatic about the virtues of this approach.

Whether or not consumption is deducted, the economic value of a life saved varies according to a variety of factors, including age (it rises during childhood and falls after a certain age because of the twin influences of life earning patterns and discounting). Other things being equal, therefore, these calculations are worth undertaking only if we believe that more resources should be devoted to saving a more "productive" life than a less "productive" life—*e.g.*, the average man in preference to the average woman of the same age, a white Protestant American in preference to a colored one, the average Englishman rather than the average Scot, a young worker rather than a baby.

To put the question this way outrages many people's feelings who do not see that the "other things" which are here assumed "equal" include one's estimate of the moral worth and human value of the different people and of the sorrow caused by their death. Without taking any position, therefore, we pass on to consider the non-economic value of a human life. By this we mean merely the amount which it is worth sacrificing in economic terms to save a life. It is less than infinity (since there are avoidable deaths), it exceeds zero (since money is spent to save lives) and it is worth ascertaining (in so far as consistent decision-making implies such a value).

The problem has been discussed by two French authors (Thedié and Abraham) with a certain Gallic elegance which does not entirely conceal the (necessary) arbitrariness of their procedure. They speak of "affective" loss and distinguish: affective injury to the family, affective injury to the rest of the nation, *pretium doloris*, and *pretium vivendi*, the last two corresponding to the prospective decedent's aversion to suffering and death respectively. Court judgments, they consider, "should . . . make it possible in each country to obtain an average opinion as regards the sums to be spent to avoid the various affective losses."

Estimates of the benefits to be had from reducing illness, relating to particular diseases, offer no new problems of principle but involve great statistical difficulties. Mushkin discusses some of the principles, making the useful distinction between the effects of disability (*e.g.*, loss of working time) and debility (*e.g.*, loss of capacity while at work). Weisbrod and Klarman also raise valuable pointers. But the fundamental difficulty—and this affects the loss through deaths arguments too—is that of the multiplicity of variables—when there are manifold influences at work on life-expectancy, productivity, and the like, how can one hope to sort out the unambiguous influence of a particular health program or any other single causative factor?

Finally, mention should be made of a different approach to all those problems, even though, as far as we are aware, it is not one which has been pursued. This stresses that the problem is essentially the *ex-ante* one of deciding how much to spend in reducing various kinds of risk. Since people in their private capacities do incur costs to reduce risks to which they and their children are exposed, it is conceivable that their valuation of diminutions in risk could be inferred from their behavior.

The Utilization of Existing
Water Supplies

JACK HIRSHLEIFER, JAMES
DE HAVEN, AND JEROME MILLIMAN

*Jack Hirshleifer is Professor of Economics
at the University of California at Los
Angeles; James De Haven is at the RAND
Corporation; and Jerome Milliman is at
Indiana University. This piece is from their
book,* Water Supply, *published in 1960.*

1. EFFICIENCY EFFECTS AND DISTRIBUTION EFFECTS

The economic effects of any proposed policy can be divided under two headings: the effects on *efficiency* and the effects on *distribution*. Efficiency questions relate to the size of the pie available; distribution questions, to who gets what share. More formally, we can think of the pie as representing the national income or community income. Someone may propose reducing income taxes in the upper brackets on the ground that the high rates now effective there seriously deter initiative and enterprise and so reduce national income; he is making an efficiency argument that the present taxes reduce the size of the national pie. Someone else may point out that such a change will help large taxpayers as against small—a distributional consideration. In the field of water supply it is possible to find examples in the West where a certain amount of water could produce goods and services more highly valued in the market place if it were shifted from agricultural to industrial uses—this is an efficiency argument. On the other hand, this shift may hurt the interests of farmers or of their customers, employees, or suppliers while helping industrial interests—all distributional considerations.

Now economics can say something of the distributional consequences of alternative possible policies, but what it says stops short of any assertion that any man's interests or well-being can be preferred to another's. The fact that economics has nothing to say on such matters does not mean, of course, that nothing important can be said. Ethics as a branch of philosophy and the entire structure of law (which to some extent embodies or applies ethical thought) are devoted to the consideration of the rights and duties of man against man, and many propositions arising out of such thought may well command almost unanimous consent in our society. Ethics may say that no one should be permitted to starve, and law that no one should be deprived of property without due process, but these are propositions outside economics.

Most of what the existing body of economic thought has to say concerns the *efficiency* effects—the effects on size of the pie—of alternative possible policies or institutional arrangements. There is, of course, a sense in which enlarging the size of the pie may be said to be good for the eaters as a group irrespective of the distribution of shares. This sense turns upon the *possibility* of dividing the enlarged pie in such a way that everybody benefits. If such a distribution of the gain is not adopted, there may or may not be good reason for the failure to do so, but the reason is presumed to be legal or ethical and so outside the sphere of economic analysis. Economics alone cannot give us answers to policy problems; it can show us how to attain efficiency and what the distributional consequences are of attaining efficiency in alternative possible ways, but it does not tell us how to distribute the gain from increased efficiency.

It is true that it is often the case that the efficiency and distributional consequences of a proposed change cannot be so neatly separated. Any particular change in the direction of efficiency will involve a certain intrinsic distribution of gains and losses, and in practice it may be unfeasible to effect a redistribution such that everyone gains. Nevertheless, we feel that a presumption in favor of changes increasing the national income is justified, while conceding that this presumption can be defeated if there are irreparable distributive consequences that are sufficiently offensive on ethical or legal grounds.

Nothing is more common in public discussions of economic affairs, however, than a consideration of distributive effects of any change to the utter exclusion of the efficiency question. The agricultural price-support policy, for example, is usually and fruitlessly discussed pro and con in terms of the interests of farmers versus the interests of consumers and taxpayers. But a policy of expensive storage of perishing commodities to hold them out of human consumption is, obviously, inefficient. Concentration upon the efficiency question might readily suggest solutions that would increase the national income and would help consumers and taxpayers a great deal while hurting farmers relatively little or not at all.

2. THE PRINCIPLE OF EQUIMARGINAL VALUE IN USE

Suppose for simplicity we first assume that the stock or the annual flow of a resource like water becomes available without cost, the only problem being to allocate the supply among the competing uses and users who desire it. Economic theory asserts one almost universal principle which characterizes a good or efficient allocation—the principle we shall here call "equimarginal value in use." The *value in use* of any unit of water, whether purchased by an ultimate or an intermediate consumer, is essentially measured by the *maximum* amount of resources (dollars) which the consumer would be willing to pay for that unit. *Marginal* value in use is the value in use of the last unit consumed, and for any consumer marginal value in use will ordinarily decline as the quantity of water consumed in any period increases. The principle, then, is that the resource should be so allocated that all consumers or users derive equal value in use from the marginal unit consumed or used.

An example of the process of equating marginal values in use may be more illuminating than an abstract proof that this principle characterizes efficient allocations. Suppose that my neighbor and I are both given rights (ration coupons, perhaps) to certain volumes of water, and we wish to consider whether it might be in our mutual interest to trade these water rights between us for other resources—we might as well say for dollars, which we can think of as a generalized claim on other resources like clam chowders, baby-sitting services, acres of land, or yachts. My neighbor might be a farmer and I an industrialist, or we might both be just retired homeowners; to make the quantities interesting, we will assume that both individuals are rather big operators. Now suppose that the last acre-foot of my periodic entitlement is worth $10 at most to me, but my neighbor would be willing to pay anything up to $50 for that right—a disparity of $40 between our marginal values in use. Evidently, if I transfer the right to him for any compensation between $10 and $50, we will both be better off in terms of our own preferences; in other words, the size of the pie measured in terms of the satisfactions yielded to both of us has increased. (Note, however, that the question of whether the compensation should be $11 or $49 is purely distributional.)

But this is not yet the end. Having given up one acre-foot, I will not be inclined to give up another on such easy terms—water has become scarcer for me, so that an additional amount given up means foregoing a somewhat more urgent use. Conversely, my neighbor is no longer quite so anxious to buy as he was before, since his most urgent need for one more acre-foot has been satisfied, and an additional unit must be applied to less urgent uses. That is, for both of us marginal values in use decline with increases of consumption (or, equivalently, marginal value in use rises if consumption is cut back). Suppose he is now willing to pay up to $45, while I am willing to sell for anything over $15. Evidently, we should trade again. Obviously, the stopping point is where the last (or marginal) unit of water is valued equally (in terms of the greatest amount of dollars we would be willing to pay) by the two of us, based on the use we can make of or the benefit we can derive from the last or marginal unit. At this point no more mutually advantageous trades are available—efficiency has been attained.

Generalizing from the illustration just given, we may say that the principle of equimarginal value in use asserts that an efficient allocation of water has been attained when no mutually advantageous exchanges are possible between any pair of claimants, which can only mean that each claimant values his last or marginal unit of water equally with the others, measured in terms of the quantity of other resources (or dollars) that he is willing to trade for an additional unit of water.

What institutional arrangements are available for achieving water allocations that meet the principle of equimarginal value in use? Our example suggests that rationing out rights to the available supply will tend to lead to an efficient result if trading of the ration coupons is freely permitted; this is true so long as it can be assumed that third parties are unaffected by the trades. More generally, any such vesting of property rights, whether originally administrative, inherited, or purchased, will tend to an efficient solution if trading is permitted. (The question of the basis underlying the original vesting of rights is a serious and important one, but it is a distributional question.) A rather important practical result is derived from this conclusion if we put the argument another way: however rights are vested, we are effectively *preventing* efficiency from being attained if the law forbids free trading of those rights. Thus, if our ration coupons are not transferable, efficiency can be achieved only if the original distribution of rights was so nicely calculated that equimarginal value in use prevailed to begin with and that thenceforth no forces operated to change these values in use. As a practical matter, these conditions could never be satisfied. Nevertheless, legal limitations on the owner's ability to sell or otherwise transfer vested water rights are very common. While at times valid justification at least in part may exist for such limitations (one example is where third parties are injured by such transfers), it seems often to be the case that these prohibitions simply inflict a loss upon all for no justifiable reason. We shall examine some instances of limitations on freedom of transfer in a later section.

It is important to note here that the market price of water rights or ration coupons, if these can be freely traded, will tend to settle at (and so to measure) the marginal value in use of the consumers in the market. Any consumer who found himself with so many coupons that the marginal value in use to him was less than market price would be trying to sell some of his rights, while anyone with marginal value in use greater than market price would be seeking to buy. The process of trading equates marginal value in use to all, and the going market price measures this value. This proposition is of very broad validity, being in no way restricted to the commodity water. It is true, technical qualifications aside, that market price measures marginal value in use to its consumers for any commodity in which free trading is permitted and perfect rights can be conveyed.

Another possible institutional device for allocating water supplies of a community would be to establish, say, a municipal water-supply enterprise which would sell water, the customers being free to take any amount desired at the price set. The principle of equimarginal value in use then, setting aside possible complications, indicates a certain pattern of pricing: the price should be equal for all and at such a level that the customers in the aggregate use up all the supply. The reason for this pattern being the best is the same as that discussed earlier: if one individual had the privilege of buying units of water for $10 when another had to pay $50, mutually advantageous trading could take place if the water (or rights to it) could be transferred. If trading possibilities are ruled out, the marginal value in use would be $10 for the favored customer and $50 for the other—the former is taking so much in terms of his needs or desires that he is employing the marginal unit of water for very low-value purposes, while high-value uses are being deprived because water is so scarce to the other customer. The efficiency effects of trading can be achieved simply by setting the price to the two customers equal at such a level that the combined demands will take the supply in hand. Since the customer is permitted to purchase any desired amount, he will continue to buy additional units so long as the marginal value in use to him exceeds the price he must pay, marginal value in use being defined in terms of the price he is willing to pay for an additional unit. Evidently, he will stop purchasing where marginal value in use equals the price—and so, if the price is equal to all customers, marginal value in use will be equal to all. Then no mutually advantageous trading will be possible, so that we have achieved an efficient allocation of the water resource.

Note that there will be a distributional consequence of the removal of a privilege to buy water at a preferential price—the former holder of the privilege will lose as compared with all others. The attainment of efficiency in the new situation means that it is *possible* to insure that everyone is better off. But whether it is or is not desirable to provide the compensation required to balance the loss of the formerly preferred customers is a distributional question.

Our discussion of the principle of equimarginal value in use has led to two rules of behavior necessary if efficiency is to be achieved in different institutional contexts: (1) If rights to water are vested as property, there should be no restrictions on the purchase and sale of such rights, so long as third parties are unaffected. (2) If water is being sold, the price should be equal to all customers. This second rule was derived, however, under a special assumption that the water became available without cost. More generally, there will be costs incurred in the acquisition and transport of water supplies to customers; taking costs into account requires a second principle for pricing of water in addition to the principle of equimarginal value in use.

3. THE PRINCIPLE OF MARGINAL-COST PRICING

In our previous discussion we assumed that a certain volume or flow of water became available without cost, the problem being to distribute just that amount among the potential customers. Normally, there will not be such a definite fixed amount but rather a situation in which another unit could always be made available by expending more resources to acquire and transport it, that is, at a certain additional or marginal cost. The question of where to stop in increasing the supplies made available is then added to the question just discussed of how to arrange for the allocation of the supplies in hand at any moment of time.

From the argument developed earlier about the allocation of a certain given supply, we can infer that, whatever the price may be, it should be equal to all users (since otherwise employments with higher marginal values in use are being foregone in favor of employments with lower values). Suppose that at a certain moment of time this price is $30 per unit. Then, if the community as a whole can acquire and transport another unit of water for, say, $20, it would clearly be desirable to do so;

in fact, any of the individual customers to whom the unit of water is worth $30 would be happy to pay the $20 cost, and none of the other members of the community is made worse off thereby. We may say that, on efficiency grounds, additional units should be made available so long as any members of the community are willing to pay the additional or marginal costs incurred. To meet the criterion of equimarginal value in use, however, the price should be made equal for all customers. So the combined rule is to make the price equal to the marginal cost and equal for all customers.

One important practical consideration is that, because of differing locations, use patterns, types of services, etc., the marginal costs of serving different customers will vary. It is of some interest to know in principle how this problem should be handled. The correct solution is to arrange matters so that for each class of customers (where the classes are so grouped that all customers *within* any single class can be served under identical cost conditions) the prices should be the same and equal to marginal cost. *Between* classes, however, prices should differ, and the difference should be precisely the difference in marginal costs involved in serving the two.

Consider, for example, a situation in which there are two customers, identical in all respects except that one can be served at a marginal cost of $10 per unit and the other at $40—perhaps because the latter has a hilltop location and requires pumped rather than gravity service. If they are both charged $10, the community will be expending $40 in resources to supply a marginal unit which the latter customer values at $10; if they both are charged $40, the former customer would be happy to lay out the $10 it costs to bring him another unit. The principle of equimarginal value in use which dictates equal prices was based on the assumption that costless transfers could take place between customers, but in this case any transfer from the gravity to the pumped customer involves a cost of $30. Another way to look at the matter is to say that the commodity provided is not the same: the customer who requires pumped water is demanding a more costly commodity than the gravity customer.

Where water is sold to customers, therefore, the principles we have developed indicate that customers served under identical cost conditions should be charged equal prices and that the commodity should be supplied and priced in such a way that the price for each class of service should equal the marginal cost of serving that class. Where marginal costs differ, therefore, prices should differ similarly.

4. LIMITATIONS ON VOLUNTARY EXCHANGE OF WATER RIGHTS

In our theoretical discussion we saw that, given any particular vesting of water rights an efficient allocation will tend to come about if free exchange of these rights between users is permitted. There is in practice, however, a wide variety of limitations upon the free exchange of water rights. Water rights are sometimes attached to particular tracts of land (i.e., the water cannot be transferred except as a package deal with the land), especially under the "riparian" principle; transfers of water rights or of uses within water rights also often must in a number of jurisdictions meet approval of some administrative agency. Some legal codes grant certain "higher" users priority or preference over other, "lower" users, transfers from "higher" to "lower" uses being hindered thereby. As a related point, "higher" uses sometimes have a right of seizure. While voluntary transfers can usually be presumed to make both parties better off, and so be in the direction of increased efficiency, no such presumption applies for compelled transfers through seizure.

The above are all instances of violation of a general proposition about property rights. If property is to be put to its most efficient use, there should be no uncertainty of tenure and no restrictions upon the use to which it may be put. When this is the case, voluntary exchange tends to make the property find the use where it is valued the highest, since this use can outbid all others on the market. Uncertainty of tenure interferes with this process, because people will be unwilling to pay much for property, however valuable, if a perfect right cannot be conveyed, and the existing holder will be wary about making those investments necessary to exploit the full value of the property if there is a risk of seizure. All restrictions upon free choice of use, whether the restriction is upon place, purpose, or transfers to other persons, obviously interfere with the market processes which tend to shift the resource to its most productive use.

The reasons underlying adoption of restrictions like those mentioned above are probably mixed, but at least one of them may have some validity: changes in water use may conceivably affect adversely the interests of third parties, such as complementary users downstream, for whom some protection seems needed. This protection should not, as it usually does, go beyond what is necessary to insure preservation of the rights of the third parties. Under California law, for example, a riparian user might attempt to sell water to a non-riparian user who can use the water more productively, none of the other riparian users being harmed thereby. However, the nonriparian purchaser gains no rights against the other riparian users, who can simply increase their diversions, leaving none for the would-be purchaser. Again, a holder of certain appropriate rights might attempt to sell his rights to another. This transfer in some cases requires approval of an administrative board which protects the rights of third parties but whose latitude goes beyond this and permits disapproval on essentially arbitrary grounds as well.

We may comment here that the growing trend to limitation of water rights to "reasonable use" is by no means a wholly obvious or desirable restriction. We might reflect on the desirability of legislation depriving people of their automobiles or their houses when it is determined in some administrative or judicial process that their use was "unreasonable." The purpose of such legislation is the prevention of certain wastes which, if only free voluntary exchange of water rights without unnecessary restrictions were permitted, would tend naturally to be eliminated by market processes (since efficient users can afford to pay more for water than it is worth to wasteful users).

The question of "higher" and "lower" uses has an interesting history. The California Water Code declares that the use of water for domestic purposes is the highest use of water and that the next highest use is for irrigation. Essentially the same statement has been attributed to the emperor Hammurabi (2250 B.C.), a remarkable demonstration of the persistence of error.

The correct idea underlying this thought seems to be that, if we had to do almost entirely without water, we would use the first little bit available for human consumption directly, and then, as more became available, the next use we would want to consider is providing food through irrigation. Where this argument goes wrong is in failing to appreciate that what we want to achieve is to make the *marginal* values in use (the values of the last units applied to any purpose) equal. It would obviously be mistaken to starve to death for lack of irrigation water applied to crops while using water domestically for elaborate baths and air conditioning; the domestic marginal value in use in such a case would be lower. Similar imbalances can make the marginal value in use in industry higher than it is in either domestic or irrigation uses. Actually, the principle of higher and lower uses is so defective that no one would for a moment consider using it consistently (first saturating domestic uses before using any water for other uses, then saturating irrigation uses, etc.). Rather, the principle enters erratically or capriciously in limiting the perfection of property rights in water applied to "lower" uses, however productive such uses may be.

5. EXISTING PRICING PRACTICES IN WATER SUPPLY

Our analysis of the principles of efficient allocation among competitive users led to the conclusion that prices should be equal for all customers served under equivalent cost conditions and that the price should be set at the marginal cost or the cost of delivering the last unit. Alternatively, we may say that the amount supplied should be such that the marginal cost equals the amount the customer is willing to pay for the marginal unit. There are considerable theoretical and practical complications in this connection which we are reserving for discussion in later chapters, but a general survey of the existing situation will be useful here for contrasting practice with the theoretical principles.

Examination of the allocation arrangements of local systems for domestic, commercial, and industrial water supply (primarily municipally owned) reveals that the great majority allocate water by charging a price for its use. The leading exceptions are in unmetered municipalities where, since water bills are not a function of consumption, water *deliveries* may be considered free to the consumer. While a certain amount is ordinarily charged as a water bill in such cities, this is a fixed sum (or "flat rate") and does not operate as a price does in leading consumers to balance the value of use against the cost of use. According to a report published by the *American City Magazine,* a survey made in 1949 of seventy-two cities discovered that 97.7 percent of the services in those cities were metered. The survey excluded, however, several of the largest cities which were partially under flat rates—New York, Chicago, Philadelphia, Buffalo, and others. Since that time, according to the report, Philadelphia has abandoned the fixed-bill system, and generally it may be said that in the United States a condition of universal metering has been approached. As of 1954, the report estimates that metering covered from 90 to 95 percent of all services. Since unmetered services usually represent the smaller domestic users, the proportion of *use* that is metered is even greater than the proportion of *services.*

In those cases, such as New York City, where some users (primarily domestic) are unmetered while others users are charged a price per unit of water used, our rule of prices equal to marginal cost is violated. An unmetered consumer will proceed to use water until its marginal value in use to him is nil to correspond to its zero price to him. This is of course wasteful, because the water system cannot provide the commodity costlessly, and hence society will lose (setting distributional considerations aside) by the excess of the cost of delivery over the value in use for such units of consumption.

It might be thought that the domestic consumers, who are the unmetered customers almost always (the only other substantial classes of use frequently unmetered are public agencies, such as park, sanitation and especially fire departments), somehow deserve a priority or preference as compared with "intermediate" economic customers like industrial or commercial services. But an intermediate consumer is essentially a final consumer once removed. If consumers are required to pay more for water used in the production of food, clothing, and other items of value than they pay for water for direct consumption, an inefficient disparity in marginal values in use between the different uses will be created. Conversely, on efficiency grounds consumers should not be required to pay *more* for domestic water and for water used in industry than for water used to grow crops, such being the effect of existing policies which commonly grant the irrigation use of water a subsidy over all other uses.

A situation in which different prices are charged to different users, or to the same user for varying quantities of the same commodity, is called one of "price discrimination." While discrimination may under certain conditions be justified on one ground or another, it has the defect of preventing the marginal values in use from being made equal between the favored and the penalized uses or users. The only exception to this statement is where discrimination is applied within the purchases of a single individual—by, for example, a declining block rate. If there are no restrictions on use, the individual concerned will continue to equate all his marginal values in the various uses to the *marginal* price (the price for the last unit or for an additional unit) he must pay for the commodity purchased. So far as his own purchases are concerned, therefore, he will still equalize his marginal values in use for all his different uses. If such a block system is used for a number of individuals, however, marginal values in use will not in general be equated between individuals; some will tend to consume an amount such that they end up in the higher-priced block, and others will end up in the lower.

All price differences for the "same" commodity are not, however, evidence of price discrimination. In fact, there should be some difference of price where an extra delivery cost or processing cost must be incurred in serving certain users. These users can be considered as buying two commodities together—the basic commodity and the special delivery or processing. If the basic commodity is to be equally priced to all users, uses requiring such additional services must be charged more.

Turning to the practical side, we should mention at once that our earlier metering discussion neglected one important consideration: the cost of metering and the associated increase in billing costs. It is clear that the additional cost of meters (especially for a great many small users) may well exceed the possible gains from the rationalization of use which would follow metering. (There would, in general, be an aggregate reduction of use as well.) While this question bears further investigation, the dominant opinion in the field of municipal water supply seems to be that universal metering produces gains that are worth the cost. By way of contrast, it appears that in Great Britain domestic use is never metered.

Even if we turn, however, to a consideration of that part of water supply that is metered, or to systems that are completely metered, we find that some non-uniform pattern of prices typically exists. There are some exceptions. In Chicago, for example, all metered users pay the same price per unit of water delivered. A more typical rate system is that of Los Angeles, where rates vary by type of use and also by amount of use (a declining or "promotional" block rate), with a service charge independent of use but based on size of connection. A rate distinction is also made in Los Angeles between firm service and service that the water department may at its convenience provide or refuse, and in some cases between gravity and pumped services.

Some of these rate differences may not be inconsistent with our theoretical discussion. The rate differential may reflect an extra cost or difficulty of delivering to the customer (or customer class, where it is not worthwhile distinguishing between individual customers) charged the higher price.

Where customers' demands vary in the degree to which they impose a peak load on the system, some differential service or demand charge can be justified. In a sense, the commodity delivered off-peak is not the same as that delivered on-peak. The common system of basing a fixed-sum demand charge on the size of service connection is, however, very crude; it provides no deterrent to the customer's contributing to the peak load. Charging a lower rate for interruptible service is somewhat more reasonable. Ideally, the situation might be handled by having differing on-peak and off-peak prices. In water enterprises storage in the distribution system usually smoothes out diurnal and weekly peaks. The seasonal peak in the summer is important, however. The Metropolitan Water District of Southern California has at times charged a premium price for summer deliveries.

Other differentiations can be justified by increased delivery costs necessary to reach certain classes of customers. A difference in rate between pumped and gravity service, for example, is eminently reasonable. We have not gone into the question of just how great the differences should be, but for the present we shall not consider such differences as violations of the principle of a common per-unit price to all.

Certain frequently encountered differences, which we may now properly call "price discrimination," are not based on any special cost of providing the service in question. In Los Angeles, for example, there is an exceptionally low rate for irrigation use. Domestic, commercial, and industrial services are not distinguished as such, but they are differentially affected by the promotional volume rates. More serious, because much more common, is the system of block rates, with reductions for larger quantities used. There is typically some saving in piping costs to large customers, since a main can be run directly to the service connection, whereas the same volume sold to many small customers would require a distribution network of pipes. Ideally, the cost of laying down the pipes to connect customers to the system should be assessed as one-time charge against the outlet served—or the lump sum could be converted into an annual charge independent of the amount of water consumed, to represent the interest and depreciation on the capital invested by the water system to serve the customer. The point is that, once the pipes are in, the unit marginal cost of serving customers is almost independent of the volume taken. A lower block rate leads therefore to wasteful use of water by large users, since small users would value the same marginal unit of water more highly if delivered to them. We may say that the promotional or block-rate system in the case of water leads to a discrimination in favor of users of water that happen to find it convenient to use a great deal of the commodity and against users that do not need as much water. The customer paying the lower price will on the margin be utilizing water for less valuable purposes than it could serve if transferred to the customer paying the higher price.

Because of the enormous fraction of water being used for irrigational purposes unusual interest attaches to the method by which water supplies of such projects are allocated to individual users. Not all irrigation water, of course, is distributed through an irrigation district or enterprise, a great deal being simply pumped or diverted by individual users. Such individual users can be considered to pay a price for water in the form of the costs actually incurred in its acquisition for irrigation purposes.

Reliable information is not available on the cost of water to irrigators, partly because of the differing methods of charging for water. The 1950 Census presented an over-all national average of $1.66 per acre-foot in 1949. This figure is not very meaningful, since it is the result of dividing water charges *per acre* by an estimate of average deliveries of water per acre. But the water charges per acre depend, for farmers served by an irrigation district or other supply enterprise, upon the terms of the "payment complex," which may include taxes and assessments, acreage charge, and service fees in addition to the water price.

Unfortunately, there do not seem to be any nationally compiled data on the methods used by irrigation enterprises to charge for water supplied. A tabulation by the Irrigation Districts Association of California indicates considerable variation in practice: some districts make no charge except by assessment of property; others charge a flat rate, either (1) a fixed amount per acre or (2), depending upon the crop, a variable amount per acre; still others charge a price per unit of water, either on a fixed or on a declining block (promotional) basis; still others have a mixture of pricing methods. Where no charge or only a flat-rate charge is made for water, the marginal price of water to the user would be zero if in fact the user can take unlimited quantities as a domestic consumer normally can (subject only to the limited size of his connection). But it seems to be fairly common practice in irrigation districts that the water is more or less rationed to the user; any "price" set is a fiscal measure to cover the operating and maintenance costs of the district and not a market price in the ordinary sense. We have seen that, with rationing of rights, efficiency can be achieved when trading is permitted. Purchase of water rights in irrigation districts normally takes place through purchase of land, which is usually freely possible (except for the so-called 160-acre limitation in Bureau of Reclamation projects), or through purchase of stock in mutual water companies. It may be remarked that a flat rate per acre varying by the type of crop grown is a kind of crude price, the higher flat rate generally corresponding to the more water-intensive crop. Irrigation districts may achieve reasonably efficient water allocations, but perhaps more often through the purchase of rights rather than the correct pricing of water itself. Where the water right cannot be detached from the land, this limitation on sale will create some inefficiency.